William Morris

The Life and Death of Jason

A Poem

William Morris

The Life and Death of Jason
A Poem

ISBN/EAN: 9783337167141

Printed in Europe, USA, Canada, Australia, Japan

Cover: Foto ©Thomas Meinert / pixelio.de

More available books at **www.hansebooks.com**

THE LIFE AND DEATH OF JASON.

LONDON: PRINTED BY W. CLOWES AND SONS, STAMFORD STREET
AND CHARING CROSS.

THE LIFE AND DEATH
OF JASON

A POEM

BY WILLIAM MORRIS.

SECOND EDITION, REVISED.

LONDON:
BELL AND DALDY.
1868.

ARGUMENT.

JASON, the son of Æson, king of Iolchos, having come to man's estate, demanded of Pelias his father's kingdom, which he held wrongfully. But Pelias answered, that if he would bring from Colchis the golden fleece of the ram that had carried Phryxus thither, he would yield him his right. Whereon Jason sailed to Colchis in the ship Argo, with other heroes, and by means of Medea, the king's daughter, won the fleece; and carried off also Medea; and so, after many troubles, came back to Iolchos again. There, by Medea's wiles, was Pelias slain; but Jason went to Corinth, and lived with Medea happily, till he was taken with the love of Glauce, the king's daughter of Corinth, and must needs wed her; whom also Medea destroyed, and fled to Ægeus at Athens; and not long after Jason died strangely.

THE LIFE AND DEATH OF JASON.

BOOK I.

Jason having grown up to manhood in the woods, is warned of what his life shall be.

IN Thessaly, beside the tumbling sea,
   Once dwelt a folk, men called the Minyæ;
For, coming from Orchomenus the old,
Bearing their wives and children, beasts and gold,
Through many a league of land they took their way,
And stopped at last, where in a sunny bay
The green Anaurus cleaves the white sea-sand,
And eastward inland doth Mount Pelion stand,
Where bears and wolves the centaurs' arrows find;
And southward is a gentle sea and kind,   10
Nigh landlocked, peopled with all kinds of fish,
And the good land yields all that man can wish.

  So there they built Iolchos, that each day
Grew great, until all these were passed away,
With many another, and Cretheus the king
Had died, and left his crown and everything
To Æson, his own son by fair Tyro;
Whom, in unhappy days and long ago,

A God had loved, whose son was Pelias.
  And so, within a while, it came to pass   20
This Pelias, being covetous and strong
And full of wiles, and deeming nought was wrong
That wrought him good, thrust Æson from his throne,
And over all the Minyæ reigned alone;
While Æson, like a poor and feeble lord,
Dwelt in Iolchos still, nor was his word
Regarded much by any man therein,
Nor did men labour much his praise to win.

  Now 'mid all this a fair young son he had;
And when his state thus fell from good to bad   30
He thought, Though Pelias leave me now alone,
Yet he may wish to make quite sure his throne
By slaying me and mine, some evil day;
Therefore the child will I straight send away,
Ere Pelias feels his high seat tottering,
And gets to know the terrors of a king,
That blood alone can deaden. Therewithal
A faithful slave unto him did he call,
And bade him from his nurses take the child
And bear him forth unto the forest wild   40
About the foot of Pelion: There should he
Blow loudly on a horn of ivory
That Æson gave him; then would come to him
A Centaur, grave of face and large of limb,
Before whom he should fall upon his knees
And, holding forth the child, say words like these:
  'O my lord Chiron, Æson sends me here

To say, if ever you have held him dear,
Take now this child, his son, and rear him up
Till we have fully drained the bitter cup 50
The fates have filled for us; and if times change
While through the peaceful oakwood here you range,
And the crown comes upon the youngling's head,
Then, though a king right fair apparelled,
Yet unto you shall he be but a slave,
Since now from fear his tender years you save;'
"And then," quoth Æson, "all these words being said,
Hold out this ring, set with a ruby red,
Adorned with dainty little images,
And this same horn, whereon, 'twixt carven trees, 60
Diana follows up the flying hart;
They shall be signs of truth upon your part.
Then leave the child with him, and come to me,
Minding what words the Centaur saith to thee;
Of whom thou needest have no whit of fear;
And, ere thou goest, bring me the child here."

   Then went the man and came again to him
With Jason, who was strong and large of **limb**
As for his years, and now upon his feet
Went firmly, and began to feel life sweet, 70
And longed for this and that, and on his tongue,
Bewildered, half articulate, speech hung.

   But Æson, when he saw the sturdy boy,
His bright round limbs and face lit up with joy
Of very life, sighed deeply, and he said:
"O child, I pray the Gods to spare thine head
The burden of a crown; were it not good

That thou shouldst live and die within this wood
That clothes the feet of Pelion, knowing nought
Of all the things by foolish men so sought;   80
For there, no doubt, is everything man needs,—
The quiver, with the iron-pointed reeds,
The cornel bow, the wood-knife at the side,
The garments of the spotted leopard's hide,
The bed of bear-skin in the hollow hill,
The bath within the pool of some green rill;
There shall the quick-eyed centaurs be thy friends,
Unto whose hearts such wisdom great Jove sends
They know the past and future, and fear nought
That by the fates upon them may be brought.   90
And when the spring brings love, then mayst thou find,
In some fair grassy place, the wood-nymphs kind,
And choose thy mate, and with her, hand in hand,
Go wandering through the blossoming sweet land;
And nought of evil there shall come to thee,
But like the golden age shall all things be;
And when upon thee falls the fated day,
Fearless and painless shalt thou pass away."

  So spoke he foolishly, nor knew indeed
How many hearts his son should make to bleed,   100
How many griefs his head, whitened with care
Long ere its time, before his death should bear.

  Now, since the moonless night and dark was come,
Time was it that the child should leave his home;
And saddled in the court the stout horse stood
That was to bear them to the Centaur's wood;
And the tried slave stood ready by his lord,

With wallet on his back, and sharpened sword
Girt to his side; to whom the horn and ring,
Fit for the belt and finger of a king,
Did Æson give, and therewith kissed the boy,
Who with his black beard played, and laughed for joy
To see the war-horse in the red torch-light.
At last, being mounted, forth into the night
They rode, and thus has Jason left his home.

All night they rode, and at the dawn, being come
Unto the outskirts of the forest wild,
They left the horse, and the still sleeping child
The slave bore in his arms, until they came
Unto the place where, living free from blame,
Chiron the old roamed through the oaken wood;
There by a flowering thorn-bush the slave stood,
And set the little Jason on the ground;
Who, waking from sweet sleep, looked all around
And 'gan to prattle; but his guardian drew
The horn from off his neck, and thereon blew
A point of hunting known to two or three,
That sounded through the forest merrily,
Then waited listening.   And meantime the sun,
Come from Eubœan cliffs, had just begun
To light the high tips of the forest grass,
And in the thorn the blackbird singing was;
But 'mid his noise the listening man could hear
The sound of hoofs, whereat a little fear
He felt within his heart, and heeded nought

The struggling of the child, who ever sought
To gain the horn all glittering of bright gold,
Wrought by the cunning Dædalus of old.

   But louder still the noise he hearkened grew,
Until at last in sight the Centaur drew,   140
A mighty grey horse, trotting down the glade,
Over whose back the long grey locks were laid,
That from his reverend head abroad did flow;
For to the waist was man, but all below
A mighty horse, once roan, now well-nigh white
With lapse of years; with oak-wreaths was he dight
Where man joined unto horse, and on his head
He wore a gold crown, set with rubies red,
And in his hand he bare a mighty bow,
No man could bend of those that battle now.   150

   So, when he saw him coming through the trees,
The trembling slave sunk down upon his knees
And put the child before him; but Chiron,
Who knew all things, cried: "Man with Æson's son,
Thou needest not to tell me who thou art,
Nor will I fail to do to him my part:
A vain thing were it, truly, if I strove,
Such as I am, against the will of Jove.
Lo now, this youngling, set 'twixt thee and me,
In days to come a mighty man shall be,   160
Well-nigh the mightiest of all those that dwell
Between Olympus and Malea; and well
Shall Juno love him till he come to die.

   "Now get thee to thy master presently,
But leave with me the red ring and the horn,

That folk may know of whom this boy was born
In days to come, when he shall leave this wild:
And lay between my arms the noble child."

  So the slave joyful, but still half afraid,
Within the mighty arms young Jason laid,   170
And gave up both the horn and the red ring
Unto the Centaur, who the horn did sling
About him; on his finger, with a smile,
Setting the ring; and in a little while
The slave departing, reached the open plain,
And straight he mounted on his horse again,
And rode on toward Iolchos all the day,
And as the sunset darkened every way,
He reached the gates, and coming to his lord,
Bid him rejoice, and told him every word   180
That Chiron said. Right glad was Æson then
That from his loins a great man among men
Should thus have sprung; and so he passed his days
Full quietly, remote from fear or praise.

  And now was Pelias mindful of the day
When from the altar's horns he drew away
Sidero's cruel hands, while Neleus smote
The golden-hilted sword into her throat,
And without fire, or barley-cake, or cup,
No pleasing victim, she was offered up   190
In Juno's temple; so he feared that he,
Though sprung from him who rules the restless sea,
Should meet an evil fate at Juno's hands:
Therefore he sent for men from many lands,

Marble and wood, and gold and brass enow,
And day by day, with many a sounding blow,
The masons wrought, until at last was reared
A temple to the Goddess that he feared;—
A wonder among temples, for the stone
That made it, and the gold that therein shone.   200
And in the midst her image Pelias set,
Wrought cunningly of purest gold, which yet
Had served him better in his treasury,
So little store the Goddess set thereby.

  Moreover to Dodona, where the doves
Amid the oak-trees murmur of their loves,
He sent a messenger to know his fate;
Who, up the temple steps, beneath the weight
Of precious things went bending; and being come
Back from the north to his Thessalian home,   210
Gave forth this answer to the doubtful king:—

  "O Pelias, fearful of so many a thing,
Sit merry o'er thy wine, sleep safe and soft,
Within thy golden bed; for surely oft
The snows shall fall before the half-shod man
Can come upon thee through the water wan."

  So at this word the king along the shore
Built many a tower, and ever more and more
Drew men unto him skilled in spear and bow;
And through the streets full often would he go   220
Beset with guards, and for the rest began
To be a terror unto every man.

  And yet indeed were all these things but vain,

For at the foot of Pelion grew his bane
In strength and comeliness from day to day,
And swiftly passed his childish years away:
Unto whom Chiron taught the worthy lore
Of elders who the wide world filled before;
And how to forge his iron arrow-heads,
And how to find within the marshy steads ·		230
The stoutest reeds, and from some slain bird's wing
To feather them, and make a deadly thing;
And through the woods he took him, nor would spare
To show him how the just-awakened bear
Came hungry from his tree, or show him how
The spotted leopard's lurking-place to know;
And many a time they brought the hart to bay,
Or smote the boar at hottest of the day.

  Now was his dwelling-place a fair-hewn cave,
Facing the south: thereto the herdsmen drave		240
Full oft to Chiron woolly sheep, and neat,
And brought him wine and garden-honey sweet,
And fruits that flourish well in the fat plain,
And cloth and linen, and would take again
Skins of slain beasts, and little lumps of gold,
Washed from the high crags: then would Chiron hold,
Upon the sunny lawns, high feast with them,
And garland all about the ancient stem
Of some great tree, and there do sacrifice
Unto the Gods, and with grave words and wise		250
Tell them sweet tales of elders passed away:
But for some wished thing every man would pray
Or ever in their hands the steel did shine,

And or the sun lit up the bubbling wine;
Then would they fall to meat, nor would they leave
Their joyances, until the dewy eve
Had given good heart unto the nightingale
To tell the sleepy wood-nymphs all his tale.

 Moreover, Chiron taught him how to cast
His hand across the lyre, until there passed   260
Such sweetness through the woods, that all about
The wood-folk gathered, and the merry rout
That called on Bacchus, hearkening, stayed awhile,
And in the chase the hunter, with a smile,
From his raised hand let fall the noisy horn,
When to his ears the sweet strange sound was borne.

 But in the night-time once did Jason wake,
And seem to see the moonlit branches shake
With huge, unwonted clamour of the chase;
Then up he sprung, but ere he went one pace   270
Unto the cave's mouth, Chiron raised his arm
And drew him back, and said; "Surely, no charm
Thou hast, my son, against Diana's sight,
Who over Pelion goes abroad this night;
Now let those go to her that she doth call,
Because no fenced town, brazen gate or wall,
No coat of mail, or seven-folded shield,
Can guard thee from the wound that ne'er is healed,
When she is angry. Sleep again, my son,
Nor wish to spoil great deeds not yet begun."   280

 Then Jason lay and trembled, while the sound
Grew louder through the moonlit woods around,
And died off slowly, going toward the sea,

Leaving the fern-owl wailing mournfully.

  Thereafter wandering lonely did he meet
A maid, with girt-up gown and sandalled feet,
Who joyously through flowering grass did go,
Holding within her hand an unstrung bow;
And, setting eyes on her, he thought, indeed,
This must be she that made Actæon bleed;   290
For, certes, ere that day he had not seen
Within that wild, one made so like a queen.

  So, doubtful, he held back, nor dared to love
Her rosy feet, or ivory knees above,
And, with half-lifted eyes, could scarcely dare
To gaze upon her eyes or golden hair,
Or hidden bosom: but she called aloud,—
"Tell me, fair youth, if thou hast seen a crowd
Of such as I go through these woods to-day?"
And when his stammering tongue no word could say, 300
She smiled upon him, and said, "Who art thou,
Who seemest fitter from some galley's prow
To lead the heroes on the merchant-town,
Than through the wilds to hunt the poor beasts down,
Or underneath the canopy to sit,
Than by the beech to watch the cushat flit?
Speak out, and fear not."

                    "O, my queen!" said he,
"Fair Goddess, as thou seemest well to be,
Give me good days and peace, and maiden's love,
And let great kings send out their sons to rove; 310
But as for me, my name is little known,
I am but Jason, who dwell here alone

With Chiron in the hollow mountain-side,
Wishful for happy days, whate'er betide."
　"Jason," she said, "all folk shall know thy name,
For verily the Gods shall give thee fame,
Whatever they keep back from thee: behold
Restless thou shalt be, as thou now art bold,
And cunning, as thou now art skilled to watch
The crafty bear, and in the toils to catch　　　　320
The grey-maned yellow lion; and now see
Thou doest my commands, for certainly
I am no mortal; so to Chiron tell
No longer is it fitting thou shouldst dwell
Here in the wilds, but in a day or two,
Clad in Magnesian garments, shalt thou go
Unto Iolchos, and there claim thine own.
And unto thee shall Chiron first make known
The story of thy father and thy kin,
That thou mayst know what right thou hast herein. 330
And say to him, I bid him do this thing,
By this same token, that the silver ring
Upon mine altar, with Sidero's blood
Is spotted still, and that the half-charred wood
My priests had lighted early on that day,
Yet lies thereon, by no flame burnt away."
Then Jason fell a-trembling, and to him
The tall green stems grew wavering and dim;
And when a fresh gust of the morning breeze
Came murmuring along the forest trees,　　　　340
And woke him as from dreaming, all alone
He stood, and with no farewell she was gone,

Leaving no traces of her dainty feet.
  But through the leaves ambrosial odours sweet
Yet floated as he turned to leave the place,
And with slow steps, and thinking on his case,
Went back to Chiron, whom at rest he found,
Half sleeping on the sunny thyme-strewn ground,
To whom he told the things that he had heard,
With flushed and eager face, for they had stirred   350
New thoughts within him of the days to come,
So that he longed to leave his woodland home.
  Then Chiron said: "O, fair son, thou shalt go,
Since now, at last, the Gods will have it so:
And know that, till thou comest to the end
Of thy loved life, shall Juno be thy friend,
Because the lovely huntress thou did see
Late in the greenwood certainly was she
Who sits in heaven beside Almighty Jove,
And noble things they do that have her love.   360
  "Now, son, to-day I rede thee not to go,
Nor yet to-morrow, for clouds great and slow
Are gathering round the hill-tops, and I think
The thirsty fields full many a draught will drink;
Therefore to-day our cups shall not be dry,
But we will sit together, thou and I,
And tales of thy forefathers shalt thou hear,
And many another, till the heavens clear."
  So was it as the Centaur said; for soon
The woods grew dark, as though they knew no noon;   370
The thunder growled about the high brown hills,
And the thin, wasted, shining summer rills

Grew joyful with the coming of the rain,
And doubtfully was shifting every vane
On the town spires, with changing gusts of wind;
Till came the storm-blast, furious and blind,
'Twixt gorges of the mountains, and drove back
The light sea breeze; then waxed the heavens black,
Until the lightning leapt from cloud to cloud,
With clattering thunder, and the piled-up crowd   380
Began to turn from steely blue to grey,
And toward the sea the thunder drew away,
Leaving the north-wind blowing steadily
The rain clouds from Olympus; while the sea
Seemed mingled with the low clouds and the rain:
And one might think that never now again
The sunny grass would make a pleasant bed
For tired limbs, and dreamy, languid head
Of sandalled nymph, forewearied with the chase.

    Meantime, within a pleasant lighted place,   390
Stretched upon warm skins, did the Centaur lie,
And nigh him Jason, listening eagerly
The tales he told him, asking, now and then,
Strange questions of the race of vanished men:
Nor were the wine-cups idle; till at last
Desire of sleep over their bodies passed,
And in their dreamless rest the wind in vain
Howled round about, with washing of the rain.   398

BOOK II.

*Jason claims his own—Pelias tells about the Golden Fleece—
Jason vows the quest thereof.*

So there they lay until the second dawn
Broke fair and fresh o'er glittering glade and lawn;
Then Jason rose, and did on him a fair
Blue woollen tunic, such as folk do wear
On the Magnesian cliffs, and at his thigh
An iron-hilted sword hung carefully;
And on his head he had a russet hood;
And in his hand two spears of cornel-wood,
Well steeled and bound with brazen bands he shook.
 Then from the Centaur's hands at last he took   10
The tokens of his birth, the ring and horn,
And so stept forth into the sunny morn,
And bade farewell to Chiron, and set out
With eager heart, that held small care or doubt.
 So lightly through the well-known woods he passed,
And came out to the open plain at last,
And went till night came on him, and then slept
Within a homestead that a poor man kept;
And rose again at dawn, and slept that night
Nigh the Anaurus, and at morrow's light   20
Rose up and went unto the river's brim;
But fearful seemed the passage unto him,
For swift and yellow drave the stream adown
'Twixt crumbling banks; and tree-trunks rough and
 brown

Whirled in the bubbling eddies here and there;
So swollen was the stream a maid might dare
To cross, in fair days, with unwetted knee.

   Then Jason with his spear-shaft carefully
Sounded the depth, nor any bottom found;
And wistfully he cast his eyes around   30
To see if help was nigh, and heard a voice
Behind him, calling out, "Fair youth, rejoice
That I am here to help, or certainly
Long time a dweller hereby shouldst thou be."

   Then Jason turned round quickly, and beheld
A woman, bent with burdens and with eld,
Grey and broad shouldered; so he laughed, and said:
"O mother, wilt thou help me? by my head,
More help than thine I need upon this day."

   "O son," she said, "needs must thou on thy way; 40
And is there any of the giants here
To bear thee through this water without fear?
Take, then, the help a God has sent to thee,
For in mine arms a small thing shalt thou be."

   So Jason laughed no more, because a frown
Gathered upon her brow, as she cast down
Her burden to the earth and came a-nigh,
And raised him in her long arms easily,
And stept adown into the water cold.

   There with one arm the hero did she hold,   50
And with the other thrust the whirling trees
Away from them; and laughing, and with ease
Went through the yellow foaming stream, and came
Unto the other bank; and little shame

Had Jason that a woman carried him,
For no man, howsoever strong of limb,
Had dared across that swollen stream to go,
But if he wished the Stygian stream to know;
Therefore he doubted not, that with some God
Or reverend Goddess that rough way he trod. 60

   So when she had clomb up the slippery bank
And let him go, well-nigh adown he sank,
For he was dizzy with the washing stream,
And with that passage mazed as with a dream.

   But, turning round about unto the crone,
He saw not her, but a most glorious one,
A lady clad in blue, all glistering
With something more than gold, crowned like the king
Of all the world, and holding in her hand
A jewelled rod.   So when he saw her stand 70
With unsoiled feet scarce touching the wet way,
He trembled sore, but therewith heard her say:—

   "O Jason, such as I have been to thee
Upon this day, such ever will I be;
And I am Juno; therefore doubt thou not
A mighty helper henceforth thou hast got
Against the swords and bitter tongues of men,
For surely mayst thou lean upon me, when
The turbulent and little-reasoning throng
Press hard upon thee, or a king with wrong 80
Would fain undo thee, as thou leanedst now
Within the yellow stream: so from no blow
Hold back thine hand, nor fear to set thine heart
On what thou deemest fits thy kingly part.

Now to the king's throne this day draw anear,
Because of old time have I set a fear
Within his heart, ere yet thou hadst gained speech,
And whilst thou wanderedst beneath oak and beech
Unthinking. And, behold! so have I wrought,
That with thy coming shall a sign be brought   90
Unto him; for the latchet of thy shoe
Rushing Anaurus late I bade undo,
Which now is carried swiftly to the sea.

   So Pelias, this day setting eyes on thee,
Shall not forget the shameful trickling blood
Adown my altar-steps, or in my wood
The screaming peacocks scared by other screams,
Nor yet to-night shall he dream happy dreams.

   Farewell, then, and be joyful, for I go
Unto the people, many a thing to show,   100
And set them longing for forgotten things,
Whose rash hands toss about the crowns of kings."

   Therewith before his eyes a cloud there came,
Sweet-smelling, coloured like a rosy flame,
That wrapt the Goddess from him; who, indeed,
Went to Iolchos, and there sowed the seed
Of bitter change, that ruins kings of men;
For, like an elder of threescore and ten,
Throughout the town she went, and, as such do,
Ever she blessed the old, and banned the new,   110
Lamenting for the passed and happy reign
Of Cretheus, wishing there were come again
One like to him; till in the market-place
About the king was many a doubtful face.

Now Jason, by Anaurus left alone,
Found that, indeed, his right-foot shoe was gone,
But, as the Goddess bade him, went his way
Half shod, and by an hour before mid-day
He reached the city gates, and entered there,
Whom the folk mocked, beholding his foot bare,   120
And iron-hilted sword, and uncouth weed :
But of no man did he take any heed,
But came into the market-place, where thronged
Much folk about Him who his sire had wronged.
But when he stood within that busy stead,
Taller he showed than any by a head,
Great limbed, broad shouldered, mightier far than all,
But soft of speech, though unto him did fall
Full many a scorn upon that day to get.

So in a while he came where there was set   130
Pelias, the king, judging the people there ;
In scarlet was he clad, and o'er his hair,
Sprinkled with grey, he wore a royal crown,
And from an ivory throne he looked adown
Upon the suitors and the restless folk.

Now, when the yellow head of Jason broke
From out the throng, with fearless eyes and grey,
A terror took the king, that ere that day
For many a peaceful year he had not felt,
And his hand fell upon his swordless belt ;   140
But when the hero strode up to the throne,
And set his unshod foot upon the stone
Of the last step thereof, and as he stood,
Drew off the last fold of his russet hood,

And with a clang let fall his brass-bound spear,
The king shrunk back, grown pale with deadly fear;
Nor then the oak-trees' speech did he forget,
Noting the one bare foot, and garments wet,
And something half remembered in his face.

 And now nigh silent was the crowded place,   150
For through the folk remembrance Juno sent,
And soon from man to man a murmur went,
And frowning folk were whispering deeds of shame
And wrong the king had wrought, and Æson's name,
Forgotten long, was bandied all about,
And silent mouths seemed ready for a shout.

 So, when the king raised up a hand, that shook
With fear, and turned a wrathful, timorous look
On his Ætolian guards, upon his ears
There fell the clashing of the people's spears;   160
And on the house-tops round about the square
Could he behold folk gathered here and there,
And see the sunbeams strike on brass and steel.
But therewithal, though new fear did he feel,
He thought, " Small use of arms in this distress,—
Needs is it that I use my wiliness;"
Then spoke aloud: "O, man, what wouldst thou here
That beardest thus a king with little fear?"

 " Pelias," he said, "I will not call thee king,
Because thy crown is but a stolen thing,   170
And with a stolen sceptre dost thou reign,
Which now I bid thee render up again,
And on his father's throne my father set,
Whom for long years the Gods did well forget,

But now, in lapse of time, remembering,
Have raised me, Jason, up to do this thing,
His son, and son of fair Alcimidé;
Yet now, since Tyro's blood 'twixt thee and me
Still runs, and thou my father's brother art,
In no wise would I hurt thee, for my part,   180
If thou wilt render to us but our own,
And still shalt thou stand nigh my father's throne."

 Then all the people, when aright they knew,
That this was Æson's son, about them drew,
And when he ended gave a mighty shout;
But Pelias cleared his face of fear and doubt,
And answered Jason, smiling cunningly:—

 "Yea, in good time thou comest unto me,
My nephew Jason; fain would I lay down
This heavy weight and burden of a crown,   190
And have instead my brother's love again,
I lost, to win a troublous thing and vain;
And yet, since now thou showest me such goodwill,
Fain would I be a king a short while still,
That everything in order I may set,
Nor any man thereby may trouble get.
And now I bid thee stand by me to-day,
And cast all fear and troublous thoughts away;
And for thy father Æson will I send,
That I may see him as a much-loved friend,   200
Now that these years of bitterness are passed,
And peaceful days are come to me at last."

 With that, from out the press grave Æson came,
E'en as he spoke; for to his ears the fame

Of Jason's coming thither had been brought;
Wherefore, with eager eyes his son he sought;
But, seeing the mighty hero great of limb,
Stopped short, with eyes set wistfully on him,
While a false honied speech the king began:

"Hail, brother Æson, hail, O happy man!   210
To-day thou winnest back a noble son,
Whose glorious deeds this fair hour sees begun,
And from my hands thou winnest back the crown
Of this revered and many-peopled town;
So let me win from thee again thy love,
Nor with long anger slight the Gods above."

Then Jason, holding forth the horn and ring,
Said to his father: "Doubtest thou this thing?
Behold the tokens Chiron gave to me
When first he said that I was sprung from thee."   220

Then little of those signs did Æson reck,
But cast his arms about the hero's neck,
And kissed him oft, remembering well the time
When as he sat beneath the flowering lime
Beside his house, the glad folk to him came
And said: "O King, all honour to thy name
That will not perish surely, for thy son
His royal life this day has just begun."

Wherefore unto him, like an empty dream,
The busy place, the king and folk did seem,   230
As on that sight at last he set his eyes,
Prayed for so oft with many a sacrifice;
And speechless for a while fain must he stand,
Holding within his hand the mighty hand;

And as the wished-for son he thus beheld,
Half mournful thoughts of swiftly-gathering eld
Came thick upon him, till the salt tears ran
On to the raiment of the goodly man;
Until at last he said: " All honour now
To Jove and all the Gods! Surely, I know, 240
Henceforth my name shall never perish; yet
But little joy of this man shall I get,
For through the wide world where will be the king
Who will not fear him; nor shall anything
Be strong against him; therefore certainly
Full seldom will he ride afield with me,
Nor will he long bear at his father's board
To sit, well-known of all, but with his sword
Will rather burst asunder banded throngs
Of evil men, healing the people's wrongs. 250

"And as for thee, O Pelias, as I may,
Will I be friend to thee from this same day;
And since we both of us are growing old,
And both our lives will soon be as tales told,
I think perchance that thou wilt let me be,
To pass these few years in felicity
That this one brings me."

      Thereon Pelias said:—
"Yea, if I hurt thee ought, then on my head
Be every curse that thou canst ever think;
And dying, of an ill draught may I drink, 260
For in my mind is nought but wish for rest.

"But on this day, I pray thee, be my guest,
While yet upon my head I wear the crown,

Which, ere this morning's flowers have fallen down,
Your head shall bear again; for in the hall,
Upon the floor the fresh-plucked rushes fall,
Even as we speak, and maids and men bear up
The kingly service; many a jewelled cup
And silver platter; and the fires roar
About the stalled ox and the woodland boar;   270
And wine we have, that ere this youngling's eyes
First saw the light, made tears and laughter rise
Up from men's hearts, making the past seem dull,
The future hollow, but the present full
Of all delights, if quick they pass away;
And we, who have been foes for many a day,
Surely, ere evening sees the pitcher dry,
May yet be friends, and talking lovingly,
And with our laughter make the pillars ring,
While this one sits revolving many a thing,   280
Saddened by that, which makes us elders glad."

 Such good words said he, but the thoughts were bad
Within his crafty breast; and still he thought
How best he might be rid of him just brought,
By sentence of the Gods, upon his head.
 Then moved the kinsmen from the market-stead
Between a lane of men, who ever pressed
About the princes, and with loud words blessed
The hero and his race, and thought no shame
To kiss his skirts; and so at last they came   290
Unto the house that rustling limes did shade,
And thereabout was many a slender maid,
Who welcomed them with music and sweet song,

And cast red roses as they went along
Before their feet; and therewith brought the three
Into the palace, where right royally
Was Jason clad, and seemed a prince indeed.
  So while the harp-string and shrill-piping reed
Still sounded, trooped the folk unto the feast,
And all were set to meat, both most and least;   300
And when with dainties they were fully fed,
Then the tall jars and well-sewn goat-skins bled,
And men grew glad, forgetting every care.
But first a golden chain and mantle fair
Pelias did on him; and then, standing up,
Poured out red wine from a great golden cup,
Unto the Gods, and prayed to them: "O ye
Who rule the world, grant us felicity
This hour, at least, nor let our sweet delight
Be marred by ought, until the silent night   310
Has come, and turned to day again, and we
Wake up once more to joy or misery,
Or death itself, if so it pleaseth you:
Is this thing, then, so great a thing to do?"
  Thereon folk shouted, and the pipes again
Breathed through the hall a sweet heart-softening strain,
And up the hall came lovely damsels, dressed
In gowns of green, who unto every guest
Gave a rose garland, nor yet hasted they,
When this was done, to pass too quick away,   320
If here and there an eager hand still held
By gown or wrist, whom the young prince beheld
With longing eyes that roved about the hall.

Now longer did the cool grey shadows fall,
And faster drew the sun unto the west,
And in the field the husbandman, opprest
With twelve hours' labour, turned unto his home,
And to the fold the woolly sheep were come;
And in the hall the folk began to tell
Stories of men of old, who bore them well,   330
And piteous tales. And Jason in mean while
Sat listening as his uncle, with a smile,
Kept pouring many a thing into his ears,
Now worthy laughter, and now meet for tears.
Until at last, when twilight was nigh gone,
And dimly through the place the gold outshone,
He bade them bring in torches, and while folk
Blinked on the glare that through the pillars broke,
He said to Jason: "Yet have I to tell
One tale I would that these should hear as well   340
As you, O Prince." And therewith did he call
The herald, bidding him throughout the hall
Cry silence for the story of the king.

And this being done, and all men listening,
He rose and said, "O noble Minyæ,
Right prosperous and honoured may ye be;
When Athamas ruled over Thebes the great,
Upon his house there fell a heavy fate,
Making his name a mere byword; for he,
Being wedded to the noble Nephele,   350
Gat on her a bold youth and tender maid,
Phryxus and Helle; but, being nought afraid

Of what the righteous Gods might do to him,
And seeing Ino, fair of face and limb
Beyond all other, needs with her must wed,
And to that end drove from his royal bed
Unhappy Nephele, who now must be
A slave, where once she governed royally;
While white-foot Ino smiling, sat alone
By Athamas upon the ivory throne.   360

 "And now, as time went on, did Ino bear
To Athamas two children hale and fair;
Therefore, the more increased her enmity
Against those two erst born of Nephele,
Who yet, in spite of all things, day by day
Grew lovelier as their sad lives wore away;
Till Ino thought, 'What help will it have been,
That through these years I have been called a queen,
And set gold raiment on my children dear,
If Athamas should die and leave me here   370
Betwixt the people and this Nephele,
With those she bore? What then could hap to me
But death or shame? for then, no doubt, would reign
Over this mighty town the children twain;
With her who once was queen still standing near,
And whispering fell words in her darlings' ear.
And then what profit would it be that they
Have won through me full many an evil day;
That Phryxus base and servile deeds doth know,
Unmeet for lords; that many a shame and woe,   380
Helle has borne, and yet is wont to stand,
Shrinking with fear, before some dreaded hand;

If still the ending of it must be this,
That I must die while they live on in bliss,
And cherish her that first lay in my bed?
Nor is there any help till they be dead.'

"Then did she fall on many an evil thought,
And going thence, with threats and money brought
The women of the land to do this thing:
In the mid-winter, yea, before the spring   390
Was in men's minds, they took the good seed corn,
And while their husbands toiled in the dark morn,
And dreaded nought, they throughly seethed it all;
Whereby this seeming portent did befall,
That neither the sweet showers of April tide,
Nor the May sunshine, gleaming far and wide
Over the meadows, made their furrows green,
Nor yet in June was any young shoot seen.

"Then drew the country folk unto the king,
Weeping and wailing, telling of the thing,   400
And praying him to satisfy the God,
Whoe'er he was, who with this cruel rod
So smote his wretched people: whereon he
Bade all his priests inquire solemnly
What thing had moved the Gods to slay them thus?
Who, hearing all this story piteous,
Because their hands had felt Queen Ino's gold,
And itched for more, this thing in answer told:—

"That great Diana with Queen Nephele
Was wroth beyond all measure, for that she,   410
Being vowed unto the Goddess, none the less
Cast by the quiver and the girt-up dress,

To wed with Athamas, the mighty king,
Therefore must she pay forfeit for the thing,
And though she still should keep her wretched life,
Yet must she give her children to the knife,
Or else this dearth should be but happiness
To what should come, for she would so oppress
The land of Thebes, that folk who saw its name
In old records, would turn the page, and blame   420
The chronicler for telling empty lies,
And mingling fables with his histories.

  "Therefore is Athamas a wretched man
To hear this tale, and doeth what he can
To save his flesh and blood, but all in vain;
Because the people, cruel in their pain,
With angry words were thronging the great hall,
And crafty Ino at his feet did fall,
Saying, 'Oh, King, I pray for these, and me,
And for my children.' Therefore, mournfully   430
He called the priests again, and bade them say,
In few words, how his children they would slay,
And when the dreadful bearer of the bow
Would best be pleased to see their young blood flow.
Who said, 'that if the thing were quickly done,
Seeing the green things were not wholly gone,
The ruined fields might give a little food,
And that high noon-tide the next day was good.
Above all other hours, to do the thing;
And thereupon they prayed unto the king,   440
To take the younglings, lest, being fled away,
They still might live and leave an evil day

To Thebes and all its folk henceforth to bear.

    "Then men were sent, who by the river fair
Found Phryxus casting nets into the stream,
Who, seeing them coming, little harm did deem
They meant him, and with welcome bade them share
The glittering heap of fishes that lay there.
But they with laughter fell at once on him,
Who, struggling wrathfully, broke here a limb   450
And there a head, but lastly on the ground
Being felled by many men, was straightly bound,
And in an iron-bolted prison laid,
While to the house they turned to seek the maid.

    "Whom soon they found, within the weaving-room,
Bent earnestly above the rattling loom,
Working not like a king's child, but a slave
Who strives her body from the scourge to save.
On her they seized, speechless for very fear,
And dragged her trembling to the prison drear,   460
Where lay her brother, and there cast her in,
Giddy and fainting, wondering for what sin
She suffered this; but, finding Phryxus laid
In the same dismal place, the wretched maid
Bewailed with him the sorrows of their life,
Praying the Gods to show the king's new wife
What sorrow was, nor let her hair grow grey
Ere in some hopeless place her body lay.

    "Now in that court a certain beast there was,
The gift of Neptune to King Athamas,   470
A mighty ram, greater than such beasts be
In any land about the Grecian sea;

And in all else a wonder to men's eyes,
For from his shoulders did two wings arise,
That seemed as they were wrought of beaten gold,
And all his fleece was such as in no fold
The shepherd sees, for all was gold indeed.
And now this beast with dainty grass to feed,
The task of Nephele had late been made,
Who, nothing of the mighty ram afraid, 480
Would bring him flowering trefoil day by day,
And comb his fleece; and her the ram would pay
With gentle bleatings, and would lick her hand,
As in his well-built palace he did stand.
For all the place was made of polished wood,
Studded with gold; and, when he thought it good,
Within a little meadow could he go,
Throughout the midst whereof a stream did flow,
And at the corners stood great linden-trees,
Hummed over by innumerable bees. 490

"So on the morning when these twain should die,
Stole Nephele to this place quietly
And loosed the ram, and led him straight away
Unto Diana's temple, where that day
Her heart should break unless the Gods were good.
There with the ram, close in a little wood,
She hid herself a-nigh the gates, till noon
Should bring those to the Lady of the Moon
She longed to see; and as the time drew nigh,
She knelt, and with her trembling hands did tie 500
About the gold beast's neck a mystic thing,
And in his ears, meanwhile, was murmuring

Words taught her by the ever-changing God,
Who on the sands at noon is wont to nod
Beside the flock of Neptune; till at last
Upon the breeze the sound of flutes went past;
Then sore she trembled, as she held the beast
By the two golden horns, but never ceased
Her mystic rhyme; and louder, and more loud
The music sounded, till the solemn crowd   510
Along the dusty road came full in sight.
First went the minstrels, clad in raiment white,
Both men and maids garlanded daintily;
And then ten damsels, naked from the knee,
Who in their hands bare bows done round with leaves,
And arrows at their backs in goodly sheaves,
Gaudily feathered, ready for the strife;
Then came three priests, whereof one bore the knife,
One a great golden bowl to hold the blood,
And one a bundle of some sacred wood;   520
And then was left a little vacant space,
And then came gold, and therewithal the face
Of beauteous Ino, flushed and triumphing,
And by her, moody and downcast, the king.

"And now her heart beat quick and fast indeed,
Because the two came, doomed that day to bleed
Over the grey bark of the hallowed wood,
Of whom went Phryxus in most manly mood,
Looking around, with mournful, steady eyes,
Upon the green fields and the braveries,   530
And all he never thought to see again.
But Helle, as she went, could not refrain

From bitter wailing for the days gone by,
When hope was mixed with certain misery;
And, when the long day's task and fear was done,
She might take pleasure sometimes in the sun,
Whose rays she saw now glittering on the knife
That in a little time should end her life.

"Now she, who in coarse raiment had been clad
For many a year, upon her body had, 540
On this ill day, a golden pearl-wrought gown,
And on her drooping head a glittering crown,
And jewelled sandals on her fainting feet,
And on her neck and bosom jewels meet
For one who should be wedded to a king;
Thus to her death went moaning this sweet thing.

"But when they drew a-nigh the temple gate
The trembling, weeping mother, laid in wait,
Let go the mighty beast upon the throng,—
Like as a hunter holds the gazehound long, 550
Until the great buck stalks from out the herd,
And then, with well-remembered hunting word,
Slips the stout leash,—so did she slip the beast,
Who dashed aside both singing-man and priest,
And girded maiden, and the startled king,
And Ino, grown all pale to see the thing,
With rising horror in her evil heart.
And thereon Phryxus, seeing the close crowd part,
And this deliverer nigh him, with wings spread
Ready for flight, and eager threatening head, 560
Without more words, upon his broad back sprung,
And drew his sister after him, who clung

D

With trembling arms about him; and straightway
They turned unto the rising of the day,
And over all rose up into the air
With sounding wings; nor yet did any dare,
As fast they flew, to bend on them a bow,
Thinking some God had surely willed it so.

"Then went the king unto his house again,
And Ino with him, downcast that the twain   570
Had so escaped her, waiting for what fate
Should bring upon her doomed head, soon or late.

"Nor long she waited; for, one evil day,
Unto the king her glittering gold array
And rosy flesh, half seen through raiment thin,
Seemed like the many-spotted leopard's skin;
And her fair hands and feet like armèd paws
The treacherous beast across the strained throat draws
Of some poor fawn; and when he saw her go
Across the hall, her footsteps soft and slow   580
And the lithe motion of her body fair
But made him think of some beast from his lair
Stolen forth at the beginning of the night.

"Therefore with fear and anger at the sight
He shook, being maddened by some dreadful God;
And stealthily about the place he trod,
Seeking his sword; and, getting it to hand,
With flaming eyes and foaming mouth did stand
Awhile, then rushed at Ino as she stood
Trembling, with cheeks all drained of rosy blood;   590
Who straightway caught her raiment up, and fled

Adown the streets, where once she had been led
In triumph by the man whose well-known cheer
Close at her heels, now struck such deadly fear
Into her heart, the forge of many a woe.

"So, full of anguish, panting did she go
O'er rough and smooth, till field and wood were passed,
And on the border of the sea at last,
With raiment torn and unshod feet, she stood,
Reddening the flowering sea-pink with her blood. 600

"But when she saw the tireless hunter nigh,
All wild and shouting, with a dreadful cry
She stretched her arms out seaward, and sprung down
Over the cliff among the seaweed brown
And washing surf, neither did any one
See ought of her again beneath the sun.

"But Athamas, being come to where she stood,
Stared vacantly awhile upon the blood,
Then, looking seaward, drew across his eyes
His fevered hand; and thronging memories 610
Came thick upon him, until dreamily
He turned his back upon the hungry sea,
And cast his sword down; and so, weaponless,
Went back, half-waking to his sore distress.

"As for the twain,—perched on that dizzy height,
The white-walled city faded from their sight,
And many another place that well they knew;
And over woods and meadows still they flew;
And to the husbandmen seemed like a flame
Blown 'twixt the earth and the sky; until they came

Unto the borders of the murmuring sea.
Nor stayed they yet, but flew unceasingly,
Till, looking back, seemed Pelion like a cloud;
And they beheld the white-topped billows crowd
Unto the eastward, 'neath the following wind.
 "And there a wretched end did Helle find
Unto her life; for when she did behold,
So far beneath, the deep green sea and cold,
She shut her eyes for horror of the sight,
Turning the sunny day to murk midnight,
Through which there floated many an awful thing,
Made vocal by the ceaseless murmuring
Beneath her feet; till a great gust of wind [blind,
Caught the beast's wings and swayed him round; then,
Dizzy, and fainting, did she grow too weak
To hold her place, though still her hands did seek
Some stay by catching at the locks of gold;
And as she fell her brother strove to hold
Her jewelled girdle, but the treacherous zone
Broke in his hand, and he was left alone
Upon the ram, that, as a senseless thing,
Still flew on toward the east, no whit heeding
His shouts and cries; but Helle, as she fell
Down through the depths, the sea-folk guarded well,
And kept her body dead, from scar or wound,
And laid it, in her golden robes enwound,
Upon the south side of the murmuring strait,
That still, in memory of her piteous fate,
Bears her sweet name; her, in a little while,
The country folk beheld, and raised a pile

Of beech and oak, with scented things around,
And, lifting up the poor corpse from the ground,
Laid it thereon, and there did everything,
As for the daughter of a mighty king.

"But through the straits passed Phryxus, sad enow,
And fearful of the wind that by his brow
Went shrieking, as, without all stop or stay,
The golden wings still bore him on his way
Above the unlucky waves of that ill sea
That foamed beneath his feet unceasingly.   660
Nor knew he to what land he was being borne,
Whether he should be set, unarmed, forlorn,
In darksome lands, among unheard-of things,
Or, stepping off from 'twixt the golden wings,
Should set foot in some happy summer isle,
Whereon the kind unburning sun doth smile
For ever, and that knows no frost or drought;
Or else, it seemed to him, he might be brought
Unto green forests where the wood-nymphs play
With their wild mates, and fear no coming day.   670
And there might he forget both crown and sword,
And e'en the names of slave, and king, and lord,
And lead a merry life, till all was done,
And 'mid the green boughs, marked by no carved stone,
His unremembered bones should waste away,
In dew, and rain, and sunshine, day by day.

"So, 'mid these thoughts, still clinging fearfully
Unto his dizzy seat, he passed the sea,

And reached a river opening into it,
Across the which the white-winged fowl did flit 680
From cliff to cliff, and on the sandy bar
The fresh waves and the salt waves were at war,
At turning of the tide. Forth flew they then,
Till they drew nigh a strange abode of men,
Far up the river, white-walled, fair, and great,
And at each end of it a brazen gate,
Wide open through the daylight, guarded well,
And nothing of its name could Phryxus tell,
But hoped the beast would stop, for to his eyes
The place seemed fair; nor fell it otherwise. 690
There stayed the ram his course, and lighted down
Anigh the western gate of that fair town,
And on the hard way Phryxus joyfully
Set foot, full dizzy with the murmuring sea,
Numbed by the cold wind; and, with little fear,
Unto the guarded gate he drew anear,
While the gold beast went ever after him.

"But they, beholding him so strong of limb,
And fair of face, and seeing the beast that trod
Behind his back, deemed him some wandering God,
So let the two-edged sword hang by the side, 701
And by the wall the well-steeled spear abide.

"But he called out to them, 'What place is this?
And who rules over you for woe or bliss?
And will he grant me peace to-day or war?
And may I here abide, or still afar
Must I to new abodes go wandering?'

"Now as he spake those words, that city's king

Adown the street was drawing toward the gate,
Clad in gold raiment worthy his estate, 710
Therefore one said: 'Behold, our king is here,
Who of all us is held both lief and dear;
Æetes, leader of a mighty host,
Feared by all folk along the windy coast.
And since this city's name thou fain wouldst know,
Men call it Æa, built long years ago,
Holpen of many Gods, who love it well.
Now come thou to the king, and straightway tell
Thy name and country, if thou art a man,
And how thou camest o'er the water wan, 720
And what the marvel is thou hast with thee;
But if thou art a God, then here will we
Build thee a house, and, reverencing thy name,
Bring thee great gifts and much-desired fame.'

"Thus spake he, fearful; but by this the king
Had reached the place, and stood there wondering
At that strange beast and fair man richly clad,
Who at his belt no sort of weapon had;
Then spoke he: 'Who art thou, in what strange wain
Hast thou crossed o'er the green and restless plain 730
Unharvested of any? And this thing,
That like an image stands with folded wing,
Is he a gift to thee from any God,
Or hast thou in some unknown country trod,
Where beasts are such-like? Howsoe'er it be,
Here shalt thou dwell, if so thou wilt, with me,
Unless some God is chasing thee, and then,
What wouldst thou have us do, who are but men,

Against the might of Gods?'
                        Then answered he:
'O king, I think no God is wrath with me,   740
But rather some one loves me; for, behold,
A while ago, just as my foe did hold
A knife against my throat, there came this ram,
Who brought me to the place where now I am
Safe from the sea and from the bitter knife.
And in this city would I spend my life,
And do what service seemeth good to thee,
Since all the Gods it pleases I should be
Outcast from friends and country, though alive;
Nor with their will have I the heart to strive   750
More than thou hast; and now as in such wise
I have been saved, fain would I sacrifice
This beast to Jove, the helper of all such,
As false friends fail, or foes oppress too much.'
  "'Yea,' said Æetes, 'so the thing shall be
In whatsoever fashion pleaseth thee;
And long time mayst thou dwell with us in bliss,
Not doing any service worse than this,
To bear in war my royal banner forth,
When fall the wild folk on us from the north.   760
Come now this eve, and hold high feast with us,
And tell us all of strange and piteous
Thy story hath.'
                        So went he with the king,
And gladly told unto him everything
That had befallen him, and in a grove,
Upon the altar of the Saving Jove,

They offered up the ram the morrow morn
That thitherward the Theban prince had born.

"And thenceforth Phryxus dwelt in Colchis long
In wealth and honour, and, being brave and strong, 770
Won great renown in many a bloody fray,
And still grew greater; and both night and day,
Within his pillared house, upon the wall
Hung the gold fell; until it did befall
That in Æetes' heart a longing grew
To have the thing, yea, even if he slew
His guest to get it; so, one evil night,
While the prince lay and dreamed about the fight,
With all armed men was every entry filled,
And quickly were the few doorkeepers killed; 780
And Phryxus, roused with clamour from his bed,
Half-armed and dizzy, with few strokes was dead.
And thus the King Æetes had his will,
And thus the GOLDEN FLEECE he keepeth still
Somewhere within his royal house of gold.

"And thus, O Minyæ, is the story told
Of things that happened forty years agone;
Nor of the Greeks has there been any one
To set the Theban's bones within a tomb,
Or to Æetes mete out his due doom; 790
And yet, indeed, it seemeth unto me
That many a man would go right willingly,
And win great thanks of men and godlike fame,
If there should spring up some great prince of name
To lead them; and I pray that such an one,

Before my head is laid beneath a stone,
Be sent unto us by the Gods above."

   Therewith he ceased; but all the hall did move
As moves a grove of rustling poplar trees
Bowed all together by the shifting breeze,   800
And through the place the name of Jason ran,
Nor, 'mid the feasters, was there any man
But toward the hero's gold-seat turned his eyes.
   Meanwhile, in Jason's heart did thoughts arise
That brought the treacherous blood into his cheek,
And he forgot his father, old and weak,
Left 'twixt the fickle people of the land
And wily Pelias, while he clenched his hand,
As though it held a sword, about his cup.
   Then, 'mid the murmuring, Pelias stood up   810
And said: "O, leaders of the Minyæ,
I hear ye name a name right dear to me—
My brother's son, who in the oaken wood
Has grown up nurtured of the Centaur good,
And now this day has come again to us,
Fair faced and mighty limbed, and amorous
Of fame and glorious deeds; nowise content
Betwixt the forest and the northern bent
To follow up the antlers of the deer,
Nor in his eyes can I see any fear   820
Of fire, or water, or the cleaving sword.
   "**Now**, therefore, if ye take him for your lord
Across the sea, most surely will ye get
Both fame and wealth, nor will men soon forget

To praise the noble city whence ye came,
Passing from age to age each hero's name."

  Then all stood up and shouted, and the king,
While yet the hall with Jason's name did ring,
Set in his hands a gleaming cup of gold,
And said: "O Jason, wilt thou well behold   830
These leaders of the people, who are fain
To go with thee and suffer many a pain
And deadly fear, if they may win at last
Undying fame when fleeting life is past?
And now, if thou art willing to be first
Of all these men, of whom, indeed, the worst
Is like a God, pour out this gleaming wine
To him with whose light all the heavens shine,
Almighty Jove."
                Then Jason poured, and said:
"O Jove, by thy hand may all these be led   840
To name and wealth! and yet, indeed, for me,
What happy ending shall I ask from thee?
What helpful friends? what length of quiet years?
What freedom from ill care and deadly fears?
Do what thou wilt, but none the less believe
That all these things and more thou shouldst receive,
If thou wert Jason, I were Jove to-day.

  "And ye who now are hot to play this play,
Seeking the fleece across an unknown sea,
Bethink ye yet of death, and misery,   850
And dull despair, before ye arm to go
Unto a savage king and folk none know,
Whence it may well hap none of ye to come

Again unto your little ones and home.
　"And do thou, Pelias, ere we get us forth,
Send heralds out, east, west, and south, and north,
And with them cunning men, of golden speech,
Thy tale unto the Grecian folk to teach;
That we may lack for neither strength nor wit,
For many a brave man like a fool will sit　　860
Beside the council board; and men there are
Wise-hearted who know little feats of war;
Nor would I be without the strength of spears,
Or waste wise words on dull and foolish ears.
　"Also we need a cunning artizan,
Taught by the Gods, and knowing more than man,
To build us a good ship upon this shore.
Then, if but ten lay hold upon the oar,
And I, the eleventh, steer them toward the east,
To seek the hidden fleece of that gold beast,　　870
I swear to Jove that only in my hand
The fleece shall be, when I again take land
To see my father's hall, or the green grass
O'er which the grey Thessalian horses pass.
　"But now, O friends, forget all till the morn
With other thoughts and fears is duly born!"

　He ceased, and all men shouted; and again
They filled their cups, and many a draught did drain.
But Pelias gazed with heedful eyes at him,
Nor drank the wine that well-nigh touched the brim　880
Of his gold cup; and, noting every word,
Thought well that he should be a mighty lord,

For now already like a king he spoke,
Gazing upon the wild tumultuous folk
As one who knows what troubles are to come,
And in this world looks for no peaceful home,—
So much he dreaded what the Gods might do.

  But Æson, when he first heard Pelias, knew
What wile was stirring, and he sat afeard,
With sinking heart, as all the tale he heard;   890
But after, hearkening what his son did say,
He deemed a God spoke through him on that day,
And held his peace; yet to himself he said:
"And if he wins all, still shall I be dead
Ere on the shore he stands beside the fleece,
The greatest and most honoured man in Greece."

  But Jason, much rejoicing in his life,
Drank and was merry, longing for the strife;
Though in his heart he did not fail to see
His uncle's cunning wiles and treachery;   900
But thought, when sixty years are gone, at most,
Then will all pleasure and all pain be lost;
Although my name, indeed, be cast about
From hall to temple, amid song and shout:
So let me now be merry with the best.

  Meanwhile, all men spoke hotly of the quest,
And healths they drank to many an honoured man,
Until the moon sank, and the stars waxed wan,
And from the east faint yellow light outshone
O'er the Greek sea, so many years agone.

BOOK III.

The Argonauts called together.

NOW the next morn, when risen was the sun,
    Men 'gan to busk them for the quest begun;
Nor long delay made Pelias, being in fear
Lest ought should stay them; so his folk did bear
News of these things throughout the towns of Greece,
Moving great men to seek the golden fleece.
    Therefore, from many a lordship forth they rode,
Leaving both wife and child and loved abode,
And many a town must now be masterless,
And women's voices rule both more and less,   10
And women's hands be dreaded, far and wide,
This fair beginning of the summer-tide.

    Now, all the folk who went upon this quest
I cannot name, but fain would hope the best
In men's remembrance ancient tales did keep
Unto our time, letting the others sleep
In nameless graves—though, mayhap, one by one,
These grew to be forgotten 'neath the sun,
Being neither poor of heart, or weak of wit,
More than those others whose crowned memories sit   20
Enthroned amid the echoing minstrelsy
Sung of old time beside the Grecian sea.

Howe'er it be, now clinging to the hem
Of those old singers, will I tell of them,
In weak and faltering voice, e'en as I can.

Now was the well-skilled Argus the first man
Who through the gates into Iolchos passed,
Whose lot in fertile Egypt first was cast,
The nurse of Gods and wonder-working men;
His father's name was Danaus, who till then 30
Had held the golden rod above the Nile,
Feared by all men for force and deadly wile.

So he, being brought to Jason, said: "O King,
Me have the Gods sent here to do the thing
Ye need the most; for truly have I seen,
'Twixt sleep and waking, one clad like a queen,
About whose head strange light shone gloriously,
Stand at my bed's foot, and she said to me:
'**Argus,** arise, when dawn is on the earth,
And go unto a city great of girth 40
Men call Iolchos, and there ask for one
Who now gets ready a great race to run
Upon a steed whose maker thou shalt be,
And whose course is the bitter trackless sea,—
Jason, the king's son, now himself a king;—
And bid him hearken, by this tokening,
That I, who send thee to him, am the same
Who in the greenwood bade him look for fame
That he desired little; and am she
Who, when the eddies rushed tumultuously 50
About us, bore him to the river side:—

And unto thee shall such-like things betide.'
"Therewith she told me many a crafty thing
About this keel that ye are now lacking,
Bidding me take thee for my king and lord,
And thee to heed my counsel as her word
As for this thing. So if ye would set forth
Before the winter takes us from the north,
I pray you let there be at my commands
Such men as are most skilful of their hands,   60
Nor spare to take lintel, rooftree, or post
Of ash or pine, or oak that helpeth most,
From whoso in this city lacketh gold;
And chiefly take the post that now doth hold
The second rafter in the royal hall,
That I may make the good ship's prow withal,
For soothly from Dodona doth it come,
Though men forget it, the grey pigeons' home.
"So look to see a marvel, and forthright
Set on the smiths the sounding brass to smite,   70
For surely shall all ye your armour need
Before these close flower-buds have turned to seed."
Then Jason gave him thanks and gifts enow,
And through the town sought all who chanced to know
The woodwright's craft, by whom was much begun,
Whilst he took gifts of wood from many an one,
And getting timber with great gifts of gold,
Spared not to take the great post used to hold
The second rafter in the royal hall
To make the new ship's goodly prow withal   80
So Argus laboured, and the work was sped

Moreover, by a man with hoary head,
Whose dwelling and whose name no man could know,
Who many a secret of the craft did show,
And 'mid their work men gazed at him askance,
Half fearful of his reverend piercing glance,
But did his bidding; yet knew not, indeed,
It was the Queen of Heaven, Saturn's seed.

  Meanwhile came many heroes to the town :—
Asterion, dweller on the windy down   90
Below Philæus, far up in the north;
Slow-footed Polyphemus, late borne forth
In chariot from Larissa, that beholds
Green-winding Peneus cleaving fertile wolds;
Erginus, son of Neptune, nigh the sea
His father set him, where the laden bee
Flies low across Mæander, and falls down
Against the white walls of a merchant town
Men call Miletus.   Behind him there came
The winner of a great and dreaded name,   100
Theseus, the slayer of the fearful beast,
Who soon in winding halls should make his feast
On youths and maidens; and with him there rode
The king Pirithous, who his loved abode
Amid the shady trees had left that tide
Where fly the centaurs' arrows far and wide.
  Black-haired was Theseus, slim, and still his cheek
Lacked all but down, for yet he had to seek
The twisted ways of Dædalus the old;

But long and twining locks of ruddy gold 110
Blew round the face of the huge forest king,
As carelessly he rode and feared no thing.

   Great joy had Jason, gazing on the twain,
Young though they were, and thought that not in vain
His quest should be, if such as these had will
The hollow of his great black ship to fill.

   Next, threading Argive ways and woody lanes,
Came Nauplius, son of Neptune, to those plains,
Crossing Anaurus dryshod, for his sire
With threats and blows drove up the land-stream higher, 120
And sucked the sea-waves back across the sands;
With him came Idmon, mighty of his hands,
But mightier that he was skilled to know
The council of the God who bears the bow,
His very father, who bore not to see
Unloved, Cyrene wandering carelessly
Beside Peneus; Iolaus came
From Argos, too, to win a deathless name;
And if thenceforth came any heroes more
I know not, and their names have died of yore. 130

   But from Arcadian forests came forth one
Who like a goddess 'mid the rowers shone,
Swift-running Atalanta, golden-haired,
Grey-eyed, and simple; with her white limbs bared,
And sandalled feet set firm upon the sand,
Amid the wondering heroes did she stand
A very maid, yet fearing not for aught;
For she, with many a vow, had dearly bought

Diana's love, and in no flowery stead
Had borne to hear love-songs, or laid her head   140
On any trembling lover's heaving breast;
Therefore of mortals was she loved the best
By Her, who through the forest goes a-nights,
And, in return for never-tried delights,
Has won a name no woman else can have.

  Next through the gates his car Oileus drave,
The Locrian king, red-haired, with fierce grey eyes
Wandering from right to left, as though some prize
He sought for in the rich Thessalian land;
Then Iphiclus beside the gates did stand,   150
His kine at all adventure left at home,
That on a doubtful voyage he might roam.

  Admetus from the well-walled Pheræ came,
Longing to add new glory to the fame
Of him whose flocks Apollo once did keep,
And then Echion, who would nowise sleep
Amid Ephesian roses, or behold
Betwixt gold cups and lovely things of gold
The white limbs of the dancing-girl, her hair
Swung round her dainty loins and bosom bare;   160
But needs must try the hollow-sounding sea,
As herald of the heroes, nor was he
Left by his brother Eurytus the strong.

  Neither did Cæneus, the Magnesian, long
Less than the others strange new lands to see,
Though wondrous things were told of him,—that he,
Once woman, now was man by Neptune's aid,
And thus had won a long-desired maid.

    From nigh Larissa came Ætalides,
Leaving a plain well-watered, set with trees,   170
That feeds much woolly sheep and lowing neat
And knoweth well the dancing maiden's feet.
Mopsus, like Idmon, knew of things to come,
And had in Lipara a rocky home.
Eurydamas, tired of the peaceful lake
Of Xynias, was come for Jason's sake
To lay his well-skilled hands upon the oar,
Dealing with greater waves than heretofore.
    Menœtius, son of Actor, from the land
Where swift Asopus runs through stones and sand, 180
Bridged by the street of Opus, next was seen.
Eribotes, who through the meadows green
Would wander oft to seek what helpeth man,
Yet cannot cure his lust, through waters wan
To seek for marvels, cometh after him.
Then a rich man, grown old, but strong of limb,
Eurytion, son of Iras, leaveth now
His husbandmen still following of the plough
In the fat Theban meadows, while he goes,
Driven by fate, to suffer biting woes.   190
    From Œchalia, Clytius the king,
And Iphitus his brother, felt the sting
That drives great men through woes to seek renown,
And left their guarded city, looking down
From rocky heights on the well-watered plain.
Right wise they were, and men say, not in vain
Before Apollo's court they claimed to be
The first who strung the fatal cornel tree,

And loosed the twanging bowstring from the ear.
   Then to the gate a chariot drew a-near,   200
Wherein two brothers sat, whereof the one
Who held the reins was mighty Telamon;
And Peleus was the other's dreaded name.
And from an island both the heroes came,
Sunny Ægina, where their father's hand
Ruled o'er the people of a fruitful land;
But they now young, rejoicing in their birth,
Dreamed not that, ere they lay beneath the earth,
Still greater heroes from their loins should come,
The doomsmen of the Trojan's godlike home.   210
   Fair Athens, and the olive groves thereby,
Phalerus left, riding through deserts dry
And rocky passes where no sweet birds sing;
And with him Butes, with the owlet's wing
Well-painted on his shield; and he, at least,
Came back no more to share the joyous feast
And pour out wine for well accomplished days,
Who, all besotted with the Syren's lays,
Must leave his mates; nor happier than he,
Tiphys the pilot came, although the sea   220
Dealt gently with the ship whose ashen helm
His hand touched; in the rich Bœotian realm
He left outlandish merceries stored up
With many a brazen bowl and silver cup
His heirs should feast from in the days to come,
When men he knew not, went about his home.
   Next Phlias came, forgetful of the hill
That bears his name, where oft the maidens fill

Their baskets with the coal-black clustering grapes,
Far on in autumn, when the parched earth gapes 230
For cool November rain and winter snow,
For there his house stood, on the shaded brow
Of that fair ridge that Bacchus loves so well.

  Then through the gates one with a lion's fell
Hung o'er his shoulders, on a huge grey steed
Came riding, with his fair Phœnician weed
Glittering from underneath the tawny hair,
Who loosely in his dreadful hand did bear
A club of unknown wood bound round with brass,
And underneath his curled black hair did pass 240
A golden circlet o'erwrought cunningly
With running beasts; so folk knew this was he
That in Amphytrion's palace first saw light,
And whose first hour began with deadly fight,
Alcmena's son, the dreadful Hercules;
The man whose shout the close Nemean trees
Had stifled, and the lion met in vain;
The ravisher of hell, the serpent's bane,
Whom neither Gods nor fate could overwhelm.

  Now was he come to this Thessalian realm 250
To serve with Jason on the wandering seas,
Half seeking fame, half wishing to appease
The wrath of her who gru 'ged him ease and rest,
Yet needs must see him of all men the best.
Laughing he went, and with him on each hand
There rode a squire from the Theban land;
Hylas was first, whose sire, Theodamas,
Had given him worthy gifts of gold and brass,

And gold-wrought arms, that he should see no more
Glittering along the green Ismenian shore.   260
With him Ephebus came, who many a year
Had backed the steed and cast the quivering spear
In Theban meadows, but whose fathers came
From Argos, and thereby had left their name.
  So through the streets like Gods they rode, but he
Who rode the midmost of the glorious three
O'ertopped them by a head; and looking down
With smiling face, whereon it seemed no frown
Could ever come, showed like the king of all.

  Now coming to the palace, by the wall   270
Sat Jason, watching while an armourer wrought
A golden crest according to his thought;
And round about the heroes were at play,
Casting the quoit; but on the well-paved way,
With clanging arms, leapt down Alcmena's son
Before the prince, and said: " I who have won
Some small renown, O Jason, in this land,
Come now to put my hand within your hand
And be your man, if wide report says true,
That even now with cinnabar and blue   280
Men paint your long ship's prow, and shave the oars
With sharpened planes; for soothly, other shores
I fain would see than this fair Grecian one,
Wherein great deeds already I have done:
And if thou willest now to hear my name,
A Theban queen my mother once became,
And had great honour; wherefore some men say

That in Amphytrion's bed my mother lay
When I was gotten; and yet other some
Say that a God upon that night did come   290
(Whose name I speak not), like unto the king,
With whom Alcmena played, but nought witting.

"Nor I, nor others know the certainty
Of all these things; but certes, royally
My brother rules at Thebes, whom all men call
Amphytrion's son, in whose well-peopled hall,
Right little loved of him and his, I eat,
Nor does he grieve to see my empty seat,
Though, since my name is Hercules, the man
Who owes me hatred hides it if he can.   300

"And now, O prince, I bid thee take my hand,
And hear me swear that till unto this land
Thou hast borne back the fleece across the sea,
Thy liege-man and thy servant I will be.
Nor have I seen a man more like a king
Than thou art, of whom minstrel folk shall sing
In days to come when men sit by the wine."

Then Jason said: "A happy lot is mine!
Surely the Gods must love me, since that thou
Art come, with me the rough green plain to plough
That no man reaps; yet certes, thou alone   311
In after days shalt be the glorious one
Whom men shall sing of when they name the fleece
That bore the son of Athamas from Greece,
When I and all these men have come to nought."

So spake he; but the great-eyed Juno brought
His words to nothing, stooping to behold

Jason's fair head, whereon the locks of gold
Curled thick and close, and his grey eager eyes,
That seemed already to behold the prize 320
In far-off Colchis: like a God he stood,
No less than he that in the darksome wood
Slew the lake-haunting, many-headed beast.

But on that day the Minyæ held a feast,
Praising the Gods, and those that they had sent
Across the sea to work out their intent.

Yea, ere the night, greater their joyance grew,
For to the throng of heroes came there two,
In nowise worse than any of the best,—
Castor and Pollux, who thought not to rest 330
In woody Lacedæmon, where the doves
Make summer music in the beechen groves,
But rather chose to hear the sea-fowl sing.
Their mother wedded Tyndarus the king.
And yet a greater name their father had,
As men deem; for that Leda, all unclad,
In cold Eurotas, on a summer morn,
Bathed her fair body, unto whom was borne,
Fleeing from seeming death, a milk-white swan,
Whom straight the naked queen, not fearing man, 340
Took in her arms, nor knew she fostered Jove,
Who rules o'er mortal men and Gods above.
So in the hall of Pelias, in their place
The twain sat down; and joy lit every face,
When both their names the sweet-voiced herald cried.

But the next morn into the town did ride
Lynceus and Idas, leaving far away
Well-walled Messene where the kestrels play
About the temples and the treasure-house.
But of these twain was Idas valorous 350
Beyond most men, and hasty of his blow;
And unto Lynceus would the darkness show
That which he lacked; and of all men was he
The luckiest to find the privity
Of gold or gems. And on the self-same day
Came Periclymenes, who folk did say
Had Proteus' gift to change from shape to shape.
 Next from Tegea, where the long green grape
Grows yellow in the dewy autumn night,
There came Ancæus, stubborn in the fight. 360
 Amphidamus and Apheus left the trees
Where sing the wood-doves to their mistresses
In the Arcadian forests; and where oft,
If through the springing brake he treadeth soft,
The happy hunter may well chance to see
Beside a hidden stream some two or three
Of tired nymphs, stripping the silken weed
From off their limbs; nor shall Acteon's meed
Betide him there among the oaken trees.
 Next came there Augeas, who at Elis sees 370
On his fat plains the sheep, and kine, and beeves,
Unnumbered as the rustling aspen leaves
Beside the river: from the grassy plain
Anigh Pellene, where the harvest wain
Scatters the grazing sheep, Amphion came,

In nowise skilled like him who bore his name,
The deathless singer, but right wise in war.
Then through the town there passed a brazen car
Bearing Euphemus, who had power to go
Dryshod across the plain no man doth sow.   380
By Tenarus he dwelt, beside the sea,
Anigh the temple of the deity
Whose son he was, the Shaker of the earth.

   Then came a fresh Ancæus, who had birth
In woody Samos, of the self-same sire
Whose heart white-footed Alta set on fire,
As on the yellow sands at dawn she went.

   Then Calydon the great a hero sent,
The fair-haired Meleager, who became,
In after-days, the glory of his name,   390
The greatest name of the Ætolian land;
While yet on him fate laid her heavy hand,
In midst of all his glory so raised up,
Who nowise now dreaded the proffered cup
Of life and death she held for him to drain,
Nor thought of death and wishes wished in vain.
With him his uncle rode, Laocoon,
No longer young, teaching his brother's son
What 'longed to ruling men and unto war.

   From Lacedæmon, Iphiclus afar   400
Had travelled, till the rich embroidered weed
His father Thestius gave him at his need
Was stained with sun and dust, but still he came
To try the sea and win undying fame.

   Then came a man long-limbed, in savage weed,

Arcas the hunter, to whose unmatched speed
All beasts that wander through the woods are slow.
In his right hand he bare the fatal bow
Of horn, and wood, and brass, but now unstrung,
And at his back a well-closed quiver hung,   410
Done round with silver bands and leopard's skin,
And fifty deaths were hidden well therein
Of men or beasts; for whoso stood before
His bended bow and angry eyes, no more
Should see the green trees and the fertile earth.

 Then came two brothers of a wondrous birth,
Zetes and Calaïs, sons of Boreas;
For he beheld Erechtheus' daughter pass
Along Ilissus, one bright windy day,
Whom from amidst her maids he bore away   420
Unto the hills of Thrace to be his bride.
Now unto them this marvel did betide,
Like men in all else, from anigh the head
Of each sprung wings, wherewith at will they sped
From land to land, 'midst of the pathless air.

 Next from Magnesia did roan horses bear
Phocus and Priasus, well skilled to cast
The whistling dart; then o'er the drawbridge passed
Ætolian Palæmonius, who not yet
Had seen men armed in anger, or steel wet   430
With blood of aught but beasts, but none the less
Was willing now to stand among the press
Of god-like men, who, with the Minyæ,
Were armed to bring the fleece across the sea.

 Then came Asclepius, whom the far-darter

Saved living from the lifeless corpse of her
He **once loved** well, but slew for treason done,
Fair-haired Coronis, whose far-seeing son
He honoured much, and taught so many a thing,
That first he knew how man may ease the sting   440
Of sickening pain, because all herbs he knew,
And what the best and worst of them could do.
So many a bitter fight with death he had,
And made the heart of many a sick man glad,
And gave new life to many a man who seemed
But dead already, wherefore people deemed
When he was dead that he was God indeed,
And on his altars many a beast did bleed.

   Acastus, Pelias' son, from wandering
Was come that self-same day unto the king,   450
And needs must go with Jason on his quest,
Careless **of** princely ease and golden rest.

   Next Neleus, growing grey, forgetting not
The double crime, had left the pleasant spot
Where wan Alpheus meets the green sea waves,
And twice a-day the walls of Pylos laves;
For he was fain to expiate the sin
Pelias shared with him, long years past within
Queen **Juno's** temple, where the brothers slew
The **old Sidero**, crying out, who knew   460
Then **first the** bitterness of such a cry
As broke from Tyro in her agony
When helpless, **bound, within the brazen** hall,
She felt unthought-of torment on her **fall,**

With none to pity her, nor knew what end
The Gods unto such misery would send.
So might Sidero feel, when fell on her
Unlooked-for death and deadly, hopeless fear;
And in their turn must Neleus o'er the sea
Go wandering now, and Pelias must be   470
A trembling liar till death seizes him.

   But now with Neleus, young but strong of limb,
His wise, far-seeing offspring, Nestor, went,
With eyes a little downward ever bent,
Thinking of this and that which he had seen;
Who, when his youth was flourishing and green,
Saw many feats of arms and ways of men,
Yet lived so long to be well honoured, when
In Troy the old the princes shared the spoil.

   Next came Laertes to share grief and toil   480
With these upon the sea; yet had he not
An easy land in Ithaca the hot,
Though Bacchus loves the ledges of the land,
And weighs the peasant in his sunburnt hand
The heavy oozing bunches, in the time
When frosts draw nigh in the rough northern clime.

   Next whom came Almenus, of nought afraid,
Well armed and hardy, whom a mortal maid
Bore unto Mars, for he, new-come from Thrace,
Beside Enipeus met her, and in chase   490
He held her long, who vainly fled from him,
Though light of foot she was, and strong of limb.

   And last of all, Orpheus the singer came,

The son of King Œager, great of fame,
Yet happier by much in this, that he
Was **loved** by heavenly Calliope,
Who bore him Orpheus **on a happy day.**
And now, through many a rough and toilsome way,
Hither he came the Minyæ to please,
And make them masters of the threatening seas,   500
Cheering their hearts, and making **their hands strong**
With **the** unlooked-for sweetness of his song.
 Now was it eve by then that Orpheus came
Into **the hall,** and when they heard his name,
And toward the high-seat of the prince he drew,
All men beholding him the singer knew,
And glad were all men there that he should be
Their mate upon the bitter, tuneless sea.
And loud they shouted, but Prince Jason said :—
"**Now, may the Gods** bring good things on thy head,
Son of Œager, but from me, indeed,   511
This gold Dædalian bowl shall be thy meed,
If thou wilt let us hear thy voice take wing
From out thine heart, and see the golden string
Quiver beneath thy fingers. But by me
First sit and feast, and happy **mayst thou be.**"
 Then, glad **at** heart, the hero took his place,
And ate and drank his **fill,** but when the space
Was cleared **of flesh and** bread, he took his lyre
And sung them of the building up of Tyre,   520
And of the fair things stored up over sea,

Till there was none of them but fain would be
Set in the ship, nor cared one man to stay
On the green earth for one more idle day.

    But Jason, looking right and left on them,
Took his fair cloak, wrought with a golden hem,
And laid it upon Orpheus, and thereto
Added the promised bowl, that all men knew
No hand but that of Dædalus had wrought,
So rich it was, and fair beyond all thought.   530
Then did he say unto the Minyæ:—
" Fair friends and well-loved guests, no more shall ye
Feast in this hall until we come again
Back to this land, well-guerdoned for our pain,
Bearing the fleece, and mayhap many a thing
Such as this god-like guest erewhile did sing,
Scarlet, and gold, and brass ; but without fail
Bearing great fame, if ought that may avail
To men who die; and our names certainly
Shall never perish, wheresoe'er we lie.   540

    " And now behold within the haven rides
Our good ship, swinging in the changing tides,
Gleaming with gold, and blue, and cinnabar,
The long new oars beside the rowlocks are,
The sail hangs flapping in the light west wind,
Nor ought undone can any craftsman find
From stem to stern ; so is our quest begun
To-morrow at the rising of the sun.
And may Jove bring us all safe back to see
Another sun shine on this fair city,   550

When **elders** and the flower-crowned maidens meet
With **tears** and singing our returning feet."

So spake he, and so mighty **was** the shout,
That the hall shook, and shepherd-folk without
The well-walled city heard it as they went
Unto the fold across the thymy bent.

BOOK IV.

The quest begun—The loss of Hylas and Hercules.

BUT through the town few eyes were sealed by sleep
When the sun rose; yea, and the upland sheep
Must guard themselves for that one morn at least,
Against the wolf; and wary doves may feast
Unscared that morning on the ripening corn.
Nor did the whetstone touch the scythe that morn;
And all unheeded did the mackerel shoal
Make green the blue waves, or the porpoise roll
Through changing hills and valleys of the sea.
   For 'twixt the thronging people solemnly   10
The heroes went afoot along the way
That led unto the haven of the bay,
And as they went the roses rained on them
From windows glorious with the well-wrought hem
Of many a purple cloth; and all their spears
Were twined with flowers that the fair earth bears;

F

And round their ladies' tokens were there set
About their helmets, flowery wreaths, still wet
With beaded dew of the scarce vanished night.

 So as they passed, the young men at the sight   20
Shouted for joy, and their hearts swelled with pride;
But scarce the elders could behold dry-eyed
The glorious show, remembering well the days
When they were able too to win them praise,
And in their hearts was hope of days to come.

 Nor could the heroes leave their fathers' home
Unwept of damsels, who henceforth must hold
The empty air unto their bosoms cold,
And make their sweet complainings to the night
That heedeth not soft eyes and bosoms white.   30
And many such an one was there that morn,
Who, with lips parted and grey eyes forlorn,
Stood by the window and forgot to cast
Her gathered flowers as the heroes passed,
But held them still within her garment's hem,
Though many a wingèd wish she sent to them.

 But on they went, and as the way they trod,
His swelling heart nigh made each man a god;
While clashed their armour to the minstrelsy
That went before them to the doubtful sea.   40

  And now, the streets being passed, they reached
   the bay,
Where by the well-built quay long Argo lay,
Glorious with gold, and shining in the sun.
Then first they shouted, and each man begun
Against his shield to strike his brazen spear;

And as along the quays they drew a-near,
Faster they strode and faster, till a cry
Again burst from them, and right eagerly
Into swift running did they break at last,
Till all the wind-swept quay being overpast, 50
They pressed across the gangway, and filled up
The hollow ship as wine a golden cup.

But Jason, standing by the helmsman's side
High on the poop, lift up his voice and cried:—
"Look landward, heroes, once, before ye slip
The tough well-twisted hawser from the ship,
And set your eager hands to rope or oar;
For now, behold, the king stands on the shore
Beside a new-built altar, while the priests
Lead up a hecatomb of spotless beasts, 60
White bulls and coal-black horses, and my sire
Lifts up the barley-cake above the fire;
And in his hand a cup of ruddy gold
King Pelias takes; and now may ye behold
The broad new-risen sun light up the God,
Who, holding in his hand the crystal rod
That rules the sea, stands by Dædalian art
Above his temple, set right far apart
From other houses, nigh the deep green sea.

"And now, O fellows, from no man but me 70
These gifts come to the God, that, ere long years
Have drowned our laughter and dried up our tears,
We may behold that glimmering brazen God
Against the sun bear up his crystal rod

Once more, and once more cast upon this land
This cable, severed by my bloodless brand."

 So spake he, and raised up the glittering steel,
That fell, and seaward straight did Argo reel,
Set free, and smitten by the western breeze,
And raised herself against the ridgy seas,   80
With golden eyes turned toward the Colchian land,
Still heedful of wise Tiphys' skilful hand.
 But silent sat the heroes by the oar,
Hearkening the sounds borne from the lessening shore;
The lowing of the doomed and flower-crowned beasts,
The plaintive singing of the ancient priests,
Mingled with blare of trumpets, and the sound
Of all the many folk that stood around
The altar and the temple by the sea.
So sat they pondering much and silently,   90
Till all the landward noises died away,
And, midmost now of the green sunny bay,
They heard no sound but washing of the seas
And piping of the following western breeze,
And heavy measured beating of the oars :
So left the Argo the Thessalian shores.

 Now Neptune, joyful of the sacrifice
Beside the sea, and all the gifts of price
That Jason gave him, sent them wind at will,
And swiftly Argo climbed each changing hill,   100
And ran through rippling valleys of the sea ;
Nor toiled the heroes unmelodiously,

For by the mast sat great Œager's son,
And through the harp-strings let his fingers run
Nigh soundless, and with closed lips for a while;
But soon across his face there came a smile,
And his glad voice brake into such a song
That swiftlier sped the eager ship along.

  "O bitter sea, tumultuous sea,
Full many an ill is wrought by thee!— 110
Unto the wasters of the land
Thou holdest out thy wrinkled hand;
And when they leave the conquered town,
Whose black smoke makes thy surges brown,
Driven betwixt thee and the sun,
As the long day of blood is done,
From many a league of glittering waves
 Thou smilest on them and their slaves.
 "The thin bright-eyed Phœnician
Thou drawest to thy waters wan, 120
With ruddy eve and golden morn
Thou temptest him, until, forlorn,
 Unburied, under alien skies
Cast up ashore his body lies.
 "Yea, whoso sees thee from his door,
Must ever long for more and more;
Nor will the beechen bowl suffice,
Or homespun robe of little price,
Or hood well-woven of the fleece
Undyed, or unspiced wine of Greece; 130
So sore his heart is set upon

Purple, and gold, and cinnamon;
For as thou cravest, so he craves,
Until he rolls beneath thy waves.
Nor in some landlocked, unknown bay,
Can satiate thee for one day.

"Now, therefore, O thou bitter sea,
With no long words we pray to thee,
But ask thee, hast thou felt before
Such strokes of the long ashen oar?   140
And hast thou yet seen such a prow
Thy rich and niggard waters plough?
"Nor yet, O sea, shalt thou be cursed,
If at thy hands we gain the worst,
And, wrapt in water, roll about
Blind-eyed, unheeding song or shout,
Within thine eddies far from shore,
Warmed by no sunlight any more.
"Therefore, indeed, we joy in thee,
And praise thy greatness, and will we   150
Take at thy hands both good and ill,
Yea, what thou wilt, and praise thee still,
Enduring not to sit at home,
And wait until the last days come,
When we no more may care to hold
White bosoms under crowns of gold,
And our dulled hearts no longer are
Stirred by the clangorous noise of war,
And hope within our souls is dead,
And no joy is remembered.   160

"So, if thou hast a mind to slay,
Fair prize thou hast of us to-day;
And if thou hast a mind to save,
Great praise and honour shalt thou have;
But whatso thou wilt do with us,
Our end shall not be piteous,
Because our memories shall live
When folk forget the way to drive
The black keel through the heaped-up sea,
And half dried up thy waters be."   170

Then shouted all the heroes, and they drove
The good ship forth, so that the birds above,
With long white wings, scarce flew so fast as they.
And so they laboured well-nigh all the day,
And ever in their ears divine words rung,
For 'midmost of them still the Thracian sung
Stories of Gods and men; the bitter life
Pandora brought to luckless men; the strife
'Twixt Pallas and the Shaker of the Earth,
The theft of Bacchus, and the wondrous birth   180
Of golden Venus. Natheless, when the sun
To fall adown the heavens had begun,
They trimmed the sails, and drew the long oars up,
And, having poured wine from a golden cup
Unto the Gods, gladdened their hearts with food;
Then, having feasted as they thought it good,
Set hands upon the oars again, and so
Toiled on, until the broad sun, growing low,
Reddened the green sea; then they held their hands

Till he should come again from unknown lands,   190
And fell to meat again, and sat so long
Over the wine-cups, cheered with tale and song,
That night fell on them, and the moon rose high,
And the fair western wind began to die,
Though still they drifted slowly towards the east;
Then with sweet sleep the others crowned their feast,
But Tiphys and the leader of the rest,
Who watched till drew the round moon to the west,
And Jason could behold beneath her light,
Far off at first, a little speck of white,   200
Which, as the grey dawn stole across the sea,
And the wind freshened, grew at last to be
Grey rocks and great, and when they nigher drew,
The skilful helmsman past all doubting knew
The land of Lemnos; therefore from their sleep
They roused their fellows, bidding them to keep
The good ship from that evil rocky shore.

  So each man set his hand unto the oar,
And, striking sail, along the coast they crept,
Till the sun rose, and birds no longer slept;   210
Then as they went they saw a sandy beach
Under the cliff, that no high wave could reach,
And in the rock a deep cave cut, whereby
A man was standing, gazing earnestly
Upon their ship, and shouting words that, tost
Hither and thither by the wind, were lost
Amid the tumbling of the ridgy sea:
Natheless, they deemed that he still prayed to be
Their fellow, and to leave those rocky shores;

Therefore, with backing of the ashen oars, 220
They stayed the ship, and beckoned unto him
To try the sea, if so be he could swim,
Because, indeed, they doubted there might be
A-nigh the place some hidden enemy;
Nor cared they much to trust their oaken keel
Too near those rocks, as deadly as sharp steel,
That lay upon their lee; but with a shout
He sprang into the sea, and beat about
The waters bravely, till he reached the ship;
And clambering up, let the salt water drip 230
From off his naked limbs, nor spoke he ought
Until before the fair prince he was brought.
But Jason, when he set his eyes on him,
And saw him famished and so gaunt of limb,
Bade them to give him food and wine enow
Before he told his tale; and still to row
Along the high cliffs eastward, nor to stay
For town or tower, or haven or deep bay.
  Then being clothed and fed, the island man
Came back to Jason, and his tale began:— 240

"O Lord, or Prince, or whoso thou mayst be,
Great thanks I give thee; yet, I pray, of me,
Ask not my name, for surely ere this day
Both name, and house, and friends have past away.
A Lemnian am I, who within the town
Had a fair house, and on the thymy down
Full many a head of sheep; and I had too
A daughter, old enough for men to woo,

A wife and three fair sons; **of** whom the first
For love and gold had now begun to thirst: 250
Full **rich** I was, and led a pleasant life,
Nor did I long for more, or doubt for strife.

"Know that in Lemnos were the Gods well served,
And duly all their awful rites observed,
Save only that no temple Venus had,
And from no altars was her heart made glad;
Wherefore for us she wove a bitter fate,
For by her power she set an evil hate
Of man, like madness in each woman's heart,
And heavy sleep on us men, for our part, 260
From which few woke, or woke in time to feel
Against their throats the pitiless sharp steel.

"**But** that there might be one to tell the thing,
Nigh dawn I woke, and turning, thought to cling
Unto the warm side of my well-loved wife,
But found nought there but a keen two-edged knife.
So, wondering much, I gat me from the bed,
And going thence, found all the floor be-bled
In my son's sleeping place, and nigh the door
His body, hacked and hewn, upon the floor: 270
Naked he was, but in his clenched right hand
Held tufts of woman's hair. Then did I stand
As in a dream a man stands, when draws nigh
The thing he fears with such wild agony,
Yet dares not flee from; but the golden sun
Came forth at last, and daylight was begun;
Then trembling I took heart to leave at last
The lonely house, but, as **I** slowly passed

Into the porch, a dreadful noise I heard,
Nor shall I be again by aught so feared,   280
How long soe'er I live, as I was then,
Because that shout was worse than cries of men
Drunken with blood; but yet as in a dream
I went to meet it, and heard many a scream
From dying men; but, as I gained the street,
Men flying for their dear lives did I meet,
And turned and fled with them, I knew not why,
But looking back in running, could espy,
With shrinking horror, what kept up the chase.

"Because, indeed, the old familiar place,   290
From house-wall unto house-wall, was now filled
With frantic women, whose thin voices shrilled
With unknown war-cries; little did they heed
If, as they tore along, their flesh did bleed
So that some man was slain, nor feared they now
If they each other smote with spear or bow,
For all were armed in some sort, and had set
On head or breast what armour they might get;
And some were naked else, and some were clad
In such-like raiment as the slain men had,   300
And some their kirtles wore looped up or rent.

"So ever at us shafts and spears they sent,
And through the street came on like a huge wave,
Until at last against the gates they drave,
And we gained on them, till some two or three,
As still the others strove confusedly,
Burst from the press, and, heading all the rest,
Ran mightily, and the last men, hard pressed,

Turned round upon them, and straightway were **slain,**
Unarmed **and** faint, and 'gan the crowd to gain   310
Upon the fleeing men, till one by one
They fell, and looked their last upon the sun,
And I alone was held in chase, until
I reached the top of a high thymy hill
Above the sea, bleeding from arm and back,
Wherein two huntsmen's arrows lightly **stack,**
Shot by no practised hands; but nigh my death
I was indeed, empty of hope and breath.

  "Yet, ere their changed hands could be laid on me,
I threw myself into the boiling sea,   320
And they turned back, nor doubted I was dead;
But I, though fearing much to show my head,
Got me, by swimming, to yon little beach,
And there the mouth of yon cave scarce could reach,
And lay there fainting till the sun was high.
Then I awoke, and, rising fearfully,
Gat into the dark cave, and there **have been,**
How long I know not, and no man **have seen;**
And as for food and drink, within the cave
Good store of sweet clear water did **I have,**   330
And in the nights I went along the **beach**
And got me shell-fish, and made shift **to reach**
Some few birds' eggs; but natheless, misery
Must soon have slain me, had not the kind sea
Sent you, O lords, to give me life again;
Therefore, I pray, ye may not wish in vain
For ought, and that with goods and happiness
The Father of all folk your lives may bless."

 Then said the prince: "And be thou strong of heart,
For, after all thy woes, shalt thou have part   340
In this our quest, if so thou willest it;
But if so be that thou wouldst rather sit
In rest and peace within a fair homestead,
That shall some king give to thee by my head,
For love of me; or else for very fear
Shall some man give thee what thou countest dear.
 "And if thou askest of us, know that we
Are children of the conquering Minyæ,
And make for Colchis o'er the watery plain,
And think we shall not fail to bring again   350
The fleece of Neptune's ram to Thessaly."
 "Prince," said the Lemnian, "I will go with thee
Whereso thou willest, neither have I will
To wait again for ruin, sitting still
Among such goods as grudging fate will give,
Even at the longest, only while I live."
 Then Jason bade them bring him arms well wrought
And robes of price; and when all these were brought,
And he was armed, he seemed a goodly man.

 Meanwhile, along the high cliffs Argo ran   360
Until a fresh land-wind began to rise,
Then did they set sail, and in goodly wise
Draw off from Lemnos, and at close of day
Again before them a new country lay,
Which when they neared, the helmsman Tiphys knew
To be the Mysian land; being come thereto,
They saw a grassy shore and trees enow,

And a sweet stream that from the land did flow;
Therefore they thought it good to land thereon
And get them water; but, the day being gone,   370
They anchored till the dawn anigh the beach,
Till the sea's rim the golden sun did reach.
But when the day dawned, most men left the ship,
Some hasting the glazed water-jars to dip
In the fresh water; others among these
Who had good will beneath the murmuring trees
To sit awhile, forgetful of the sea.
And with the sea-farers there landed three
Amongst the best, Alcmena's godlike son,
Hylas the fair, and that half-halting one,   380
Great Polyphemus.   Now both Hercules
And all the others lay beneath the trees,
When all the jars were filled, nor wandered far;
But Hylas, governed by some wayward star,
Strayed from them, and up stream he set his face,
And came unto a tangled woody place,
From whence the stream came, and within **that wood**
Along its bank wandered in heedless mood,
Nor knew **it haunted of the sea-nymphs fair,**
Whom on that morn the heroes' noise did scare   390
From their abiding-place anigh the **bay;**
But these now hidden in the water lay
Within the wood, and thence could they behold
The fair-limbed Hylas, with his hair of gold,
And mighty arms down-swinging carelessly,
And fresh face, ruddy from the wind-swept sea;
Then straight they loved him, and, being fain to have

His shapely body in the glassy wave,
And taking counsel there, they thought it good
That one should meet him in the darksome wood, 400
And by her wiles should draw him to some place
Where they his helpless body might embrace.

So from the water stole a fair nymph forth,
And by her art so wrought, that from the north
You would have thought her come, from where a queen
Rules over lands summer alone sees green;
For she in goodly raiment, furred, was clad,
And on her head a golden fillet had,
Strange of its fashion, and about her shone
Many a fair jewel and outlandish stone. 410

So in the wood, anigh the river side,
The coming of the Theban did she bide,
Nor waited long, for slowly pushing through
The close-set saplings, o'er the flowers blue
He drew nigh, singing, free from any care;
But when he saw her glittering raiment fair
Betwixt the green tree-trunks, he stayed a space,
For she, with fair hands covering up her face,
Was wailing loud, as though she saw him not,
And to his mind came old tales half forgot, 420
Of women of the woods, the huntsman's bane.

Yet with his fate indeed he strove in vain;
For, going further forward warily,
From tree-trunk unto tree-trunk, he could see
Her ivory hands, with wrist set close to wrist,
Her cheek as fair as any God has kissed,
Her lovely neck and wealth of golden hair,

That from its fillet straggled here and there,
And all her body writhing in distress,
Wrapped in the bright folds of her golden dress. 430

   Then forthwith he drew near her eagerly,
Nor did she seem to know that he was nigh,
Until almost his hand on her was laid;
Then, lifting up a pale wild face, she said,
Struggling with sobs and shrinking from his hand:—
"O, fair young warrior of a happy land,
Harm not a queen, I pray thee, for I come
From the far northland, where yet sits at home
The king, my father, who, since I was wooed
By a rich lord of Greece, had thought it good 440
To send me to him with a royal train,
But they, their hearts being changed by hope of gain,
Seized on my goods, and left me while I slept;
Nor do I know, indeed, what kind God kept
Their traitorous hands from slaying me outright;
And surely yet, the lion-haunted night
Shall make an end of me, who erewhile thought
That unto lovelier lands I was being brought,
To live a happier life than heretofore.

   "But why think I of past times any more, 450
Who, a king's daughter once, am now grown fain
Of poorest living, through all toil and pain,
If so I may but live: and thou, indeed,
Perchance art come, some God, unto my need;
For nothing less thou seemest, verily.
But if thou art a man, let me not die,
But take me as thy slave, that I may live.

For many a gem my raiment has to give,
And these weak fingers surely yet may learn
To turn the mill, and carry forth the urn 460
Unto the stream, nor shall my feet unshod,
Shrink from the flinty road and thistly sod."

She ceased; but he stooped down, and stammering
" Mayst thou be happy, O most lovely maid,   [said :
And thy sweet life yet know a better day·
And I will strive to bring thee on thy way,
Who am the well-loved son of a rich man
Who dwells in Thebes, beside Ismenus wan."
Therewith he reached his hand to her, and she
Let her slim palm fall in it daintily; 470
But with that touch he felt as through his blood
Strange fire ran, and saw not the close wood,
Nor tangled path, nor stream, nor aught but her
Crouching before him in her gold and fur,
With kind appealing eyes raised up to his,
And red lips trembling for the coming kiss.

But ere his lips met hers did she arise,
Reddening with shame, and from before his eyes
Drew her white hand, wherewith the robe of gold
She gathered up, and from her feet did hold, 480
Then through the tangled wood began to go,
Not looking round; but he cared not to know
Whither they went, so only she was nigh.
So to her side he hurried fearfully,
She nought gainsaying, but with eyes downcast
Still by his side betwixt the low boughs past,

G

Following the stream, until a space of green
All bare of trees they reached, and there-between
The river ran, grown broad and like a pool,
Along whose bank a flickering shade and cool   490
Grey willows made, and all about they heard
The warble of the small brown river bird.
And from both stream and banks rose up a haze
Quivering and glassy, for of summer days
This was the chiefest day and crown of all.

   There did the damsel let her long skirts fall
Over her feet, but as her hand dropped down,
She felt it stopped by Hylas' fingers brown,
Whereat she trembled and began to go
Across the flowery grass with footsteps slow,   500
As though she grew aweary, and she said,
Turning about her fair and glorious head:
"Soft is the air in your land certainly,
But under foot the way is rough and dry
Unto such feet as mine, more used to feel
The dainty stirrup wrought of gold and steel,
Or tread upon the white bear's fell, or pass
In spring and summer o'er such flowery grass
As this, that soothly mindeth me too much
Of that my worshipped feet were wont to touch,   510
When I was called a queen; let us not haste
To leave this sweet place for the tangled waste,
I pray thee, therefore prince, but let us lie
Beneath these willows while the wind goes by,
And set our hearts to think of happy things,
Before the morrow pain and trouble brings."

She faltered somewhat as she spoke, but he
Drew up before her and took lovingly
Her other hand, nor spoke she more to him,
Nor he to her awhile, till, from the rim
Of his great shield, broke off the leathern band
That crossed his breast, whether some demon's hand
Snapped it unseen, or some sharp, rugged bough
Within the wood had chafed it even now;
But clattering fell the buckler to the ground,
And, startled at the noise, he turned him round,
Then, grown all bold within that little space,
He set his cheek unto her blushing face,
And smiling, in a low voice said:

       "O sweet,
Call it an omen that this, nowise meet
For deeds of love, has left me by its will,
And now by mine these toys that cumber still
My arms shall leave me."

      And therewith he threw
His brass-bound spear upon the grass, and drew
The Theban blade from out its ivory sheath,
And loosed his broad belt's clasp, that like a wreath
His father's Indian serving-man had wrought,
And cast his steel coat off, from Persia brought;
And so at last being freed of brass and steel,
Upon his breast he laid her hand to feel
The softness of the fine Phœnician stuff
That clad it still, nor yet could toy enough
With that fair hand; so played they for a space,
Till softly did she draw him to a place

Anigh the stream, and they being set, he said:
  "**And what** dost thou, O love? art thou afraid
To cast thine armour off, as I have done,
Within this covert where the fiery sun
Scarce strikes upon one jewel of your gown?"

  Then she spake, reddening, with her eyes cast down:
"O prince, behold me as I am to-day,   551
But if o'er many a rough and weary way
It hap unto us both at last to come
Unto the happy place that is thine home,
Then let me be as women of thy land
When they before the sea-born goddess stand,
And not one flower hides them from her sight."

  But with that word she set her fingers white
Upon her belt, and he said amorously:
"**Ah**, God, whatso thou wilt must surely be,   560
But would that I might die or be asleep
Till we have gone across the barren deep,
And you and I together, hand in **hand**,
Some day, ere sunrise lights the quiet land,
Behold once more the seven gleaming gates."

  "O love," she said, "and such a fair time waits
Both thee and **me**; but now to give thee rest,
Here, in the noontide, were it not the best
To soothe thee with some gentle murmuring song,
Sung to such notes as to our folk belong;   570
Such as my maids awhile ago would sing
When on my bed a-nights I lay waking?"

  "Sing on," he said, "but let me dream of bliss
If I should sleep, nor yet forget thy kiss."

She touched his lips with hers, and then began
A sweet song sung not yet to any man.

"I know a little garden close
Set thick with lily and red rose,
Where I would wander if I might
From dewy dawn to dewy night, 580
And have one with me wandering.

"And though within it no birds sing,
And though no pillared house is there,
And though the apple boughs are bare
Of fruit and blossom, would to God,
Her feet upon the green grass trod,
And I beheld them as before.

"There comes a murmur from the shore,
And in the place two fair streams are,
Drawn from the purple hills afar, 590
Drawn down unto the restless sea;
The hills whose flowers ne'er fed the bee,
The shore no ship has ever seen,
Still beaten by the billows green,
Whose murmur comes unceasingly
Unto the place for which I cry.

"For which I cry both day and night,
For which I let slip all delight,
That maketh me both deaf and blind,
Careless to win, unskilled to find, 600
And quick to lose what all men seek.

"Yet tottering as I am, and weak,
Still have I left a little breath

　　　　To seek within the jaws of death
　　　　An entrance to that happy place,
　　　　To seek the unforgotten face
　　　　Once seen, once kissed, once reft from me
　　　　Anigh the murmuring of the sea."

　　She ceased her song, that lower for a while
And slower too had grown, and a soft smile　　　　610
Grew up within her eyes as still she sung.
Then she rose up and over Hylas hung,
For now he slept; wherewith the God in her
Consumed the northern robe done round with fur
That hid her beauty, and the light west wind
Played with her hair no fillet now did bind,
And through her faint grey garment her limbs seemed
Like ivory in the sea, and the sun gleamed
In the strange jewels round her middle sweet,
And in the jewelled sandals on her feet.　　　　620
　　So stood she murmuring till a rippling sound
She heard, that grew until she turned her round
And saw her other sisters of the deep
Her song had called while Hylas yet did sleep,
Come swimming in a long line up the stream,
And their white dripping arms and shoulders gleam
Above the dark grey water as they went,
And still before them a great ripple sent.
　　But when they saw her, toward the bank they drew,
And landing, felt the grass and flowers blue　　　　630
Against their unused feet; then in a ring
Stood gazing with wide eyes, and wondering

At all his beauty they desired so much.
And then with gentle hands began to touch
His hair, his hands, his closed eyes; and at last
Their eager naked arms about him cast,
And bore him, sleeping still, as by some spell,
Unto the depths where they were wont to dwell;
Then softly down the reedy bank they slid,
And with small noise the gurgling river hid   640
The flushed nymphs and the heedless sleeping man.

  But ere the water covered them, one ran
Across the mead and caught up from the ground
The brass-bound spear, and buckler bossed and round,
The ivory-hilted sword, and coat of mail,
Then took the stream; so what might tell the tale,
Unless the wind should tell it, or the bird
Who from the reed these things had seen and heard?

  Meanwhile, the ship being watered, and the day
Now growing late, the prince would fain away;   650
So from the ship was blown a horn to call
The stragglers back, who mustered one and all,
But Theban Hylas; therefore, when they knew
That he was missing, Hercules withdrew
From out the throng, if yet perchance his voice
Hylas might hear, and all their hearts rejoice
With his well-known shout in reply thereto;
With him must Polyphemus likewise go,
To work out the wise counsel of the fates,
Unhappy, who no more would see the gates   660
Of white-walled fair Larissa, or the plain

Burdened by many an overladen wain.
    For, while their cries and shouts rang through the
        wood,
The others reached the ship, and thought it good
To weigh the anchor, and anigh the shore,
With loosened sail, and run-out ready oar,
To trim the ship for leaving the fair bay;
And therefore, Juno, waiting for that day,
And for that hour, had gathered store of wind
Up in the hills to work out all her mind,   670
Which, from the Mysian mountains now let slip,
Tearing along the low shore, smote the ship
In blinding clouds of salt spray mixed with rain.
    Then vainly they struck sail, and all in vain
The rowers strove to keep her head to wind,
And still they drifted seaward, drenched and blind.
    But, 'mid their struggling, suddenly there shone
A light from Argo's high prow, and thereon
Could their astonished, fearful eyes behold
A figure standing, with wide wings of gold,   680
Upright, amid the weltering of the sea,
Calm 'midst the noise and cries, and presently
To all their ears a voice pierced, saying: "No more,
O Jove-blessed heroes, strive to reach the shore,
Nor seek your lost companions, for of these
Jove gives you not the mighty Hercules
To help you forward on your happy way,
But wills him in the Greek land still to stay,
Where many a thing he has for him to do,
With whom awhile shall Polyphemus go,   690

Then build in Mysia a fair merchant-town,
And when long years have passed, there lay him down:
And as for Hylas, never think to see
His body more, who yet lies happily
Beneath the green stream where ye were this morn,
And there he praises Jove that he was born,
Forgetting the rough world, and every care;
Not dead, nor living, among faces fair,
White limbs, and wonders of the watery world.

  "And now I bid ye spread the sail ye furled,   700
And make on towards the straits while Juno sends
Fair wind behind you, calling you her friends."

  Therewith the voice ceased, and the storm was still,
And afterward they had good wind at will,
To help them toward the straits, but all the rest,
Rejoicing at the speeding of their quest,
Yet wondered much whence that strange figure came,
That on the prow burnt like a harmless flame;
Yea, some must go and touch the empty space
From whence those words flew from the godlike face;
But Jason and the builder, Argus, knew   711
Whereby the prow foretold things strange and new,
Nor wondered aught, but thanked the Gods therefore,
As far astern they left the Mysian shore.

BOOK V.

The death of Cyzicus—Phineus freed from the Harpies.

NOW, driven by the oar, and feeling well
  The wind that made the fair white sail outswell,
Thessalian Argo flew on toward the place
Where first the rude folk saw dead Helle's face;
There, fearful of the darkness of the night,
Without the rocks they anchored till the light,
And when the day broke, sped them through the
    straits
With oars alone, and through the narrow gates
Came out into Propontis, where with oar
And sail together, within sight of shore,   10
They went, until the sun was falling down,
And then they saw the white walls of a town,
And made thereto, and soon being come anigh,
They found that on an isle the place did lie,
And Tiphys called it Cyzicum, a place
Built by a goodly man of a great race,
Himself called Cyzicus, Euzorus' son,
Who still in peace ruled over many an one,
Merchants and other, in that city fair.
  Therefore, they thought it good to enter there,   20
And going softly, with sails struck, at last
Betwixt the two walls of a port they passed,

And on the quays beheld full many a man
Buying and selling, nigh the water wan.
 So, as they touched the shore, an officer
Drew nigh unto them, asking who they were;
And when he knew, he cried: " O heroes, land,
For here shall all things be at your command;
And here shall you have good rest from the sea."
Therewith he sent one to go speedily   30
And tell the king these folks were landed there.
 Then passed the heroes forth upon the fair
Well builded quays; and all the merchant folk
Beholding them, from golden dreams awoke,
And of the sword and clattering shield grew fain,
And glory for awhile they counted gain.
 But Jason and his fair folk passing these
Came to a square shaded about by trees,
Where they beheld the crowned king glorious stand
To wait them, who took Jason by the hand   40
And led him through the rows of linden trees
Unto his house, the crown of palaces;
And there he honoured them with royal feast
In his fair hall, hung round with man and beast
Wrought in fair Indian cloths, and on soft beds,
When they grew weary, did they lay their heads.
 But he, when on the morn they would away,
Full many a rich gift in their keel did lay,
And while their oars were whitening the green sea,
Within his temple he prayed reverently   50
For their good hap to Jove the Saving God.
Hapless himself that these had ever trod

His quiet land; for, sailing all the day,
Becalmed at last at fall of night they lay;
And lying there, an hour before midnight
A black cloud rose that swallowed up the light
Of moon and stars, and therefrom leapt a wind
That drave the Argo, tottering and blind,
Back on her course, and, as it died, at last
They heard the breakers roaring, and so cast 60
Their anchors out within some shallow bay,
They knew not where, to wait until the day.

   There, as they waited, they saw beacons flame
Along the coast, and in a while there came
A rout of armed men thereto, as might seem
By shouts and clash of arms that now 'gan gleam
Beneath the light of torches that they bore.
Then could the heroes see that they from shore
Were distant scarce a bowshot, and the tide
Had ebbed so quick the sands were well-nigh dried 70
Betwixt them and the foremost of the foe,
Who, ere they could push off, began to go
Across the wet beach, and with many a cry
The biting arrows from their bows let fly.
Nor were the heroes slow to make return,
Aiming where'er they saw the torches burn.

   So passed the night with little death of men;
But when the sky at last grew grey, and when
Dimly the Argo's crew could see their foes,
Then overboard they lept, that they might close 80
With these scarce seen far-fighting enemies,
And so met man to man, crying their cries,

In deadly shock, but Jason, for his part,
Rushing before the rest, put by a dart
A tall man threw, and closing with him, drave
His spear through shield and breast-plate weak to save
His heart from such an arm; then straight he fell
Dead on the sands, and with a wailing yell
The others, when they saw it, fled away,
And gat them swiftly to the forest grey   90
The yellow sands fringed like a garment's hem,
Nor gave the seafarers much chase to them,
But on the hard sand all together drew.

And now, day growing, they the country knew
And found it Cyzicum, and Jason said:
"Fellows, what have we done? by likely-head
An evil deed, and luckless, but come now,
Draw off the helmet from this dead man's brow
And name him." So when they had done this thing
They saw the face of Cyzicus the king.   100

But Jason, when he saw him, wept, and said:
"Ill hast thou fared, O friend, that I was led
To take thy gifts and slay thee; in such guise,
Blind and unwitting, do fools die and wise,
And I myself may hap to come to die
By that I trusted, and like thee to lie
Dead ere my time, a wonder to the world.
But, O poor king, thy corpse shall not be hurled
Hither and thither by the heedless wave,
But in an urn thine ashes will I save,   110
And build a temple when I come to Greece

A rich man, with the fair-curled golden fleece,
And set them there, and call it by thy name,
That thou mayst yet win an undying fame."

   Then hasted all the men, and in a while,
'Twixt sea and woodland, raised a mighty **pile,**
And there they burned him, but for spices **sweet**
Could cast thereon but wrack from 'neath **their feet,**
And wild wood flowers and resin from the pine;
And when the pile grew low, with odorous wine   120
They quenched the ashes, and the king's they set
Within a golden vessel, that with fret
Of twining boughs and gem-made flowers was wrought
That they from Pelias' treasure-house had brought.
Then, since the sun his high meridian
Had left, they pushed into the waters wan,
And so, with hoisted sail and stroke of oar,
Drew off from that unlucky fateful shore.

   Now eastward with a fair **wind as they went,**
And towards the opening of the ill sea bent   130
Their daring course, Tiphys arose and said:

   "Heroes, it seems to me that hardihead
Helps mortal men but little, if thereto
They join not wisdom; now needs must we go
Into the evil sea through blue rocks twain
No keel hath ever passed, although in vain
Some rash men trying it of old, have been
Pounded therein, as poisonous herbs and green
Are pounded by some witch-wife on the shore
Of Pontus,—for these two rocks evermore   140

Each against each are driven, and leave not
Across the whole strait such a little spot
Safe from the grinding of their mighty blows,
As that through which a well-aimed arrow goes
When archers for a match shoot at the ring.
 "Now, heroes, do I mind me of a king
That dwelleth at a sea-side town of Thrace
That men call Salmydessa, from this place
A short day's sail, who hidden things can tell
Beyond all men; wherefore, I think it well   150
That we for counsel should now turn thereto,
Nor headlong to our own destruction go."
 Then all men said that these his words were good,
And turning, towards the Thracian coast they stood,
Which yet they reached not till the moonlit night
Was come, and from the shore the wind blew light;
Then they lay to until the dawn, and then
Creeping along, found an abode of men
That Tiphys knew to be the place they sought.
Thereat they shouted, and right quickly brought   160
Fair Argo to the landing-place, and threw
Grapnels ashore, and landing forthwith drew
Unto the town, seeking Phineus the king.
But those they met and asked about this thing
Grew pale at naming him, and few words said;
Natheless, they being unto the palace led,
And their names told, soon were they bidden in
To where the king sat, a man blind and thin,
And haggard beyond measure, who straightway
Called out aloud: "Now blessed be the way   170

That led thee to me, happiest of all
Who from the poop see the prow rise and fall
And the sail bellying, and the glittering oars;
And blessed be the day whereon our shores
First felt thy footsteps, since across the sea
My hope and my revenge thou bring'st with thee."

 Then Jason said: "Hail, Phineus, that men call
Wisest of men, and may all good befall
To thee and thine, and happy mayst thou live;
Yet do we rather pray thee gifts to give,   180
Than bring thee any gifts, for, soothly, we
Sail, desperate men and poor, across the sea."

 Then answered Phineus: "Guest, I know indeed
What gift it is that on this day ye need,
Which I will not withhold; and yet, I pray,
That ye will eat and drink with me to-day,
Then shall ye see how wise a man am I,
And how well-skilled to scape from misery."

 Therewith he groaned, and bade his folk to bring
Such feast as 'longed unto a mighty king,   190
And spread the board therewith; who straight obeyed,
Trembling and pale, and on the tables laid
A royal feast most glorious in show.

 Then said the king: "I give you now to know
That the Gods love me not, O guests; therefore,
Lest your expected feast be troubled sore,
Eat by yourselves alone, while I sit here
Looking for that which scarcely brings me fear
This day, since I so long have suffered it."

 So, wondering at his words, they all did sit   200

At that rich board, and ate and drank their fill;
But yet with little mirth indeed, for still
Within their wondering ears the king's words rang,
And his blind eyes, made restless by some pang,
They still felt on them, though no word he said.
  At last he called out: "Though ye be full fed,
Sit still at table and behold me eat,
Then shall ye witness with what royal meat
The Gods are pleased to feed me, since I know
As much as they do both of things below   210
And things above."
                    Then, hearkening to this word,
The most of them grew doubtful and afeard
Of what should come; but now unto the board
The king was led, and nigh his hand his sword,
Two-edged and ivory-hilted, did they lay,
And set the richest dish of all that day
Before him, and a wine-crowned golden cup,
And a pale, trembling servant lifted up
The cover from the dish; then did they hear
A wondrous rattling sound that drew anear,   220
Increasing quickly: then the gilded hall
Grew dark at noon, as though the night did fall,
And open were all doors and windows burst,
And such dim light gleamed out as lights the cursed,
Unto the torments behind Minos' throne:
Dim, green, and doubtful through the hall it shone,
Lighting up shapes no man had seen, before
They fell, awhile ago, upon that shore.

For now, indeed, the trembling Minyæ
Beheld the daughters of the earth and sea, 230
The dreadful snatchers, who like women were
Down to the breast, with scanty coarse black hair
About their heads, and dim eyes ringed with red,
And bestial mouths set round with lips of lead,
But from their gnarled necks there began to spring
Half hair, half feathers, and a sweeping wing
Grew out instead of arm on either side,
And thick plumes underneath the breast did hide
The place where joined the fearful natures twain.
Grey feathered were they else, with many a stain 240
Of blood thereon, and on bird's claws they went.

These through the hall unheard-of shrieking sent,
And rushed at Phineus, just as to his mouth
He raised the golden cup to quench his drouth,
And scattered the red wine, and buffeted
The wretched king, and one, perched on his head,
Laughed as the furies laugh, when kings come down
To lead new lives within the fiery town,
And said: "O Phineus, thou art lucky now
The hidden things of heaven and hell to know; 250
Eat, happy man, and drink." Then did she draw
From off the dish a goblet with her claw,
And held it nigh his mouth, the while he strove
To free his arm, that one hovering above,
Within her filthy vulture-claws clutched tight,
And cried out at him: "Truly, in dark night
Thou seest, Phineus, as the leopard doth."   [both
  Then cried the third: "Fool, who would fain have

Delight and knowledge, therefore, with blind eyes
Clothe thee in purple, wrought with braveries,   260
And set the pink-veined marble 'neath thy throne;
Then on its golden cushions sit alone,
Hearkening thy chain-galled slaves without singing
For joy, that they behold so many a thing."

   Then shrieked the first one in a dreadful voice:—
" And I, O Phineus, bid thee to rejoice,   [this—
That 'midst thy knowledge still thou know'st not
Whose flesh the lips, wherewith thy lips I kiss,
This morn have fed on." Then she laughed again,
And fawning on him, with her sisters twain   270
Spread her wide wings, and hid him from the sight,
And mixed his groans with screams of shrill delight.

   Now trembling sat the seafarers, nor dared
To use the weapons from their sheaths half-bared,
Fearing the Gods, who there, before their eyes,
Had shown them with what shame and miseries
They visit impious men: yet from the board
There started two, with shield and ready sword,
The Northwind's offspring, since, upon that day,
Their father wrought within them in such way,   280
They had no fear: but now, when Phineus knew,
By his divine art, that the godlike two
Were armed to help him, then from 'twixt the wings
He cried aloud: " O, heroes, more than kings,
Strike, and fear not, but set me free to-day,
That ye within your brazen chests may lay
The best of all my treasure-house doth hold,
Fair linen, scarlet cloth, and well-wrought gold."

Then shrieked the snatchers, knowing certainly
That now the time had come when they must fly 290
From pleasant Salmydessa, casting off
The joys they had in shameful mock and scoff.
So gat they from the blind king, leaving **him**
Pale and forewearied in his every limb;
And, flying through the roof, they set them **down**
Above the hall-doors, 'mid the timbers **brown,**
Chattering with fury. **Then** the fair dyed wings
Opened upon the shoulders of the kings,
And on their heels, and shouting, they uprose,
And poised themselves in air to meet their foes. 300

Then here and there those loathly things did fly
Before the brazen shields, and swords raised high,
But as they flew unlucky words they cried.

The first said: "Hail, O folk who wander **wide,**
Seeking a foolish thing across the sea,
Not **heeding** in what case your houses be,
Where now perchance the rovers cast the brand
Up to the roof, and leading by the hand
The fair-limbed **women with their fettered feet**
Pass down the sands, their hollow ship to meet." 310

"Fair hap **to him who weds** the sorceress,"
The second cried, "and may the just Gods bless
The slayer of his kindred and his name."

"**Luck to the** toilsome seeker after fame,"
The third one from the open hall-door cried,
"**Fare** ye **well,** Jason, still unsatisfied,
Still seeking for a better thing than best,

A fairer thing than fairest, without rest;
Good speed, O traitor, who shall think to wed
Soft limbs and white, and find thy royal bed   320
Dripping with blood, and burning up with fire;
Good hap to him who henceforth **ne'er** shall tire
In seeking good that ever flies his hand
Till he lies buried in **an alien land!"**

So screamed the monstrous fowl, but now the twain
Sprung from the north-wind's loins to be their bane,
Drew nigh unto them; **then, with** huddled wings,
Forth from the hall they gat, but evil things
In flying they gave forth with weakened voice,
Saying unto them: "O ye men, rejoice,   330
Whose bodies worms shall feed on soon or late,
Blind slaves, and foolish **of** unsparing fate,
Seeking for that which ye can never get,
Whilst life and death **alike ye** do forget
In needless strife, until on some sure day,
Death takes your scarcely tasted life away."

Quivering their voices ceased as on they **flew**
Before the swift wings of the godlike two
Far over land and sea, until they were
Anigh the isles called Strophades, and there,   340
With tired wings, all voiceless did they light,
Trembling to see anigh the armour bright
The wind-born brothers bore, but as these drew
Their gleaming swords and towards the monsters flew,
From out the deep rose up a black-haired man,
Who, standing on the white-topped waves that ran

On towards the shore, cried: "Heroes, turn again,
For on this islet shall ye land in vain,
But without sorrow leave the chase of **these**
Who henceforth 'mid the rocky Strophades 350
Shall dwell for ever, servants unto me,
Working my will, therefore rejoice that ye
Win gifts and honour for your deed to-day."

 Then, even as he spoke, they saw but grey,
White headed waves rolling where he had stood,
Whereat they sheathed their swords, and through their blood
A tremor ran, for now they knew that he
Was Neptune, shaker of the earth and sea;
Therefore they turned them back unto the hall
Where yet the others were, and ere nightfall 360
Came back to Salmydessa and the king,
And lighting down they told him of the thing.

 Who, hearing them, straight lifted up his voice,
And 'midst the shouts cried: "Heroes, now rejoice
With me who am delivered on this day
From that which took all hope and joy away;
Therefore to feast again, until the **sun**
Another glad day for us has begun,
And then, indeed, if ye must try the sea,
With gifts and counsel shall ye go from me; 370
Such as the Gods have given me to give,
And happy lives and glorious may ye live."

 Then did they fall to banqueting again,
Forgetting all forebodings and all pain;
And when that they had ate and drank enow,

With songs and music, and a goodly show,
Their hearts were gladdened, for before their eyes
Played youths and damsels with strange fantasies,
Clad as in Saturn's time folk used to be,
With green leaves gathered from the summer tree, 380
When all the year was summer everywhere,
And every man and woman blest and fair.

  So, set 'twixt pleasure and some soft regret,
All cares of mortal men did they forget,
Except the vague desire not to die,
The hopeless wish to flee from certainty,
That sights and sounds we love will bring on us
In this sweet fleeting world and piteous.

BOOK VI.

The passage of the Symplegades—The heroes come to Æa.

BUT on the morrow did they get them gone,
   Gifted with gold and many a precious stone,
And many a bale of scarlet cloth and spice,
And arms well wrought, and goodly robes of price.
But chiefly to the wind-born brothers strong
Did gifts past telling on that morn belong.

  Now as they stood upon the windy quay,
Ready their hands upon the ropes to lay,
Phineus, who 'midst his mighty lords was there,
Set high above them in a royal chair, 10

Said: "Many a gift ye have of me to-day
Within your treasuries at home to lay,
If so it be that through hard things and pain
Ye come to the horse-nurturing land again;
Natheless, one more gift shall ye have of me,
For lacking that, beneath the greedy sea,
The mighty tomb of mariners and kings,
Doubt not to lay down these **desired things,**
Nor think to come to Thessaly at all."
And therewith turning, he began to call   20
Unto his folk to bring what they had there.
Then one brought forward a cage great and fair,
Wherein they saw a grey, pink-footed dove.

   Then said the king: "The very Gods above
Can scantly help you more than now I do,
For listen; as upon this day ye go
Unto the narrow ending of the sea,
Anigh the clashing rocks lie patiently,
And let the keenest-eyed among you stand
Upon the prow, **and** let loose from **his hand**   30
This dove, who from my mouth to-day has heard
So many a mystic and compelling word,
He cannot choose, being loosed, but fly down straight
Unto the opening of that dreadful gate;
So let the keen-eyed watch, and if so be
He comes out safe into the evil sea,
Then bend unto the oars, nor fear at all
Of aught that from the clashers may befall;
But if he perish, then turn back again,
And know the Gods have made your passage vain. 40

Thereafter, if ye will, come back to me,
And if ye find nought in my treasury
That ye desire, yet ye at least shall have
A king and a king's son to be your slave;
And all things here still may ye bind and loose,
And from our women freely may ye choose,
Nor spare the fairest or most chaste to kiss,
And in fair houses shall ye live in bliss."

"O king," said Jason, "know that on this day
I will not be forsworn, but by some way 50
Will reach the oak-grove and the Golden Fleece,
Or, failing, die at least far off from Greece,
Not unremembered; yet great thanks we give
For this thy gift and counsel, and will strive
To come to Colchis through the unknown land
And whatso perils wait us, if Jove's hand
Be heavy on us, and the great blue gates
Are shut against us by the unmoved fates.
Farewell, O king, and henceforth, free from ill,
Live happy as thou mayest, and honoured still." 60

Then turned he, shouting, to the Minyæ,
Who o'er the gangways rushed tumultuously,
And from the land great Argo straightway thrust,
And gat them to their work, hot with the lust
Of fame and noble deeds, and happy prize.
But the bird Lynceus took, unto whose eyes
The night was as the day, and fire as air.

Then back into his marble palace fair
The king turned, thinking well upon the way
Of what had happed since morn of yesterday. 70

Now from the port passed Argo, and the wind
Being fair for sailing, quickly left behind
Fair Salmydessa, the kind, gainful place;
And so, with sail and oar, in no long space
They reached the narrow ending of the sea,
Where the wind shifted, blowing gustily
From side to side, so that their flapping **sail**
But little in the turmoil could avail;
And now at last did they begin to hear
The pounding of the rocks; but nothing clear   80
They saw them; for the steaming clouds of spray,
Cast by the meeting hammers every way,
Quite hid the polished bases from their sight;
Unless perchance the eyes of Lynceus might
Just now and then behold the deep blue shine
Betwixt the scattering of the silver brine;
But sometimes 'twixt the clouds the sun would pass
And show the high rocks glittering like glass,
Quivering, as far beneath the churned-up waves
Were ground together the strong arched caves,   90
Wherein none dwelt, no, not the giant's brood,
Who fed the green sea with his lustful blood,
Nor were sea-devils even nurtured there,
Nor dared the sea-worm use them for its lair.

   And now the Minyæ, as they drew anear,
Had been at point to turn about for fear,
Each man beholding his pale fellow's face,
Whose speech was silenced in that dreadful place
By the increasing clamour of the sea
And adamantine rocks; then verily   100

Was Juno good at need, who set strange fire
In Jason's heart, and measureless desire
To be the first of men, and made his voice
Clear as that herald's, whose sweet words rejoice
The Gods within the flowery fields of Heaven,
And gave his well-knit arm the strength of seven.
So then, above the crash and thundering,
The Minyæ heard his shrill, calm voice, crying:—
"Shall this be, then, an ending to our quest?
And shall we find the worst, who sought the best? 110
Far better had ye sat beside your wives,
And 'mid the wine-cups lingered out your lives,
Dreaming of noble deeds, though trying none,
Than as vain boasters, with your deed undone,
Come back to Greece, that men may sing of you.
Are ye all shameless?—are there not a few
Who have slain fear, knowing the unmoved fates
Have meted out already what awaits
The coward and the brave? Ho! Lynceus! stand
Upon the prow, and let slip from your hand   120
The wise king's bird; and all ye note, the wind
Is steady now, and blowing from behind
Drives us on toward the clashers, and I hold
The helm myself; therefore, lest we be rolled
Broadside against these horrors, take the oar,
And hang here, half a furlong from the shore,
Nor die of fear, until at least we know
If through these gates the Gods will let us go:
And if so be they will not, yet will we
Not empty-handed come to Thessaly,   130

But strike for Æa through this unknown land,
Whose arms reach out to us on either hand."

Then they for shame began to cast off fear,
And, handling well the oars, kept Argo near
The changing, little-lighted, spray-washed **space**
Whereunto Lynceus set his eager face,
And loosed the dove, who down the west **wind flew**;
Then all the others lost her, dashing through
The clouds of spray, but Lynceus noted how
She reached the open space, just as a blow   140
Had spent itself, and still the hollow sound
Of the last clash was booming all around;
And eagerly he noted how the dove
Stopped 'mazed, and hovered for awhile above
The troubled sea, then stooping, darted through,
As the blue gleaming rocks together drew;
Then scarce he breathed, until a joyous shout
He gave, as he beheld her passing out
Unscathed, above the surface of the sea,
While back again the rocks drew sluggishly.   150

Then back their poised oars whirled, and straight
    they drave
Unto the opening of the spray-arched cave;
But Jason's eyes alone, of all the crew,
Beheld the sunny sea and cloudless blue,
Still narrowing, but bright from rock to rock.

Now as they neared, came the next thundering shock
That deafened all, and with an icy cloud
Hid man from man; but Jason, shouting loud,

Still clutched the tiller; and the oars, grasped tight
By mighty hands, drave on the ship forthright   160
Unto the rocks, until, with blinded eyes,
They blinked one moment at those mysteries
Unseen before, the next they felt the sun
Full on their backs, and knew their deed was done.

  Then on their oars they lay, and Jason turned,
And o'er the rocks beheld how Iris burned
In fair and harmless many-coloured flame,
And he beheld the way by which they came
Wide open, changeless, of its spray-clouds cleared;
And though in his bewildered ears he heard   170
The tumult yet, that all was stilled he knew,
While in and out the unused sea-fowl flew
Betwixt them, and the now subsiding sea
Lapped round about their dark feet quietly.
  So, turning to the Minyæ, he cried:—
"See ye, O fellows, the gates opened wide,
And chained fast by the Gods, nor think to miss
The very end we seek, or well-earned bliss
When once again we feel our country's earth,
And 'twixt the tears of elders, and the mirth   180
Of young men grown to manhood since we left,
And longing eyes of girls, the fleece, once reft
From a king's son of Greece, we hang again
In Neptune's temple, nigh the murmuring main."

  Then all men, with their eyes now cleared of brine,
Beheld the many-coloured rainbow shine
Over the rocks, and saw it fade away,

And saw the opening cleared of sea and spray,
And saw the green sea lap about the feet
Of those blue hills, that never more should meet, 190
And saw the wondering sea-fowl fly about
Their much-changed tops; then, with a mighty shout,
They rose rejoicing, and poured many a cup
Of red wine to the Gods, and hoisting up
The weather-beaten sail, with mirth and song,
Having good wind at will, they sped along.

 Three days with good hap and fair wind they went,
That ever at their backs Queen Juno sent,
But on the fourth day, about noon, they drew
Unto a new-built city no man knew;   200
No, not the pilot; so they thought it good
To arm themselves, and thus in doubtful mood
Brought Argo to the port, and being come nigh,
A clear-voiced herald from the land did cry:
"Whoso ye be, if that ye come in peace,
King Lycus bids you hail, but if from Greece
Ye come, and are the folk of whom we hear
Who make for Colchis, free from any fear
Then doubly welcome are ye, here take land,
For everything shall be at your command."   210
 So without fear they landed at that word,
And told him who they were, which when he heard,
Through the fair streets he brought them to the king,
Who feasted them at night with everything
That man could wish; but when on the next day
They gathered at the port to go away,

The wind was foul and boisterous, so perforce
There must they bide, lest they should come to worse.

 And there for fourteen days did they abide,
And for their pastime oft would wander wide   220
About the woods, for slaying of the beasts
Whereby to furnish forth the royal feasts;
But on a day, a closely-hunted boar,
Turning to bay, smote Idmon very sore
So that he died; poor wretch, who could foresee
Full many an unknown thing that was to be,
And yet not this, whose corpse they burnt with fire
Upon a purple-covered spice-strewn pyre,
And set his ashes in a marble tomb.
Neither could Tiphys there escape his doom,   230
Who, after suffering many a bitter storm,
Died bitten of a hidden crawling worm,
As through the woods he wandered all alone.
Now he being burned, and laid beneath a stone,
The wind grew fair for sailing, and the rest
Bade farewell to the king, and on their quest
Once more were busied, and began to plough
The unsteady plain; for whom Erginus now,
Great Neptune's son, the brass-bound tiller held.

 Now leaving that fair land, nought they beheld 240
For seven days but sea and changeful sky,
But on the eighth, keen could Lynceus espy
A land far off, and nigher as they drew
A low green shore, backed up by mountains blue,
Cleft here and there, all saw, 'twixt hope and fear,

For now it seemed to them they should be near
The wished-for goal of Æa, and the place
Where in the great sea Phasis ends his race.

 Then, creeping carefully along the beach,
The mouth of a green river did they reach,   250
Cleaving the sands, and on the yellow bar
The salt waves and the fresh waves were at war,
As Phryxus erst beheld them, but no man
Among them ere had sailed that water wan,
Now that wise Tiphys lay within his tomb.

 Natheless they, wrapt in that resistless doom
The fates had woven, turned from off the sea
Argo's fair head, and rowing mightily
Drave her across the bar, who with straight keel
The eddying stream against her bows did feel.   260

 So, with the wind behind them, and the oars
Still hard at work, they went betwixt the shores
Against the ebb, and now full oft espied
Trim homesteads here and there on either side,
And fair kine grazing, and much woolly sheep,
And skin-clad shepherds, roused from mid-day sleep,
Gazing upon them with scared wondering eyes.
So now they deemed they might be near their prize;
And at the least knew that some town was nigh,
And thought to hear new tidings presently,   270
Which happed indeed, for on the turn of tide,
At ending of a long reach, they espied
A city wondrous fair, which seemed indeed
To bar the river's course; but, taking heed
And drawing nigher, soon found out the case,

That on an island builded was the place
The more part of it; but four bridges fair
Set thick with goodly houses everywhere,
Crossed two and two on each side to the land,
Whereon was built, with walls on either hand,   280
A towered outwork, lest that war should fall
Upon the land, and midmost of each wall
A noble gate; moreover did they note
About the wharves full many a ship and boat.
And they beheld the sunlight glistering
On arms of men and many a warlike thing,
As nigher to the city they were borne,
And heard at last some huge deep booming horn
Sound from a tower o'er the watery way,
Whose last loud note was taken up straightway   290
By other watchers further and more near.

  Now when they did therewith loud shouting hear,
Then Jason bade them arm for what might come,
"For now," quoth he, "I deem we reach the home
Of that great marvel we are sworn to seek,
Nor do I think to find these folk so weak
That they with few words and a gift or two
Will give us that for which they did forego
Fair fame, the love of Gods, and praise of men;
Be strong and play the man, I bid you then,   300
For certes in none other wise shall ye
Come back again to grassy Thessaly."

  Then loud they shouted, clean forgetting fear,
And strong Erginus Argo straight did steer
On to the port; but through the crowded waist

Ran Jason to the high prow, making haste
To be the first to look upon that throng.
Shieldless he was, although his fingers strong
About a sharpened brass-bound spear did meet,
And as the ashen oars swept on, his feet   310
Moved lightly to their cadence under him;
So stood he like a God in face and limb.

Now drawing quickly nigh the landing-place,
Little by little did they slack their pace,
Till half a bowshot from the shore they lay,
Then Jason shouted: "What do ye to-day
All armed, O warriors? and what town is this
That hero by seeming ye have little bliss
Of quiet life, but, smothered up in steel,
Ye needs must meet each harmless merchant keel 320
That nears your haven, though perchance it bring
Good news, and many a much-desired thing
That ye may get good cheap? and such are we,
But wayfarers upon the troublous sea,
Careful of that stored up within our hold,
Phœnician scarlet, spice, and Indian gold,
Deep dying-earths, and woad and cinnabar,
Wrought arms and vessels, and all things that are
Desired much by dwellers in all lands;
Nor doubt us friends, although indeed our hands 330
Lack not for weapons, for the unfenced head,
Where we have been, soon rests among the dead."

So spake he with a smiling face, nor lied;
For he, indeed, was purposed to have tried

To win the fleece neither by war or stealth;
But by an open hand and heaps of wealth,
If so it might be, bear it back again,
Nor with a handful fight a host in vain.

  But being now silent, at the last he saw
A stir among those folk, who 'gan to draw   340
Apart to right and left, leaving a man
Alone amidst them, unarmed, with a wan
And withered face, and black beard mixed with grey
That swept his girdle, who these words did say :—

  " O seafarers, I give you now to know
That on this town oft falleth many a foe,
Therefore not lightly may folk take the land
With helm on head, and naked steel in hand;
Now, since indeed ye folk are but a few,
We fear you not, yet fain would that we knew   350
Your names and countries, since within this town
Of Æa may a good man lay him down
And fear for nought, at least while I am king,
Æetes, born to heed full many a thing."

  Now Jason, hearing this desired name
He thought to hear, grown hungrier yet for fame,
With eager heart, and fair face flushed for pride,
Said : " King Æetes, if not over wide
My name is known, that yet may come to be,
For I am Jason of the Minyæ,   360
And through great perils have I come from Greece
And now, since this is Æa, and the fleece
Thou slayedst once a guest to get, hangs up
Within thine house, take many a golden cup,

And arms, and dyestuffs, cloth, and spice, and gold,
Yea, all the goods that lie within our hold;
Which are not mean, for neither have we come
Leaving all things of price shut up at home,
Nor have we seen the faces of great kings
And left them giftless; therefore take these things 370
And be our friend; or, few folk as we are,
The Gods and we may bring thee bitter care."

   Then spake Æetes: "Not for any word,
Or for the glitter of thy bloodless sword,
O youngling, will I give the fleece to thee,
Nor yet for gifts,—for what are such to me?
Behold, if all thy folk joined hand to hand
They should not, striving, be enough to stand
And girdle round my bursting treasure-house;
Yet, since of this thing thou art amorous,   380
And I love men, and hold the Gods in fear,
If thou and thine will land, then mayst thou hear
What great things thou must do to win the fleece;
Then, if thou wilt not dare it, go in peace.
But come now, thou shalt hear it amidst wine
And lovely things, and songs well-nigh divine,
And all the feasts that thou hast shared erewhile
With other kings, to mine shall be but vile.
Lest thou shouldst name me, coming to thy land,
A poor guest-fearing man, of niggard hand."   390

   So spake he outwardly, but inly thought,
"Within two days this lading shall be brought
To lie amongst my treasures with the best,
While 'neath the earth these robbers lie at rest."

But Jason said: "King, if these things be such
As man may do, I shall not fear them much,
And at thy board will I feast merrily
To-night, if on the morrow I must die;
And yet, beware of treason, since for nought
Such lives as ours by none are lightly bought. 400

"Draw on, O heroes, to the shore, if ye
Are willing still this great king's house to see."
Thereat was Argo brought up to the shore,
And straight all landed from her, less and more,
And the king spake to Jason honied words,
And idle were all spears, and sheathed all swords,
As toward the palace they were gently brought.
But Jason, smiling outwardly, yet thought
Within his heart: "All this is fair enow,
Yet do I think it but an empty show; 410
Natheless, until the end comes, will not I,
Like a bad player, spoil the bravery
By breaking out before they call my turn,
And then of me some mastery they may learn."

Amidst these thoughts, between the fair streets led,
He noted well the size and goodly-head
Of all the houses, and the folk well clad,
And armed as though good store of wealth they had,
Peering upon them with a wondering gaze.
At last a temple, built in ancient days 420
Ere Æa was a town, they came unto;
Huge was it, but not fair unto the view
Of one beholding from without, but round

The ancient place they saw a spot of ground
Where laurels grew each side the temple door,
And two great images set up before
The brazen doors, whereof the one was She,
Who draws this way and that the fitful sea;
The other the great God, the Life of man,   429
Who makes the brown earth green, the green earth wan,
From spring to autumn, through quick following days,
The lovely archer with his crown of rays.

  Now over against this temple, towering high
Above all houses, rose majestically
Æetes' marble house: silent it stood,
Brushed round by doves, though many a stream of blood
Had trickled o'er its stones since it was built,
But now, unconscious of all woe and guilt,
It drank the sunlight that fair afternoon.

  Then spake Æetes: "Stranger, thou shalt soon   440
Hear all thou wouldst hear in my house of gold;
Yet ere thou enterest the door, behold
That ancient temple of the Far Darter,
And know that thy desire hangeth there,
Against the gold wall of the inmost shrine,
Guarded by seven locks, whose keys are thine
When thou hast done what else thou hast to do,
And thou mayst well be bold to come thereto."

  "King," said the prince, "fear not, but do thy part,
Nor look to see me turn back faint of heart,   450
Though I may die as my forefathers died,
Who, living long, their loved souls failed to hide

From death at last, however wise they were.
But verily, O King, thy house is fair,
And here I think to see full many a thing
Men love; so, whatso the next day may bring,
Right merrily shall pass these coming hours
Amidst fair things and wine-cups crowned with
    flowers."

"Enter, O guests," the king said, and doubt not
Ye shall see things to make the heart grow hot   460
With joy and longing."
                    As he spoke, within
Blew up the horns, as when a king doth win
His throne at last, and from behind, the men
Who hedged the heroes in, shouted as when
He stands up on his throne, hidden no more.
Then those within threw open wide the door,
And straight the king took Jason by the hand,
And entered, and the Minyæ did stand
In such a hall as there has never been
Before or afterwards, since Ops was queen.   470

The pillars, made the mighty roof to hold,
The one was silver and the next was gold,
All down the hall; the roof, of some strange wood
Brought over sea, was dyed as red as blood,
Set thick with silver flowers, and delight
Of intertwining figures wrought aright.
With richest webs the marble walls were hung,
Picturing sweet stories by the poets sung
From ancient days, so that no wall seemed there,
But rather forests black and meadows fair,   480

And streets of well-built towns, with tumbling seas
About **their** marble wharves and palaces;
And fearful crags and mountains; and all trod
By changing feet of giant, nymph and God,
Spear-shaking warrior and slim-ankled maid.

 The floor, moreover, of the place was laid
With coloured stones, wrought like **a flowery mead**;
And ready to the hand for every need,
Midmost the hall, two fair streams trickled down
O'er **wondrous gem-like** pebbles, green and brown, 490
Betwixt smooth banks of marble, **and** therein
Bright-coloured fish shone through the water thin.

 Now, 'midst these wonders were there tables spread,
Whither the wondering seafarers were led,
And there with meat and drink full delicate
Were feasted, and strange dainty things they ate,
Of unused savour, and drank godlike wine;
While from the golden galleries, divine,
Heart-softening music breathed about the place;
And 'twixt the pillars, at a gentle pace, 500
Passed lovely damsels, raising voices sweet
And shrill unto the music, while their feet
From thin dusk raiment now and then would gleam
Upon the polished edges of the stream.

 Long sat the Minyæ there, and for their parts
Few **words they said, because,** indeed, their hearts,
O'er-burdened with delight, still dreaded death;
Nor did **they think** that **they** might long draw breath
In such an **earthly** Paradise as this,
But **looked to find sharp** ending **to** their bliss. 510

BOOK VII.

*Jason first sees Medea—The magic **potion of Medea**.*

SO long they **sat,** until at last the sun
    Sank in the sea, and noisy day was done.
Then bade Æetes light the place, that they
Might turn grim-looking night into the day;
Whereon, the scented torches being brought,
As men with shaded eyes the shadows sought,
Turning to Jason, spake the king these words:—
   "**Dost thou** now wonder, guest, that with sharp
      swords
And mailèd breasts of men I fence myself,
Not as a pedler guarding his poor pelf,   10
But as a God shutting the door of heaven.
Behold! O Prince, for threescore years and seven
Have I dwelt here in bliss, nor dare I give
The fleece to thee, lest I should cease to live;
Nor dare I quite this treasure to withhold,
Lest to the Gods I seem grown over-bold;
For many a cunning man I have, to tell
Divine foreshowings of the oracle,
And thus they warn me. Therefore shalt thou hear
What well may fill a hero's heart with fear;   20
But not from my old lips; that thou mayst have,
Whether thy life thou here wilt spill or save,

At least one joy before thou comest to die :—
Ho ye, bid in my lady presently!"

But Jason, wondering what should come of this,
With heart well steeled to suffer woe or bliss,
Sat waiting, while within the music ceased,
But from without a strain rose and increased,
Till shrill and clear it drew anigh the hall,
But silent at the entry did it fall;   30
And through the place there was no other sound
But falling of light footsteps on the ground,
For at the door a band of maids was seen,
Who went up towards the dais, a lovely queen
Being in their midst, who, coming nigh the place
Where the king sat, passed at a gentle pace
Alone before the others to the board,
And said: "Æetes, father, and good lord,
What is it thou wouldst have of me to-night?"

"O daughter," said Æetes, "tell aright   40
Unto this king's son here, who is my guest,
What things he must accomplish, ere his quest
Is finished, who has come this day to seek
The golden fell brought hither by the Greek,
The son of Athamas, the unlucky king,
That he may know at last for what a thing
He left the meadowy land and peaceful stead."

Then she to Jason turned her golden head,
And reaching out her lovely arm, took up
From off the board a rich fair-jewelled cup,   50
And said: "O prince, these hard things must ye do:—
First, going to their stall, bring out the two

Great brazen bulls, the king my father feeds
On grass of Pontus and strange-nurtured seeds;
Nor heed what they may do, but take the plough
That in their stall stands ever bright enow,
And on their gleaming necks cast thou the yoke,
And drive them as thou mayst, with cry and stroke,
Through the grey acre of the God of War.   59

"Then, when turned up the long straight furrows are,
Take thou the sack that holds the serpents' teeth
Our fathers slew upon the sunless heath;
There sow those evil seeds, and bide thou there
Till they send forth a strange crop, nothing fair,
Which garner thou, if thou canst 'scape from death.

" But if thereafter still thou drawest breath,
Then shalt thou have the seven keys of the shrine
Wherein the beast's fair golden locks yet shine;
But yet sing not the song of triumph then,
Or think thyself the luckiest of men;   70
For just within the brazen temple-gates
The guardian of the fleece for ever waits,—
A fork-tongued dragon, charmed for evermore
To writhe and wallow on the precious floor,
Sleepless, upon whose skin no steel will bite.

" If then with such an one thou needs must fight,
Or knowest arts to tame him, do thy worst,
Nor, carrying off the prize, shalt thou be curst
By us or any God. But yet, think well
If these three things be not impossible   80
To any man; and make a bloodless end
Of this thy quest, and as my father's friend

Well gifted, in few days return in peace,
Lacking for nought, forgetful of the fleece."

Therewith she made an end; but while she spoke
Came Love unseen, and cast his golden yoke
About them both, and sweeter her **voice grew,**
And softer ever, as betwixt them flew,
With fluttering wings, the new-born, strong desire:
And when her eyes met his grey eyes, on fire   90
With **that** that burned her, then with sweet new shame
Her fair face reddened, and there went and came
Delicious tremors through her. But he said :—
" A bitter song thou singest, royal maid,
Unto a sweet tune; yet doubt not that I
To-morrow this so certain death will **try;**
And dying, may perchance not pass unwept,
And with sweet memories may my name be kept,
That men call Jason of the Minyæ."
   Then said she, trembling : "Take, then, this of me,
And drink in token that thy life is passed,   101
And that thy reckless hand the **die has** cast."
   Therewith she reached the cup to him, but he
Stretched out his hand, and took it joyfully,
As with the cup he touched her dainty hand,
Nor was she loth, awhile with him to stand,
Forgetting all else in that honied pain.
   At last she turned, and with head raised again
He drank, and swore for nought to leave that **quest**
Till he had reached the worst end or the best;   110
And down the hall the clustering Minyæ

Shouted for joy his godlike face to see.
But she, departing, made no further sign
Of her desires, but, while with song and wine
They feasted till the fevered night was late,
Within her bower she sat, made blind by fate.

But, when all hushed and still the palace grew,
She put her gold robes off, and on her drew
A dusky gown, and with a wallet small
And cutting wood-knife girt herself withal, 120
And from her dainty chamber softly passed
Through stairs and corridors, until at last
She came down to a gilded watergate,
Which with a golden key she opened straight,
And swiftly stept into a little boat,
And, pushing off from shore, began to float
Adown the stream, and with her tender hands
And half-bared arms, the wonder of all lands,
Rowed strongly through the starlit gusty night
As though she knew the watery way aright. 130
So, from the city being gone apace,
Turning the boat's head, did she near a space
Where, by the water's edge, a thick yew wood
Made a black blot on the dim gleaming flood:
But when she reached it, dropping either oar
Upon the grassy bank, she leapt ashore
And to a yew-bough made the boat's head fast.
Then here and there quick glances did she cast
And listened, lest some wanderer should be nigh.
Then by the river's side she tremblingly 140

Undid the bands that bound her yellow hair
And let it float about her, and made bare
Her shoulder and right arm, and, kneeling down,
Drew off her shoes, and girded up her gown,
And in the river washed her silver feet
And trembling hands, and then turned round to meet
The yew-wood's darkness, gross and palpable,
As though she made for some place known full well.

  Beneath her feet the way was rough enow,
And often would she meet some trunk or bough,   150
And draw back shrinking, then press on again
With eager steps, not heeding fear or pain;
At last an open space she came unto,
Where the faint glimmering starlight, shining through,
Showed in the midst a circle of smooth grass,
Through which, from dark to dark, a stream did pass,
And all around was darkness like a wall.
  So, kneeling there, she let the wallet fall,
And from it drew a bundle of strange wood
Wound all about with strings as red as blood;   160
Then breaking these, into a little pyre
The twigs she built, and swiftly kindling fire,
Set it alight, and with her head bent low
Sat patiently, and watched the red flames grow
Till it burned bright and lit the dreary place;
Then, leaving it, she went a little space
Into the shadow of the circling trees
With wood-knife drawn, and whiles upon her knees
She dropt, and sweeping the sharp knife around,

Took up some scarce-seen thing from off the ground 170
And thrust it in her bosom, and at last
Into the darkness of the trees she passed.

  Meanwhile, the new fire burned with clear red flame,
Not wasting aught; but when again she came
Into its light, within her caught-up gown
Much herbs she had, and on her head a crown
Of dank night-flowering grasses, known to few.

  But, casting down the mystic herbs, she drew
From out her wallet a bowl polished bright,
Brazen, and wrought with figures black and white, 180
Which from the stream she filled with water thin,
And, kneeling by the fire, cast therein
Shreddings of many herbs, and setting it
Amidst the flames, she watched them curl and flit
About the edges of the blackening brass.
But when strange fumes began therefrom to pass,
And clouds of thick white smoke about her flew,
And colourless and sullen the fire grew,
Unto her fragrant breast her hand she set,
And drew therefrom a bag of silken fret, 190
And into her right palm she gently shook
Three grains of something small that had the look
Of millet seeds, then laid the bag once more
On that sweet hidden place it kissed before.
And, lifting up her right hand, murmured low:—

  "O Three-formed, Venerable, dost thou know
That I have left to-night my golden bed
On the sharp pavement of thy wood to shed

Blood from my naked feet, and from mine eyes
Intolerable tears; to pour forth sighs 200
In **the** thick darkness, as with footsteps weak
And trembling knees I prowl about to seek
That which I need forsooth, but fear to find?
What wouldest thou, my Lady? art thou blind,
Or sleepest thou, or dost thou, dread one, **see**
About me somewhat that misliketh thee?
What crown but thine is on mine unbound hair,
What jewel on my arms, or have I care
Against the flinty windings of thy wood
To guard my feet? or have I thought it good 210
To come before thee with unwashen hands?

  "And this my raiment: Goddess, from three lands
The fleeces it was woven with were brought
Where deeds of thine in ancient days were wrought,
Delos, and Argos, and the Carian mead;
Nor was it made, O Goddess, with small heed;
By **unshod** maidens was the yarn well spun,
And at the moonrise the close web begun,
And finished at the dawning of the light.

  " Nought hides me from the unseen eyes of night 220
But this alone, what dost thou then to me,
That at my need my flame sinks wretchedly,
And all is vain I do? Ah, is it so
That to some other helper I must go
Better at need; wilt thou then take my part
Once more, and pity my divided heart?
For never was I vowed to thee alone,
Nor didst thou bid me take the tight-drawn zone,

And follow through the twilight of the trees
The glancing limbs of trim-shod huntresses.　　230
Therefore, look down upon me, and see now
These grains of what thou knowest, I will throw
Upon the flame, and then, if at my need
Thou still wilt help me, help; but if indeed
I am forsaken of thee utterly,
The naked knees of Venus will I try;
And I may hap ere long to please her well
And one more story they may have to tell
Who in the flowery isle her praises sing."

So speaking, on the dulled fire did she fling　　240
The unknown grains; but when the Three-formed heard
From out her trembling lips that impious word,
She granted all her asking, though she knew
What evil road Medea hurried to
She fain had barred against her on that night.
So, now again the fire flamed up bright,
The smoke grew thin, and in the brazen bowl,
Boiling, the mingled herbs did twine and roll,
And with new light Medea's wearied eyes
Gleamed in the fireshine o'er those mysteries;　　250
And, taking a green twig from off the ground,
Therewith she stirred the mess, that cast around
A shower of hissing sparks and vapour white,
Sharp to the taste, and 'wildering to the sight;
Which when she saw, the vessel off she drew,
As though the ending of her toil she knew,
And cooling for awhile she let it stand,

But at the last therein she laid her hand,
And when she drew it out she thrust the same
Amidst the fire, but neither coal or flame   260
The tender rosy flesh could harm a whit,
Nor was there mark or blemish left on it.

  Then did she pour whatso the bowl did hold
Into a fair gemmed phial wrought of gold
She drew out from the wallet, and straightway
Stopping the mouth, in its own place did lay
The well-wrought phial, girding to her side
The wallet that the precious thing did hide;
Then all the remnants of the herbs she cast
On to the fire, and straight therefrom there passed   270
A high white flame, and when that sunk, outright
The fire died into the voiceless night.

  But toward the river did she turn again,
Not heeding the rough ways or any pain,
But running swiftly came unto her boat,
And in the mid-stream soon was she afloat,
Drawn onward toward the town by flood of tide.

  Nor heeded she that by the river side
Still lay her golden shoes, a goodly prize
To some rough fisher in whose sleepy eyes   280
They first should shine, the while he drew his net
Against the yew wood of the Goddess set.

  But she, swept onward by the hurrying stream,
Down in the east beheld a doubtful gleam
That told of dawn; so bent unto the oar

In terror lest her folk should wake before
Her will was wrought; nor failed she now to hear
From neighbouring homesteads shrilly notes and clear
Of waking cocks, and twittering from the sedge
Of restless birds about the river's edge;   290
And when she drew between the city walls,
She heard the hollow sound of rare footfalls
From men who needs must wake for that or this
While upon sleepers gathered dreams of bliss,
Or great distress at ending of the night,
And grey things coloured with the gathering light.
  At last she reached the gilded water-gate,
And though nigh breathless, scarce she dared to wait
To fasten up her shallop to the stone,
Which yet she dared not leave; so this being done,   300
Swiftly by passages and stairs she ran,
Trembling and pale, though not yet seen by man,
Until to Jason's chamber door she came.

  And there awhile indeed she stayed, for shame
Rose up against her fear; but mighty love
And the sea-haunting rose-crowned seed of Jove
O'ermastered both; so trembling, on the pin
She laid her hand, but ere she entered in
She covered up again her shoulder sweet,
And dropped her dusky raiment o'er her feet;   310
Then entering the dimly-lighted room,
Where with the lamp dawn struggled, through the
    gloom,
Seeking the prince she peered, who sleeping lay

Upon his gold bed, and abode the day
Smiling, still clad in arms, and round his sword
His fingers met; then she, with a soft word,
Came nigh him, and from out his slackened hand
With slender rosy fingers drew the brand,
Then kneeling, laid her hand upon his breast,
And said: "O Jason, wake up from thy rest,   320
Perchance from thy last rest, and speak to me."

Then fell his light sleep from him suddenly,
And on one arm he rose, and clenched his hand,
Raising it up, as though it held the brand,
And on this side and that began to stare.

But bringing close to him her visage fair,
She whispered: "Smite not, for thou hast no sword,
Speak not above thy breath, for one loud word
May slay both thee and me.   Day grows apace;
What day thou knowest! Canst thou see my face?   330
Last night thou didst behold it with such eyes,
That I, Medea, wise among the wise,
The safeguard of my father and his land,
Who have been used with steady eyes to stand
In awful groves alone with Hecate,
Henceforth must call myself the bond of thee,
The fool of love; speak not, but kiss me, then,
Yea, kiss my lips, that not the best of men
Has touched ere thou.   Alas, quick comes the day!
Draw back, but hearken what I have to say,   340
For every moment do I dread to hear
Thy wakened folk, or our folk drawing near;
Therefore I speak as if with my last breath,

Shameless, beneath the shadowing wings of death,
That still may let us twain again to meet,
And snatch from bitter love the bitter sweet
That some folk gather while they wait to die.

"Alas, I loiter, and the day is nigh!
Soothly I came to bring thee more than this,
The memory of an unasked fruitless kiss   350
Upon thy death-day, which this day would be
If there were not some little help in me."

Therewith from out her wallet did she draw
The phial, and a crystal without flaw
Shaped like an apple, scored with words about,
Then said: "But now I bid thee have no doubt.
With this oil hidden by these gems and gold
Anoint thine arms and body, and be bold,
Nor fear the fire-breathing bulls one whit,
Such mighty virtue have I drawn to it,   360
Whereof I give thee proof." Therewith her hand
She thrust into the lamp-flame that did stand
Anigh the bed, and showed it him again
Unscarred by any wound or drawn with pain,
Then said: "Now, when Mars' plain is ploughed at
        last
And in the furrows those ill seeds are cast,
Take thou this ball in hand and watch the thing;
Then shalt thou see a horrid crop upspring
Of all-armed men therefrom to be thy bane,
Were I not here to make their fury vain.   370
Draw not thy sword against them as they rise,
But cast this ball amid them, and their eyes

Shall serve **them then** but little to see thee,
And each of others' weapons slain shall be.
  "Now will my father hide his rage at heart,
And praise thee much that thou hast played thy part,
And bid thee to a banquet on this night,
And pray thee wait until to-morrow's light
Before thou triest the Temple of the Fleece.
Trust not to him, but see that unto Greece   380
The ship's prow turns, and all is ready there.
And at the banquet let thy men forbear
The maddening wine, and bid them arm them all
For what upon this night may chance to fall.
  "But I will get by stealth the keys that hold
The seven locks which guard the Fleece of Gold;
And while we try the fleece, let thy men steal,
How so they may, unto thy ready keel,
Thus art thou saved alive with thy desire.
  "But what thing will be left to me but fire?   390
The fire of fierce despair within my heart,
The **while** I reap my guerdon for my part,
Curses and torments, and in no long space
Real fire of pine-wood in some rocky place,
Wreathing around my body **greedily**,
A dreadful beacon o'er the leaden **sea**."

  But Jason drew her to him, and he said:—
"Nay, **by** these tender hands and golden head,
That saving things for me have wrought to-night,
I know not what; by this unseen delight   400
Of thy fair body, may I rather burn,

Nor may the flame die ever if I turn
Back to my hollow ship, and leave thee here,
Who in one minute art become so dear,
Thy limbs so longed for, that at last I know
Why men have been content to suffer woe
Past telling, if the Gods but granted this,
A little while such lips as thine to kiss,
A little while to drink such deep delight.
  "What wouldst thou? Wilt thou go from me?
     The light   410
Is grey and tender yet, and in your land
Surely the twilight, lingering long, doth stand
'Twixt dawn and day."
                    "O Prince," she said, "I came
To save your life. I cast off fear and shame
A little while, but fear and shame are here.
The hand thou holdest trembles with my fear,
With shame my cheeks are burning, and the sound
Of mine own voice: but ere this hour comes round,
We twain will be betwixt the dashing oars,
The ship still making for the Grecian shores.   420
Farewell, till then, though in the lists to-day
Thyself shalt see me, watching out the play."

  Therewith she drew off from him, and was gone,
And in the chamber Jason left alone,
Praising the heavenly one, the Queen of Jove,
Pondered upon this unasked gift of love,
And all the changing wonder of his life.
  But soon he rose to fit him for the strife,

And ere the sun his orb began to lift
O'er the dark hills, with fair Medea's gift   430
His arms and body he anointed well,
And round about his neck he hung the spell
Against the earth-born, the fair crystal ball
Laid in a purse, and then from wall to wall,
Athwart the chamber paced full eagerly,
Expecting when the fateful time should be.

  Meanwhile, Medea coming to her room
Unseen, lit up the slowly parting gloom
With scented torches: then bound up her hair,
And stripped the dark gown from her body fair,   440
And laid it with the brass bowl in a chest,
Where many a day it had been wont to rest,
Brazen and bound with iron, and whose key
No eye but hers had ever happed to see.

  Then wearied, on her bed she cast her down,
And strove to think; but soon the uneasy frown
Faded from off her brow, her lips closed tight
But now, just parted, and her fingers white
Slackened their hold upon the coverlet,
And o'er her face faint smiles began to flit,   450
As o'er the summer pool the faint soft air:
So instant and so kind the God was there.

BOOK VIII.

The taming of the brazen bulls—The destruction of the Earth-born.

NOW when she woke again the bright sun glared
  In at the window, and the trumpets blared,
Shattering the sluggish air of that hot day,
For fain the king would be upon his way.
Then straight she called her maidens, who forthright
Did due observance to her body white,
And clad her in the raiment of a queen,
And round her crown they set a wreath of green.
  But she descending, came into the hall,
And found her father clad in royal pall,   10
Holding the ivory rod of sovereignty,
And Jason and his folk were standing by.
  Now was Æetes saying : "Minyæ,
And you, my people, who are here by me,
Take heed, that by his wilful act to-day
This man will perish, neither will I slay
One man among you. Nay, Prince, if you will,
A safe return I give unto you still."
  But Jason answered, smiling in his joy :—
"Once more, Æetes, nay. Against this toy   20
My life is pledged, let all go to the end."
Then, lifting up his eyes, he saw his friend,

Made fresh, and lovelier by her quiet rest,
And set his hand upon his mailèd breast,
Where in its covering lay the crystal ball.
  But the king said: " Then let what will fall, fall!
Since time it is that we were on the way;
And thou, O daughter, shalt be there to-day,
And see thy father's glory once more shown
Before our folk and those the wind has blown   30
From many lands to see this play played out."
  Then raised the Colchians a mighty shout,
And doubtful grew the Minyæ of the end,
Unwitting who on that day was their friend.
But down the hall the king passed, who did hold
Medea's hand, and on a car of gold
They mounted, drawn anigh the carven door,
And spearmen of the Colchians went before
And followed after, and the Minyæ
Set close together followed solemnly,   40
Headed by Jason, at the heels of these.
  So passed they through the streets and palaces
Thronged with much folk, and o'er the bridges passed,
And to the open country came at last,
Nor there went far, but turning to the right,
Into a close they came, where there were dight
Long galleries about the fateful stead,
Built all of marble fair and roofed with lead,
And carved about with stories of old time,
Framed all about with golden lines of rhyme.   50
Moreover, midmost was an image made
Of mighty Mars who maketh kings afraid,

That looked down on an altar builded fair,
Wherefrom already did a bright fire glare
And made the hot air glassy with its heat.
 So in the gallery did the king take seat
With fair Medea, and the Colchians stood
Hedging the twain in with a mighty wood
Of spears and axes, while the Minyæ
Stood off a space the fated things to see.   60
 Ugly and rugged was that spot of ground,
And with an iron wall was closed around,
And at the further end a monstrous cage
Of iron bars, shut in the stupid rage
Of those two beasts, and therefrom ever came
The flashing and the scent of sulphurous flame,
As with their brazen, clangorous bellowing
They hailed the coming of the Colchian king;
Nor was there one of the seafaring men
But trembled, gazing on the deadly pen,   70
But Jason only, who before the rest
Shone like a star, having upon his breast
A golden corslet from the treasury
Of wise King Phineus by the doubtful sea,
By an Egyptian wrought who would not stay
At Salmydessa more than for a day,
But on that day the wondrous breast-plate wrought,
Which, with good will and strong help, Jason bought;
And from that treasury his golden shoe
Came, and his thighs the king's gift covered too;   80
But on his head his father's helm was set
Wreathed round with bay leaves, and his sword lay yet

Within the scabbard, while his ungloved hand
Bore nought within it but an olive wand.
 Now King Æetes well beholding him,
Fearless of mien and so unmatched of limb,
Trembled a little in his heart as now
He bade the horn-blowers the challenge blow,
But thought, " what strength can help him, or what art,
Or which of all the Gods be on his part." 90
Impious, who knew not through what doubtful days,
E'en from his birth, and perilous rough ways
Juno had brought him safely, nor indeed
Of his own daughter's quivering lips took heed,
And restless hands wherein the God so wrought,
The wise man seeing her had known her thought.
 Now Jason, when he heard the challenge blow,
Across the evil fallow 'gan to go
With face beyond its wont in nowise pale,
Nor footstep faltering, if that might avail 100
The doomed man aught; so to the cage he came,
Whose bars now glowed red hot with spouted flame,
In many a place; nor doubted any one
Who there beheld him that his days were done,
Except his love alone, and even she,
Sickening with doubt and terror, scarce could see
The hero draw the brazen bolt aside
And throw the glowing wicket open wide.

 But he alone, apart from his desire,
Stood unarmed, facing those two founts of fire, 110

Yet feared not aught, for hope and fear were dead
Within his heart, and utter hardihead
Had Juno set there; but the awful beasts
Beholding now the best of all their feasts,
Roared in their joy and fury, till from sight
They and the prince were hidden by the white,
Thick rolling clouds of sulphurous pungent smoke,
Through which upon the blinded man they broke.
  But when within a yard of him they came,
Baffled they stopped, still bellowing, and the flame   120
Still spouting out from nostril and from mouth,
As from some island mountain in the south
The trembling mariners behold it cast;
But still to right and left of him it passed,
Breaking upon him as cool water might,
Nor harming more, except that from his sight
All corners of the cage were hidden now,
Nor knew he where to seek the brazen plough;
As to and fro about the quivering cage
The monsters rushed in blind and helpless rage.   130
  But as he doubted, to his eyes alone
Within the place a golden light outshone,
Scattering the clouds of smoke, and he beheld
Once more the Goddess who his head upheld
In rough Anaurus on that other tide;
She, smiling on him, beckoned, and 'gan glide
With rosy feet across the fearful floor,
Breathing cool odours round her, till a door
She opened to him in the iron wall,
Through which he passed, and found a grisly stall   140

Of iron still, and at one end of it,
By glimmering lamps with greenish flame half lit,
Beheld the yoke and shining plough he sought;
Which, seizing straight, by mighty strength he
    brought
Unto the door, nor found the Goddess there,
  Who in the likeness of a damsel fair,
Colchian Metharma, through the spearmen passed,
Bearing them wine, and causeless terror cast
Into their foolish hearts, nor spared to go
And 'mid the close seafaring ranks to sow   150
Good hope of joyful ending, and then stood
Behind the maid unseen, and brought the blood
Back to her cheeks and trembling lips and wan,
With thoughts of things unknown to maid or man,
  Meanwhile upon the foreheads of the twain
Had Jason cast the yoke with little pain,
And drove them now with shouts out through the door
Which in such guise ne'er had they passed before,
For never were they made the earth to till,
But rather, feeding fat, to work the will   160
Of some all-knowing man; but now they went
Like any peasant's beasts, tamed by the scent
Of those new herbs Medea's hand had plucked,
Whose roots from evil earth strange power had sucked.
  Now in the open field did Jason stand
And to the plough-stilts set his unused hand,
And down betwixt them lustily he bent;
Then the bulls drew, and the bright ploughshare sent
The loathly fallow up on the right side,

Whilst o'er their bellowing shrilly Jason cried :— 170
"Draw nigh, O King, and thy new ploughman see,
Then mayst thou make me shepherd, too, to thee;
Nor doubt thou, doing so, from out thy flock
To lose but one, who ne'er shall bring thee stock,
Or ram or ewe, nor doubt the grey wolf, King,
Wood-haunting bear, dragon, or such like thing.
Ah the straight furrow! how it mindeth me
Of the smooth parting of the land-locked sea
Over against Eubœa, and this fire
Of the fair altar where my joyful sire 180
Will pour out wine to Neptune when I come
Not empty-handed back unto my home."

Such mocks he said; but when the sunlight broke
Upon his armour through the sulphurous smoke,
And showed the lengthening furrow cutting through
The ugly farrow as anigh they drew,
The joyful Minyæ gave a mighty shout;
But pale the king sat with brows knit for doubt,
Muttering: "Whose counsel hast thou taken, then,
To do this thing, which not the best of men 190
Could do unholpen of some sorcery?
Whoso it is, wise were he now to die
Ere yet I know him, since for many a day
Vainly for death I hope to hear him pray."

   Meanwhile, askance Medea eyed the king,
Thinking nought safe until that everything
Was finished in the Colchian land, and she
No more beheld its shores across the sea;

But he, beholding her pale visage, thought
Grief like to his such paleness on her brought,
And turning to her, said: "How pale thou art!
Let not this first foil go unto thine heart
Too deeply, since thou knowest certainly,
One way or other this vain fool must die."
"Father," she said, "a doubt is on me still,
Some God this is come here our wealth to spill;
Nor is this first thing easier than the rest."
Then stammering, she said: "Were it not best
To give him that which he must have at last,
Before he slays us." But Æetes cast
A sharp glance at her, and a pang shot through
His weary heart as half the truth he knew.
But for one moment, and he made reply
In passionate words: "Then, daughter, let me die!
And, ere I die, beheld thee led along
A wretched slave to suffer grief and wrong
In far-off lands, and Æa at thy back
Nought but a huge flame hiding woe and wrack,
Before from out my willing open hand
This wonder, and the safeguard of my land
A God shall take; and such this man is not.
What! dost thou think because his eyes are hot
On tender maidens he must be a God?
Or that because firmly this field he trod
Well-fenced with magic? Were he like to me,
Grey-haired and lean, what Godhead wouldst thou see
In such an one? Hold, then, thy peace of this,
And thou shalt see thy God full widely miss

The mark he aims at, when from out the earth
Spring up those brothers of an evil birth." 230
 And therewithal he gazed at her, and thought
To see the rosy flush by such words brought
Across her face; as in the autumn eve,
Just as the sun's last half begins to leave
The shivering world, both east and west are red.—
But calm and pale she turned about her head,
And said: "My father, neither were these words
My words, nor would I struggle with my lords;
Thou art full wise; whatso thine heart would have
That do, and heed me not, who fain would save 240
This glory of thy kingdom and of thee.
But now look up, and soothly thou shalt see
Mars' acre tilled: the field is ready then,
Bid them bring forth the seed that beareth men."
 Again with her last words the shouts out-broke
From the seafarers, for, beside the yoke,
Before Mars' altar did Prince Jason stand,
Holding the wand of olive in his hand,
And on the new-turned furrow shone the sun
Behind him, and his half-day's work was done. 250

 And now another marvel: for, behold,
As at the furrow's end he slacked his hold
Upon the plough-stilts, all the bellowing
Wherewith the beasts had made the grim close ring,
Fell suddenly, and all the fire died
That they were wont erewhile to scatter wide
From mouth and nostril, and their loins and knees

Stiffened, and they grew nought but images
Lifelike but lifeless, wonderful but dead,
Such as he makes, who many a day hath fed   260
His furnace with the beechwood, when the clay
Has grown beneath his deft hands day by day
And all is ready for the casting, then
Such things as these he makes for royal men.

But 'mid the shouts turned Jason to the king,
And said: "Fair sir, behold a wondrous thing,
And since these beasts have been content to stay
Before Mars' altar, from this very day
His should they be if they were mine to give."

"O Jason," said the king, "well mayst thou live   270
For many a day, since thou this deed hast done,
But for the Gods, not unto any one
Will I give gifts; but let them take from me
What once they gave, if so the thing must be.
But do thou take this sack from out my hand
And cast its seed about the new-tilled land,
And watch the issue; and keep words till then,
I counsel thee, O luckiest of men."

Then Jason took the sack, and with it went
About that field new turned, and broadcast sent   280
The white teeth scattering, but or ere he came
Back to the altar, and the flickering flame,
He heard from 'neath the earth a muttered sound
That grew and grew, till all that piece of ground
Swelled into little hillocks, like as where
A stricken field was foughten, but that there

Quiet the heroes' bones lie underneath
The quivering grasses and the dusky heath;
But now these heaps the labouring earth upthrew
About Mars' acre, ever greater grew, 290
And still increased the noise, till none could hear
His fellow speak, and paleness and great fear
Fell upon all; and Jason only stood
As stands the stout oak in the poplar wood
When winds are blowing.
      Then he saw the mounds
Bursten asunder, and the muttered sounds
Changed into loud strange shouts and warlike clang,
As with freed feet at last the earth-born sprang
On to the tumbling earth, and the sunlight
Shone on bright arms clean ready for the fight. 300

 But terribly they showed, for through the place
Not one there was but had his staring face,
With great wide eyes, and lips in a set smile,
Turned full on Jason, who, for a short while,
Forgot indeed Medea's warning word,
And from its golden sheath half drew his sword,
But then, remembering all, cried valiantly:
"New born ye are—new slain too shall ye be,
Take this, and round about it read your doom,
And bid them make new dwellings in the tomb, 310
Wherefrom ye came, nor ever should have passed."

 Therewith the ball among the host he cast,
Standing to watch what next that folk would do.
But he the ball had smitten turned unto
The one who stood by him and like a cup

Shattered his head; then the next lifted up
His axe and slew the slayer, and straightway
Among the rest began a deadly fray.

 No man gave back a foot, no breathing space
One took or gave within that dreadful place,   320
But where the vanquished stood there was he slain,
And straight the conquering arm was raised again
To meet its match and in its turn to fall.
No tide was there of fainting and recall,
No quivering pennon o'er their heads to flit,
Nor name or eager shout called over it,
No groan of pain, and no despairing cry
From him who knows his time has come to die,
But passionless each bore him in that fight,
Scarce otherwise than as a smith might smite   330
On sounding iron or bright glittering brass.

 So, little by little, did the clamour pass
As one by one each fell down in his place,
Until at last, midmost the bloody space,
One man was left, alive but wounded sore,
Who, staring round about and seeing no more
His brothers' spears against him, fixed his eyes
Upon the queller of those mysteries.
Then dreadfully they gleamed, and with no word,
He tottered towards him with uplifted sword.   340
But scarce he made three paces down the field,
Ere chill death reached his heart, and on his shield
Clattering he fell. So satiate of fight
Quickly the earth-born were, and their delight
With what it fed on perished, and one hour

Ripened the deadly fruit of that fell flower.
  Then Jason, mocking, cried unto the king:—
" O wonderful, indeed, must be the thing
Thou guardest with such wondrous guards as these;
Make no delay, therefore, but bring the keys   350
That I may see this dear delight of all."
  But on Æetes' face a change did fall,
As though a mask had been set over it,
And smiles of little meaning 'gan to flit
O'er his thin lips, as he spake out at last:—
" No haste, dear guest, for surely now is passed
All enmity from 'twixt us, since I know
How like a God thou art; and thou shalt go
To-morrow to thy ship, to make for Greece;
And with no trial more, bear back the fleece   360
Along our streets, and like no conquered thing,
But with much scattered flowers and tabouring,
Bearing with it great gifts and all my love;
And in return, I pray thee, pray to Jove,
That I may have a few more years of life,
And end at last in honour, free from strife.
And now to-night be merry, and let time
Be clean forgotten, and bring Saturn's clime
And golden days upon our flower-crowned brows,
For of the unseen future what man knows?"   370
  " O King," said Jason, " for these words I praise
Thy wisdom much, and wish thee happy days.
And I will give thee honour as I can,
Naming thee ever as a noble man
Through all the lands I come to: and will take

Thy gifts, indeed, and thou, for Jason's sake,
Shalt have gifts too, whatso thy soul may wish,
From out our keel that has escaped the fish."

So spake those wary foes, fair friends in look,
And so in words great gifts they gave and took,   380
And had small profit, and small loss thereby.
Nor less Medea feigned, but angrily
Regarded Jason, and across her brow
Drew close her veil, nor doubted the king now
Her faith and loyalty.

So from the place
Back toward the town they turned at a soft pace,
In guise of folk that hold high festival,
Since straightly had Æetes bid that all
Should do the strangers pleasure on that day.
But warily went Jason on the way,
And through his folk spread words, to take   390
    good heed
Of what might come, and ready be at need,
Nor yet to take Æetes for their friend,
Since even then he plotted how to end
Their quest and lives: therefore he bade them spare
The wine that night, nor look on damsels fair;
But that, the feast done, all should stealthily
Get to the quay, and round about to sea
Turn Argo's head, and wait like hounds in slip,
Holding the oars, within the hollow ship.   400

"Nor doubt," said he, "that good and glorious
The end shall be, since all the Gods for us
Are fighting certainly: but should death come

Upon me in this land, then turn back home,
Nor wait till they shall lay your bones with mine,
Since now I think to go unto the shrine,
The while ye wait, and take therefrom the fleece,
Not all unholpen, and depart in peace,
While yet the barbarous king beholds us dead
In dreams alone, or through his waking head 410
The vile plots chase each other for our death."

   These things he said, but scarce above his breath,
Unto wise Nestor, who beside him went,
Who unto Butes straight the message sent,
And he to Phlias, so the words at last
Throughout the wondering seafarers had passed,
And so were all made ready for the night.

   But on that eve, with manifold delight,
Æetes feasted them in his fair hall;
But they, well knowing what might chance to fall, 420
Sat saying little, nor drank deep of wine;
Until at last the old king gave the sign
To break the feast up, and within a while
All seemed asleep throughout the mighty pile.

   All seemed asleep, but now Medea went
With beating heart to work out her intent,
Scarce doubtful of the end, since only two
In all the world, she and Æetes, knew
Where the keys were, far from the light of day,
Beneath the palace. So, in garments grey, 430
Like the soft creeping twilight did she go,
Until she reached a passage far below

The river, past whose oozing walls of ston
She and the king alone had ever gone.

  Now she, who thus far had come through the dark,
Stopped, and in haste striking a little spark
From something in her hand, lit up a lamp,
Whose light fell on an iron door, with damp
All rusted red, which with a key of brass
She opened, and there through made haste to pass, 440
Shuddering a little, as her feet 'gan tread
Upon a dank cold floor, though overhead
High-arched the place was, fairly built enow.

  But she across the slippery floor did go
Unto the other wall, wherein was built
A little aumbrye, with a door o'er-gilt,
That with the story of King Athamas,
And Phryxus, and the ram all carven was.
There did she draw forth from her balmy breast
A yellow flowering herb, that straight she pressed 450
Upon the lock, low muttering the while;
But soon across her face there passed a smile,
As backward in the lock the bolts did turn,
And the door opened ; then a golden urn
She saw within the aumbrye, whereon she
Drew out the thing she sought for eagerly,
The seven keys with sere-cloth done about.
Then through the dreary door did she pass out,
And made it fast, and went her way once more
Through the black darkness on from floor to floor. 460

  And so, being come to Jason, him she found
All armed, and ready ; therefore, with no sound,

She beckoned him to follow, and the twain
Passed through the brazen doors, locked all in vain,
Such virtue had the herb Medea bore,
And passing, did they leave ajar each door,
To give more ease unto the Minyæ.

  So out into the fresh night silently
The lovers passed, the loveliest of the land;
But as they went, neither did hand touch hand,   470
Or face seek face; for, gladsome as they were,
Trembling with joy to be at last so near
The wished-for day, some God yet seemed to be
'Twixt the hard past and their felicity.

BOOK IX.

*The Fleece taken from the temple—The departure of Argo—
The death of Absyrtus.*

BUT when they reached the precinct of the God,
    And on the hallowed turf their feet now trod,
Medea turned to Jason, and she said:—
"O love, turn round, and note the goodlihead
My father's palace shows beneath the stars.
Bethink thee of the men grown old in wars,
Who do my bidding; what delights I have,
How many ladies lie in wait to save
My life from toil and carefulness, and think
How sweet a cup I have been used to drink,   10
And how I cast it to the ground for thee.

Upon the day thou weariest of me,
I wish that thou mayst somewhat think of this,
And 'twixt thy new-found kisses, and the bliss
Of something sweeter than thine old delight,
Remember thee a little of this night
Of marvels, and this starlit, silent place,
And these two lovers standing face to face."

"O love," he said, "by what thing shall I swear,
That while I live thou shalt not be less dear   20
Than thou art now?"

"Nay, sweet," she said, "let be;
Wert thou more fickle than the restless sea,
Still should I love thee, knowing thee for such;
Whom I know not, indeed, but fear the touch
Of Fortune's hand when she beholds our bliss,
And knows that nought is good to me but this.

"But now be ready, for I long full sore
To hear the merry dashing of the oar,
And feel the freshness of the following breeze
That sets me free, and sniff the rough salt seas.   30
Look! yonder thou mayst see armed shadows steal
Down to the quays, the guiders of thy keel;
Now follow me, though little shalt thou do
To gain this thing, if Hecate be true
Unto her servant. Nay, draw not thy sword,
And, for thy life, speak not a single word
Until I bid thee, else may all be lost,
And of this game our lives yet pay the cost."

Then toward the brazen temple-door she went,

Wherefrom, half-open, a faint gleam was sent;　40
For little need of lock it had forsooth,
Because its sleepless guardian knew no ruth,
And had no lust for precious things or gold,
Whom, drawing near, Jason could now behold,
As back Medea thrust the heavy door,
For prone he lay upon the gleaming floor,
Not moving, though his restless, glittering eyes
Left them no hope of wile or of surprise.
Hideous he was, where all things else were fair;
Dull-skinned, foul-spotted, with lank rusty hair　50
About his neck; and hooked yellow claws
Just showed from 'neath his belly and huge jaws,
Closed in the hideous semblance of a smile.
Then Jason shuddered, wondering with what guile
That fair king's daughter such a beast could tame,
And of his sheathed sword had but little shame.

But being within the doors, both mantle grey
And heavy gown Medea cast away,
And in thin clinging silk alone was clad,
And round her neck a golden chain she had,　60
Whereto was hung a harp of silver white.
Then the great dragon, at that glittering sight,
Raised himself up upon his loathly feet,
As if to meet her, while her fingers sweet
Already moved amongst the golden strings,
Preluding nameless and delicious things;
But now she beckoned Jason to her side,
For slowly towards them 'gan the beast to glide,
And when close to his love the hero came,

She whispered breathlessly: "On me the blame 70
If here we perish; if I give the word,
Then know that all is lost, and draw thy sword,
And manlike die in battle with the beast;
So dying shalt thou fail to see at least
This body thou desiredst so to see,
In thy despite here mangled wretchedly.
Peace, for he cometh, O thou Goddess bright,
What help wilt thou be unto me this night?"

So murmured she, while ceaselessly she drew
Her fingers through the strings, and fuller grew 80
The tinkling music, but the beast drawn nigh
Went slower still, and turning presently
Began to move around them in a ring.
And as he went, there fell a strange rattling
Of his dry scales; but as he turned, she turned,
Nor failed to meet the eyes that on her burned
With steadfast eyes, and, lastly, clear and strong
Her voice broke forth in sweet melodious song :—

"O evil thing, what brought thee here
  To be a wonder and a fear 90
  Unto the river-haunting folk?
Was it the God of Day that broke
  The shadow of thy windless trees,
  Gleaming from golden palaces,
  And shod with light, and armed with light,
  Made thy slime stone, and day thy night,
  And drove thee forth unwillingly
  Within his golden house to lie?

"Or was it the slim messenger,
Who, treading softly, free from fear,   100
Beguiled thee with his smiling face
From out thy dim abiding place,
To follow him and set thee down
Midst of this twice-washed royal town?
"Or, was it rather the dread Lord
Who slayeth without spear or sword,
And with the flower-culling maid
Of Enna, dwelleth in the shade,
Who, with stern voice compelling thee,
Hath set thee here, our bane to be?   110
"Or was it Venus, seeking far
A sleepless guard 'gainst grief and war,
Who, journeying through thy dismal land,
Beside the heavy lake did stand,
And with no word, but very sight
Of tender limbs and bosom white,
Drew forth thy scaly feet and hard,
To follow over rock and shard?
"Or rather, thy dull, waveless lake
Didst thou not leave for her dread sake,   120
Who, passing swift from glade to glade,
The forest-dwellers makes afraid
With shimmering of her silver bow
And dreadful arrows? Even so
I bid thee now to yield to me,
Her maid, who overmastered thee,
The three-formed dreadful one who reigns
In heaven and the fiery plains,

But on the green earth best of all.
"Lo, now thine upraised crest let fall,   130
Relax thy limbs, let both thine eyes
Be closed, and bestial fantasies
Fill thy dull head till dawn of day
And we are far upon our way."

As thus she sung the beast seemed not to hear
Her words at first, but ever drew anear,
Circling about them, and Medea's face
Grew pale unto the lips, though still the place
Rung with the piercing sweetness of her song;
But slower soon he dragged his length along,   140
And on his limbs he tottered, till at last
All feebly by the wondering prince he passed,
And whining to Medea's feet he crept,
With eyes half closed, as though well-nigh he slept,
And there before her laid his head adown;
Who, shuddering, on his wrinkled neck and brown
Set her white foot, and whispered: "Haste, O love!
Behold the keys; haste! while the Gods above
Are friendly to us; there behold the shrine
Where thou canst see the lamp of silver shine.   150
Nay, draw not death upon both thee and me
With fearless kisses; fear, until the sea
Shall fold green arms about us lovingly,
And kindly Venus to thy keel be nigh."
Then lightly from her soft side Jason stept,
While still upon the beast her foot she kept,
Still murmuring gently many an unknown word,

As when through half-shut casements the brown bird
We hearken when the night is come in June,
And thick-leaved woods are 'twixt us and his tune. 160

   But Jason, going swiftly with good heart,
Came to the wished-for shrine built all apart
Midmost the temple, that on pillars stood
Of jasper green, and marble red as blood,
All white itself and carven cunningly
With Neptune bringing from the wavy sea
The golden shining ram to Athamas;
And the first door therof of silver was,
Wrought over with a golden glittering sun
That seemed well-nigh alike the heavenly one. 170
Such art therein the cunningest of men
Had used, which little Jason heeded then,
But thrusting in the lock the smallest key
Of those he bore, it opened easily;
And then five others, neither wrought of gold,
Or carved with tales, or lovely to behold,
He opened; but before the last one **stayed**
His hand, wherein the heavy key he weighed,
And pondering, in low muttered words he said:—
   "The prize is reached, which yet I somewhat dread
To draw unto me; since I know indeed, 181
That henceforth war and toil shall be my meed.—
Too late to fear, it was too late, the hour
I left the grey cliffs and the beechen bower,
So here I **take hard life and deathless praise**,
Who once desired nought but quiet days,

And painless life, not empty of delight;
I, who shall now be quickener of the fight,
Named by a great name—a far-babbled name,
The ceaseless seeker after praise and fame.   190
   "May all be well, and on the noisy ways
Still may I find some wealth of happy days."

   Therewith he threw the last door open wide,
Whose hammered iron did the marvel hide,
And shut his dazzled eyes, and stretched his hands
Out toward the sea-born wonder of all lands,
And plunged them deep within the locks of gold,
Grasping the fleece within his mighty hold.

   Which when Medea saw, her gown of grey
She caught up from the ground, and drew away   200
Her wearied foot from off the rugged beast,
And while from her soft strain she never ceased,
In the dull folds she hid her silk from sight,
And then, as bending 'neath the burden bright,
Jason drew nigh, joyful, yet still afraid,
She met him, and her wide grey mantle laid
Over the fleece, whispering: "Make no delay;
He sleeps, who never slept by night or day
Till now; nor will his charmed sleep be long.
Light-foot am I, and sure thine arms are strong;   210
Haste, then! No word! nor turn about to gaze
At me, as he who in the shadowy ways
Turned round to see once more the twice-lost face."

   Then swiftly did they leave the dreadful place,

Turning no look behind, and reached the street,
That with familiar look and kind did greet
Those wanderers, mazed with marvels and with
    fear.
And so, unchallenged, did they draw anear
The long white quays, and at the street's end now
Beheld the ships' masts standing row by row   220
Stark black against the stars: then cautiously
Peered Jason forth, ere they took heart to try
The open starlit place; but nought he saw
Except the night-wind twitching the loose straw
From half-unloaded keels, and nought he heard
But the strange twittering of a caged green bird
Within an Indian ship, and from the hill
A distant baying: yea, all was so still,
Somewhat they doubted, natheless forth they passed,
And Argo's painted sides they reached at last.   230
  On whom down-looking, scarce more noise they
    heard
Than from the other ships; some muttered word,
Some creaking of the timbers, as the tide
Ran gurgling seaward past her shielded side.
Then Jason knelt, and whispered: "Wise be ye,
O fair companions on the pathless sea,
But come, Erginus, Nestor, and ye twain
Of Lacedæmon, to behold my gain;
Take me amongst you, neither be afraid
To take withal this gold, and this fair maid.   240
  Yare!—for the ebb runs strongly towards the sea,
The east wind drives the rack to Thessaly,

M

And lightly do such kings as this one sleep
If now and then small watch their servants keep."

   Then saw Medea men like shadows grey,
Rise from the darksome decks, who took straightway
With murmured joy, from Jason's outstretched hands,
The conquered fleece, the **wonder of all lands,**
While with strong arms he raised the royal **maid,**
And **in** their hold the precious burthen **laid,**   259
And scarce her dainty feet could touch the deck,
Ere **down he** leapt, and little now did reck
That loudly clanged his armour therewithal.

   But, turning townward, did Medea call:—
"**O noble Jason, and** ye heroes strong,
To sea, to sea! nor pray ye loiter long;
For surely shall ye see the beacons flare
Ere in mid stream ye are, and running fair
On toward the sea with tide, and oar, and sail.
My father wakes, **nor bides** he to bewail   266
His loss and me; I see his turret **gleam**
As he goes towards the beacon, and down stream
Absyrtus lurks **before** the sandy bar
In mighty keel **well manned and dight for war.**"

   But as she spoke, rattling the cable **slipped**
From out the hawse-hole, and the long oars **dipped**
As from the quays the heroes pushed away,
And in the loosened sail the **wind** 'gan play;
But e'en as they unto the stroke leaned back,
And Nauplius, catching at the main-sheet **slack**   270
Had drawn it taut, out flared the beacon **wide,**
Lighting the waves, and they heard folk who cried:

"Awake, awake, awake, O Colchian folk!"
And all about the blare of horns outbroke,
As watch-tower answered watch-tower down the
    stream,
Where far below they saw the bale-fires gleam;
And galloping of horses now they heard,
And clang of arms, and cries of men afeared,
For now the merchant mariners who lay
About the town, thought surely an ill day   280
Had dawned upon them while they slept at ease,
And, half awake, pushed madly from the quays
With crash of breaking oars and meeting ships,
And cries and curses from outlandish lips;
So fell the quiet night to turmoil sore,
While in the towers, over the uproar,
Melodiously the bells began to ring.

  But Argo, leaping forward to the swing
Of measured oars, and, leaning to the breeze,
Sped swiftly 'twixt the dark and whispering trees;   290
Nor longer now the heroes silence kept,
So joyously their hearts within them leapt,
But loud they shouted, seeing the gold fell
Laid heaped before them, and longed sore to tell
Their fair adventure to the maids of Greece;
And as the mingled noises did decrease
With added distance, and behind them night
Grew pale with coming of the eastern light,
Across the strings his fingers Orpheus drew,
And through the woods his winged music flew:—   300

"O surely, now the fisherman
Draws homeward through the water wan
Across the bay we know so well,
And in the sheltered chalky dell
The shepherd stirs; and now afield
They drive the team with white wand peeled,
Muttering across the barley-bread
At daily toil and dreary-head.
"And midst them all, perchance, my love
Is waking, and doth gently move   310
And stretch her soft arms out to me,
Forgetting thousand leagues of sea;
And now her body I behold,
Unhidden but by hair of gold,
And now the silver water kiss,
The crown of all delight and bliss.
And now I see her bind her **hair**
And do upon her raiment fair,
And now before the altar stand,
With incense in her **outstretched hand,**   320
To supplicate the Gods for me;
Ah, one day landing from the sea,
Amid the maidens shall I hear
Her voice in praise, and see her near,
Holding the gold-wrapt laurel crown,
'Midst of the shouting, wondering **town!**"

So sung he joyously, nor knew that they
Must wander yet for many an evil day
Or ever the dread Gods should let them **come**

Back to the white walls of their long-left home. 330
But on the shouting heroes gazed adown
The foundress of their triumph and renown,
And to her lover's side still drew anear,
With heart now swelled with joy, now sick with fear,
And cheeks now flushed with love, now pale and wan,
As now she thought upon that goodly man,
And now on the uncertain, dreadful Gods,
And now upon her father, and the odds
He well might raise against the reckless crew,
For all his mighty power full well she knew; 340
No wonder therefore if her heart grew cold,
And if her wretched self she did behold,
Led helpless through some old familiar place,
With none to turn on her a pitying face,
Unto the death in life, she still might win;
And yet, if she should 'scape the meed of sin
This once, the world was fair and bright enough,
And love there was to lead her o'er the rough
Of life, and love to crown her head with flowers,
And fill her days and nights with happy hours. 350

Now swift beneath the oar-strokes Argo flew,
While the sun rose behind them, and they drew
Unto the river's mouth, nor failed to see
Absyrtus' galley waiting watchfully
Betwixt them and the white-topped turbid bar.
Therefore they gat them ready now for war,
With joyful hearts, for sharp they sniffed the sea,

And saw the great waves tumbling green and free
Outside the bar upon the way to Greece,
The rough green way to glory and sweet peace.   360

   Then to the prow gat Jason, and the maid
Must needs be with him, though right sore afraid,
As nearing now the Colchian ship, they hung
On balanced oars; but the wild Arcas strung
His deadly bow, and clomb into the top.

   Then Jason cried: " Absyrtus, will ye stop
Our peaceful keel, or let us take the sea?
Soothly, have we no will to fight with thee
If we may pass unfoughten, therefore say,
What is it thou wilt have this dawn of day?"   370

   Now on the other prow Absyrtus stood,
His visage red with eager wrathful blood,
And in his right hand shook a mighty spear,
And said : " O seafarers, ye pass not here,
For gifts or prayers, but if it must be so,
Over our sunken bulwarks shall ye go ;
Nor ask me why, for thus my father wills,
Yet, as I now behold you, my heart thrills
With wrath indeed ; and hearken for what cause,
That ye against all friendship and good laws   380
Bear off my sister with you ; wherefore now
Mars give you courage and a brazen brow !
That ye may try this dangerous pass in vain,
For soothly, of your slaughter am I fain."

   Then Jason wrathfully threw up his head,
But ere the shout came, fair Medea said,
In trembling whisper thrilling through his ear :—

"Haste, quick upon them! if before is fear,
Behind is death!" Then Jason turning, saw
A tall ship staggering with the gusty flaw,   390
Just entering the long reach where they were,
And heard her horns through the fresh morning air.
 Then lifted he his hand, and with a cry
Back flew the balanced oars full orderly,
And toward the doomed ship mighty Argo passed;
Thereon Absyrtus shouted loud, and cast
His spear at Jason, that before his feet
Stuck in the deck; then out the arrows fleet
Burst from the Colchians; and scarce did they spare
Medea's trembling side and bosom fair;   400
But Jason, roaring as the lioness
When round her helpless whelps the hunters press,
Whirled round his head his mighty brass-bound spear,
That flying, smote the Prince beneath the ear,
As Arcas' arrow sunk into his side.
Then falling, scarce he met the rushing tide,
Ere Argo's mighty prow had thrust apart
The huddled oars, and through the fair ship's heart
Had thrust her iron beak, and the green wave
Rushed in as rush the waters through a cave   410
That tunnels half a sea-girt lonely rock.
Then drawing swiftly backward from the shock,
And heeding not the cries of fear and woe,
They left the waters dealing with their foe;
And at the following ship threw back a shout,
And seaward o'er the bar drave Argo out.
 Then joyful felt all men as now at last

From hill to green hill of the sea they passed;
But chiefly joyed Medea, as now grew
The Colchian hills behind them faint and blue,   420
And like a white speck showed the following ship.
There 'neath the canopy, lip pressed to lip,
They sat and told their love, till scarce he thought
What precious burden back to Greece he brought
Besides the maid, nor for his kingdom cared,
As on her beauty with wet eyes he stared,
And heard her sweet voice soft as in a dream,
When all seems gained, and trouble dead does seem.

  So passed this day, and she no less forgot
That wreck upon the bar, the evil spot,   430
Red with a brother's blood, where long was stayed
The wrathful king as from the stream he weighed
The bleeding body of his well-loved son.

  Lo in such wise their journey was begun,
And so began short love and long decay,
Sorrow that bides and joy that fleets away.

BOOK X.

Argo cut off from the straits—The entry of the river—The passage northward.

NIGHT came, but still on by the stars they sailed
  Before the wind, till at the dawn it failed,
And faded soon the sunrise hue away,
Leaving the heavens colourless and grey,
And dull and lightless the decreasing swell
About the watery ways now rose and fell,
And Lynceus, looking back, no more beheld
The galley that so long the chase had held.
Then were all glad, and toiled on at the oar,
When now the drooping sails would help no more. 10
  But soon before their way it seemed as though
A curtain hung they needs must journey through,
A low black mist so brooded o'er the sea.
Then did they hold their hands, but presently,
Moving to meet them, did it hide from sight
The dog-vane and the maintop gilded bright,
Yea in heart-chilling waves it so enwound
The seafarers, that each man gazed around
And saw but shadows where his fellows were.
So with the windless swell did Argo fare   20
Two days with furled sails purposeless and blind,
And bearing heavy hearts; the third, the wind

Sprung up at daybreak, and straight drove away
That hideous mist, that after sunrise lay
A heavy purple bank down in the west.

 Then by the sun his way Erginus guessed,
For on no side could they see any land;
But as upon the helm he set his hand
Such mighty light blazed out upon the prow,
That faint and yellow did the sunlight show   30
Beside it, and amidst it they beheld
The figure that ere now their hands had held
Anigh the Mysian shore; and now it said:—
 "O heroes, wherefore haste ye to be dead?
Behold, while through the heart of yonder fog
I, Argo, drifted as an unsteered log,
Æetes passed us going towards the straits,
And now is lying ready by the gates;
Nor with one ship alone, but with ten keels,
Raised from his subject kings and commonweals,   40
Abides your coming, hoping soon to see
Your bodies on the shore lie wretchedly,
While to the Gods he offers bulls and sheep;
But your fair helper, and your joy will keep,
That she in Æa unavenged may burn.
 "But now the Gods, taking your swift return
Away from you, yet will not let you die;
But bid you, taking heart, turn presently
Unto the northern shore of this ill sea;
There by a mighty river shall ye be,   50
Along whose sides dwell the Sarmatian folk,

Knowing no arts, untaught to bear the yoke
Of equal laws; into this river's mouth
Straight must ye enter, and forget the south,
And many unknown lands and unknown seas,
And deadly forests, vocal with no breeze,
Shall ye go wandering through, but long time past,
Unto the seas ye know shall come at last,
And passing by the western garden fair
Toward the Italian shore, shall ye find there 60
Circe the wise, the wonder of all lands,
Thy father's sister, lady, at whose hands
Of late-wrought guilt shall ye be purified.

"And so, by many troubles being tried,
Unto Iolchos shall ye all come back
Except some few; nor there find any lack
Of much-desired wealth and babbling praise,
And so each man depart unto such days
As the fates grant him, be they good or ill,
With death at last according to their will." 70

With these last words she vanished quite away,
And these, left floating on that dawn of day
Felt severed utterly from hoped-for things;
Like some caged eagle that, with fluttering wings,
Beats at his bars, beholding far away
His windy eyrie up the mountain grey.
—A while ago, and every man nigh saw
The long white walls rise sunny without flaw
From out the curled white edges of the sea;
Yea, almost felt as if they well might be 80
In fair Iolchos that same afternoon.

And now how many and many a glittering moon
Must fill her horns up, while their lives are spent
In unknown lands mid helpless drearyment!

  But as his fellows, speechless and amazed,
Upon the weary sea so stood and gazed,
Spake Jason to them: "Heroes, tell me where
Your hearts are gone, since helpless thus ye stare
On that which helpeth not? in no such wise
A while ago, before Æetes' eyes   90
Ye smote the Colchian ship; with other heart
Ye drave the dark blue clashers far apart;
No eyes I saw like these upon the day,
When with the Colchian spears on every way,
Unto Mars' acre on a doubtful quest
We passed, and dared the worst to get the best.
  "What will ye? Is it then so hard a thing
That we, through many countries wandering,
Shall see unheard-of things, nor fail to come
When yet our blood is warm, back to our home?   100
Be merry, think upon the lives of men,
And with what troubles threescore years and ten
Are crowded oft, yea, even unto him
Who sits at home, nor fears for life and limb,
But trembles the base slave unto a slave;
Or holding trifles he is fain to save,
Sits pleasureless and wearing out his life,
Or with vain words wages disgraceful strife
That leads nowhither, till forgotten death
Seizes the babbler, choking out his breath.   110

"But ye—forget all—get ye to the oar,
And steer rejoicing to the northern shore,
Since we shall win such glory and renown,
That, coming home again to our fair town,
Those left behind shall count us all for lords,
And tremble, gazing at our sheathed swords.
Fair is the wind, the sunny dawn is clear,
Nor are we bound for Pluto's kingdom drear,
But for fair forests, plentiful of beasts,
Where, innocent of craft, with joyous feasts   120
The wise folk live as in the golden age,
Not reddening spears and swords in useless rage;
Nor need they houses, but in fair-wrought cave
Their bodies from the winter's cold they save;
Nor labour they at all, or weave, or till,
For everything the kind land bears at will.
Doubt not at all that they will welcome us
As very Gods, with all things plenteous."

So spake he, knowing nought of that same land;
Natheless, they noting him as he did stand   130
Beside Erginus, with unclouded face,
Took heart again, and to the oars apace
Thy gat and toiled, forgetting half the word
That from great Argo's sprite ere now they heard,
Nor thinking of the ills that they might meet,
But of the day when their returning feet
Should bear them, full of knowledge, wealth, and fame,
Up to the royal hall wherefrom they came.

But Jason in his heart thought: "Now, indeed, 140
Of home and fame full little is my need,
The days will change, and time will bring a day
When through my beard are sprinkled locks of grey,
And love no more shall be enough for me,
And no fair woman much delight shall be;
But little do we want when we are young,
The bended knee and flattering double tongue,
Which we, grown old, and drained of half our fire,
Knowing them false, do yet so much desire."

But for his love, she, set quite free from fear
Of frightful death, held life itself so dear, 150
That where she went she scarcely heeded yet,
For still she seemed to see the black pile set
For her undoing by the temple-gate;
And seemed to see the thronging people wait
For her, who there to make the tragedy
Alone was wanting: then she saw anigh
His face, and with her fingers felt him toy,
And therewithal trembled for very joy,
And set aside for that time all her care,
So sweet was love, and life so blithe and fair. 160

Now northward Argo steered for two days more,
Until at last they came in sight of shore,
And creeping on, they found a river-mouth,
That a long spit of land fenced from the south,
And turned due west: and now, at ebb, full strong
Turbid and yellow rolled its stream along,
That scarce could Argo stem it; wherefore they,

It being but early, anchored till mid-day,
And as they waited, saw an eddy rise
Where sea joined river, and before their eyes
The battle of the waters did begin.
So, seeing the mighty ocean best therein,
Weighing their anchor, they made haste to man
Both oars and sails, and therewith plying, ran
With the first wave of the great conquering flood
Far up the stream, on whose banks forests stood,
Darkening the swirling water on each side.
   And now between them swiftly did they glide,
And now no more they smelt the fresh salt sea,
Or heard the steady wind pipe boisterously
Through the strained rigging, neither with their feet
Set wide, the pitching of their ship to meet,
Went to and fro; for all was quiet now
But gurgling of the stream beside the prow,
And flapping of the well-nigh useless sail,
And from the black woods some faint dismal wail,
Whether of man or beast they know not well.

   Then o'er their hearts a melancholy fell,
And they began to think they might forget
The quest whereon their hearts had once been set,
Now half accomplished, and all wealth and fame,
All memory of the land wherefrom they came,
Their very names, indeed, to wander on,
Unseen, unheard of, till their lives were done.
   In such-like thoughts they anchored for the night,
Nor slept they much, but wishing for daylight,

About the deck they paced, or sat them down
In longing thought of some fair merchant-town.
  So sadly passed the weary night away,
That, dreary, yet was noisier than the day ;   200
For all about them evil beasts 'gan stir
At nightfall, and great soft-winged bats would whirr
About their raiment and their armour bright.
And when the moon rose, and her crescent white
Made the woods blacker, then from either shore
They heard the thundering of the lion's roar,
Now coming nigher, dying now away ;
And once or twice, as in the stream they lay
A spear-cast from the shore, could they behold
The yellow beast stalk forth, and, stark and bold,   210
Stand in the moonlight on the muddy beach.
Then, though they doubted not their shafts could reach
His kingly heart, they held their hands, for here
All seemed as in a dream, where deadly fear
Is mingled with the most familiar thing ;
And in the cup we see the serpent's sting,
And common speech we answer with a scream.
Moreover, sounds they heard they well might deem
To be men's voices ; but whatso they were,
Unto the river side they drew not near,   220
Nor yet of ought like man did they have sight.
  So dawned the day ; but like another night
Unto their wearied eyes it seemed to be,
Amid that solitude, where tree joined tree
For ever, as it seemed ; and natheless, they
Ran out the oars and gat them on their way

Against the ebb, and little help the flood
Gave them that day; but yet for bad or good
They laboured on, though still with less intent,   229
More hopeless past the changeless woods they went.

  But every day, more and more sluggishly
And shorter time, the water from the sea
Ran up, and failed ere eve of the third day,
Though slower took the downward stream its way,
Grown wide and dull, and here and there the wood
Would draw away and leave some dismal rood
Of quaggy land about the river's edge,
Where 'mid the oozes and decaying sedge
There wallowed ugly, nameless, dull-scaled things.

  These now the weary company of kings,   240
As they passed by, could not endure to see
Unscathed of arrows, turning lazily
Blue-gleaming slimy sides up in the sun,
Whose death swift Atalanta first begun.
For as anigh the prow she chanced to stand,
Unto her bow did she set foot and hand,
And strung it, and therefrom an arrow sent
That through the belly of a monster went,
Legged like a lizard, maned with long lank hair.
He, screaming, straight arose from out his lair,   250
With many another of his kith and kin,
And swiftly getting to the water thin,
Made for the ship; and though upon the way
Some few among them lost the light of day,
Smit by Thessalian arrows, yet the most
The narrow strip of water fairly crossed,

And scaled the ship's sides, and therewith began
A fearful battle betwixt worm and man.
Not long it dured; though Ceneus through the mail
Was bitten, and one monster's iron tail   260
Smote down Asterion, whom Eribotes
Made shift to save; but chiefly amid these
She who had been the first to raise the strife
Was hard bested, and scarce escaped with life.

One worm 'twixt ship and shore her arrow slew,
But ere her amazonian axe she drew,
Another monster had got slimy hold
Of her slim ankles, and cast fold on fold
About her legs, and binding thigh to thigh,
Wrapt round her sides, enfolding mightily   270
Her foiled right hand, then raised aloft his crest
Against her unembraced tender breast;
But she, with one unarmed hand yet left free,
Still strove to ward the blow, but giddily,
Because the deadly rings still tighter grew
About her heart; yet as she fell, there flew
A feathered javelin swiftly from the left,
By Arcas desperately cast, that cleft
The monster's head, and dulled his glittering eyes.

Then the glad Minyæ with joyous cries   280
Cleared Argo's decks of all the monstrous things,
As from the maiden's limbs the slimy rings
Slacked and fell off: but she, so saved from death,
Sat weary by the mast, and drew glad breath,
And vowed the grey and deadly thing should shine,
Wrought all of gold, within Diana's shrine,

In woody fair Arcadia. But the rest,
When they with poured-out wine the Gods had blest,
And flayed the slain worms, gat them to the oar,
And 'gainst the sluggish stream slid past the shore.

    But swifter the next day the river ran
With higher banks, and now the woods began
To be of trees that in their land they knew,
And into clumps of close-set beeches grew,
And oak-trees thinly spread, and there-between
Fair upland hillocks well beset with green;
And 'neath the trees great herds of deer and neat,
And sheep, and swine, fed on the herbage sweet,
Seeming all wild as though they knew not man,
For quite untented here and there they ran,
And while two great bucks raised the armed brow
Each against each (since time of fight was now)
About them would the swine squeal, and the sheep
In close-drawn flock their faint republic keep,
With none to watch: nor saw they fence or fold,
Nor any husbandry did they behold,
But the last men their wearied eyes had seen
Were those strong swimmers in the Phasis green.

    So seeing now these beasts in such plenty,
It seemed good unto the Minyæ
To make provision thereof for their need.
And drawing Argo up through sedge and reed,
They made her fast, while divers took the land.
Arcas the hunter, Idas strong of hand,
White Atalanta, wise Eurytion,
Far-seeing Lynceus, and the Sminthian's son,

Keen Theseus, with Pirithous his mate,
Clitius, whose swift shaft smote as sure as fate,
Ætalides, the runner of the plain,
Phocus, whose sling was seldom whirled in vain,   320
Cæneus the cragsman, Periclimenes,
And Apheus, haunter of the close-set trees.

   So forth these set, and none of them had lack
Of spear or bow, or quiver at the back,
As through the land they went with wary mirth,
For they rejoiced once more to feel the earth
Beneath their feet, while on their heads fell down
The uncupped acorn, and the long leaves brown,
For on that land the sad mid-autumn lay,
And earlier came the sunset day by day.   330

   But now unto their hunting gave they heed,
And of the more part happy was the speed,
And soon to Argo did they turn again,
Laden with that they had set forth to gain,
Of deer and beasts the slaughtered carcases
Upborne on interwoven boughs of trees.

   With whom came Theseus not, nor Arcas came,
Nor yet Ætalides (who had the fame
Next Atalanta among all the rest
For swiftness, she being easily the best).   340
There waiting till the night, yet none the more
Came down those three unto the river's shore,
Nor through the night: but swift Ætalides
At dawn they saw come running through the trees,
With Arcas far behind, and Theseus slim
The last of all, but straining every limb

To be their equal: empty-handed they
Came back to Argo on that dawn of day,
And on being asked, a short tale had to tell.
 Unto their part to chase a great buck fell,   350
That led them far, and he at last being lost,
They sat them down with nought to pay the cost
Of all their travail, so being set, they heard
A hubbub of strange voices, and afeard
Leapt to their feet, and presently they saw
Strange folk, both men and women, toward them draw,
Who spread about them as to stop their flight
On all hands more than they durst lightly fight.
 So being thus trapped they fain had spoke them fair,
But knowing not their tongue, they yet had care   360
To speak with smiles as though they feared not aught,
Asking for food by signs, which soon was brought;
No flesh, but roots and nuts, whereof they ate,
And so by signs until the day grew late
They dealt together, making clear indeed
Each unto each but little of their need;
At last of their departure were they fain,
But, being stayed, they durst not strive in vain
For fear of worse; but now, the night being come,
The wild folk seemed to think that place their home 370
Just as another, and there gat to sleep,
Nor yet upon the Greeks a watch did keep
To stop their going; "So," said Arcas, "we
An hour after midnight, warily
Stole from among them, neither gave they chase,
Being still asleep, like beasts, in that same place;

And for their semblance, neither were they clad,
Nor in their hands a spear or sword they had,
Or any brass or iron, but long slings,
And scrips of stones, and ugly stone-set things   380
Most like to knives, and clubs of heavy wood;
Soft-voiced they were, and gentle of their mood,
And goodly made as such wild folk may be,
But tanned with sun and wind; there did we see
Old men and young, and women old and young,
With many children scattered there among,
All naked, and with unshorn yellow hair
Blowing about; and sooth we deem they were
Houseless and lawless, without town or king,
Knowing no Gods, and lacking everything."   390

   So said he, but Medea spoke, and said:—
"O heroes, surely by all likelihead
These are the folk of whom I erst heard tell
In Æa, where to me it oft befell
To speak with many men from many lands,
Long ere ye crossed the Phasis' yellow sands.

   " Of these I learned more tongues of speaking men
Than ye might deem men spoke, who told me then
Of such as these, that ye have seen but now.
And yet indeed some Gods these folk do know,   400
The Sun, the Moon, the mother of the earth,
And more perchance, and days they have of mirth
When these they honour; yea, and unto these
Within their temples, groves of ancient trees,
Clad but in leaves, and crowned in solemn wise,
They offer strangers up in sacrifice,

Which was your doom had not the Gods been **kind**,
Who for **your** bodies other graves will find."

 But when they heard her, glad they were indeed
That they from such a bondage had been freed.   410
And, day being fully come, they loosed **from shore**,
And 'gainst the stream all bent unto the oar.
All day they toiled, and every mile **of way**
Still swifter grew the stream, so on that day
Few leagues they made; and still the banks were fair,
But rising into scarped cliffs here and there,
Where screamed the great ger-falcon as they passed,
And whence the sooty swifts about the mast
Went sweeping, with shrill cries at that new sight.
 Nought happed that day worth record, but at
  night,   420
When they were moored, and sound of splashing oars
Had ceased, and stiller grew the upland shores,
Another sound they heard besides the **stream**
That gurgled past them, that to them did seem
Like sound of feet of men who pass to war,
Rising and falling as the wind from far
Would bear it on or drop it in the dark.
So, while with strained ears, they stood to hark
The murmur, as folk use, scarce sure they heard
That which already inward fear had stirred,   430
Erginus spoke: "O heroes, fear ye nought,
This is not death, though ye to toil are brought;
This noise is but the river as it falls
Over its mountainous and iron walls,

Which, being once passed, both calm and deep will be
The pent-up stream, and Argo easily
Will stem it; but or ere we come thereto,
Needs must we heave her up and make her go
Over the hard earth, till the falls are past.
Eat therefore now, and sleep, that ye may last   440
Through this and other toils, and so may come
Through many labours, back unto your home."

So, landing, many a pine-torch did they light,
And made the dusky evening strange and bright,
And there a mighty fire did they pile,
And set the flesh thereto, and in a while,
When all was ready, did they offer up
That which the Gods claimed, pouring out a cup
Of red wine to them from a new-pierced skin.
Then in that lonely land did they begin   450
Their feast, and first the flesh to Jason gave,
And next to her who all their souls did save,
Far up the Phasis on that other day,
And then unto the swift Arcadian May
The guarded treasure of the trim-shod queen.
Then to the godlike singer, set between
The twin Laconian stars, and then to these;
And then to Arcas, haunter of the trees,
Theseus, Pirithous, Erginus true,
The north-wind's sons, the cleavers of the blue;   460
And all the kings being satisfied in turn,
With vain desires 'gan their hearts to burn,
So stirred within them wine and changing speech.

But unto him his harp did Orpheus reach,
And smote the strings, and through the ancient trees
Rang the heart-piercing honied melodies:—

    " Alas! for Saturn's days of gold,
Before the mountain men were bold
To dig up iron from the earth
Wherewith to slaughter health and mirth,   470
And bury hope far underground.
When all men needed did abound
In every land; nor must they toil,
Nor wear their lives in strife to foil
Each other's hands, for all was good,
And no man knew the sight of blood.
    " With all the world man had no strife,
No element against his life
Was sworn and bitter; on the sea,
Dry-shod, could all walk easily;   480
No fire there was but what made day,
Or hidden in the mountains grey;
No pestilence, no lightning flash,
No over-mastering wind, to dash
The roof upon some trembling head.
    " Then the year changed, but ne'er was dead,
Nor was the autumn-tide more sad
Than very spring; and all unclad
Folk went upon the harmless snow,
For not yet did midwinter know   490
The biting frost and icy wind,
The very east was soft and kind.

"And on the crown of July days,
All heedless of the mid-day blaze,
Unshaded by the rosy bowers,
Unscorched beside the tulip flowers,
The snow-white naked girl might stand;
Or fearless thrust her tender hand
Amidst the thornless rose-bushes.
"Then, 'mid the twilight of the trees 500
None feared the yellow beast to meet;
Smiling to feel their languid feet
Licked by the serpent's forkèd tongue.
For then no clattering horn had rung
Through those green glades, or made afraid
The timid dwellers in the shade.
No lust of strength nor fear of death
Had driven men, with shortened breath,
The stag's wide-open eyes to watch;
No shafts to slay, no nets to catch, 510
Were yet; unyoked the neat might play
On untilled meads, and mountains grey,
Unshorn, the silly sheep might rove.
"Nor knew that world consuming love,
Mother of hate, or envy cold,
Or rage for fame, or thirst for gold,
Or longing for the ways untried,
That ravening and unsatisfied,
Draw shortened lives of men to Hell.

"Alas! what profit now to tell 520
The long unweary lives of men

Of past days—threescore years and ten,
Unbent, unwrinkled, beautiful,
Regarding not death's flower-crowned skull,
But with some damsel intertwined
In such love as leaves hope behind.
 " Alas, the vanished days of bliss!
Will no God send some dream of this,
That we may know what it has been?

 " Oh, thou, the chapleted with green, 530
Thou purple-stained, but not with blood,
Who on the edge of some cool wood
Forgettest the grim Indian plain,
And all the strife and all the pain,
While in thy sight the must foams out,
And maid and man, with cry and shout,
Toil while thou **laughest,** think of us,
And drive away these piteous,
Formless and wailing thoughts, that press
About our hour of happiness. 540
 " Lyæus, King! **by** thee alone
To song may change our tuneless moan,
The murmur of the bitter sea
To ancient tales be changed by thee.
By thee the unnamed smouldering fire
Within our hearts turns to desire
Sweet, amorous, half satisfied;
Through thee the doubtful years untried
Seem fair to us and fortunate,
In spite of death, **in spite of** fate." 550

He ceased, and bent his head above the wine;
Then, as he raised his eyes they saw them shine
In the red torchlight with unwilling tears,
And their hearts too, with thoughts of vanished years
Were pensive, as at ending of his song
They heard the bubbling river speed along,
Nor did they miss that doubtful noise to hear
The rising night-wind through the branches bear,
Till sleep fell on them, and the watch alone
Waked in that place, and heard the distant moan 560
Grow louder as the dead night stiller grew,
And fuller of all fear, till daylight drew
A faint wan streak between the thinner trees,
And in their yellowing foliage the breeze
Made a new sound, that through their waking dream
Like to the surging sea well-nigh did seem.

But the full day being come, all men awake,
Fresh hold upon the oars began to take,
Stemming the stream, that now at every mile
Swifter and shallower ran, and in a while 570
Above all noises did they hear that roar,
And saw the floating foam borne past the shore,
So but ten leagues they made upon that day;
And on the morrow, going on their way,
They went not far, for underneath their keel
Some once or twice the hard rock did they feel,
And looking on ahead, the stream could see
White with the rapids; therefore warily
Some mile or two they went at a slow pace

And stayed their course where they beheld a place 580
Soft-sloping to the river; and there all,
Half deafened by the noises of the fall
And bickering rapids, left the ashen oar,
And spreading over the well-wooded shore
Cut rollers, laying on full many a stroke,
And made a capstan of a mighty oak,
And so drew Argo up, with hale and how,
On to the grass, turned half to mire now.

Thence did they toil their best, in drawing her
Beyond the falls, whereto being come anear, 590
They trembled when they saw them, for from sight
The rocks were hidden by the spray-clouds white,
Cold, wretched, chilling, and the mighty sound
Their heavy-laden hearts did sore confound;
For parted from all men they seemed, and far
From all the world, shut out by that great bar.

Moreover, when with toil and pain, at last
Unto the torrent's head they now had passed,
They sent forth swift Ætalides to see
What further up the river there might be. 600
Who going twenty leagues, another fall
Found, with great cliffs on each side, like a wall,
But 'twixt the two, another unbarred stream
Joined the main river; therefore did they deem,
When this they heard, that they perforce must try
This smoother branch; so somewhat heavily
Argo they launched again, and gat them forth
Still on toward the winter and the north.

BOOK XI.

The passage northward continued— Argo drawn over-land—The winter by the northern river.

NOW might the Minyæ hoist up to the breeze
 Their well-wrought sail, for barren of all trees
The banks were now become, not rising high
Above the deep green stream that sluggishly
Strove with the strenuous Argo's cleaving stem.
 So after all their toil was rest to them
A little while, and on the deck they sat,
Not wholly sad, and talked of this and that,
Or watched the restless fishes turn and wind,
Or the slim kestrel hanging in the wind,   10
Or the wild cattle scouring here and there
About the plain; for in a plain they were,
Edged round with hills, with quaggy brooks cleft
     through,
That 'mid their sedges toward the river drew,
And harboured noisome things, and death to man.
But looking up stream, the green river ran
Unto their eyes, from out the mountains high,
For 'twixt no pass could they behold the sky,
Though at the mountain's foot, far through the plain,
They saw the wandering river shine again,   20
Then vanish wholly, therefore through their case,
With fear did they the jealous Gods appease.

Natheless, for two days did they speed along,
Not toiling aught, and cheered with tale and song,
But the third noonday, bringing them anear
The mountains, turned to certain grief their fear,
For now they saw the stream, grown swift but deep,
Come from a cavern in the mountain steep,
Nor would it help them aught upon that tide
To heave the swift ship out on either side,   30
For all that plain the mountain ridge bestrode,
And scarcely could a horseman find a road
Through any pass into the further land.

  Then 'mid the downcast men did Jason stand,
And lifting up his voice, said: "Minyæ,
Why right and left upon this plain look ye,
Where dwell but beasts or beast-like men alone?
Look rather to that heap of rugged stone,
Pierced with the road that leadeth to the north.
Yea, if from very hell this stream runs forth,   40
Let us go thither, bearing in our hands
This golden, hard-won marvel of all lands.
Yet, since not death it bears, but living things,
Shall we not reach thereby the sea that rings
The whole world round, and so make shift to reach
Sunny Eubœa, and fair Argo beach
Before Iolchos, having lost no whit
Of all our gains? Or else here must we sit
Till hunger slays us on some evil day,
Or wander till our raiment falls away   50
From off our bodies, and we, too, become
Like those ye saw, not knowing any home,

Voiceless, desiring nought but daily food,
And seeking that like beasts within the wood,
Each for himself. And all our glory gone,
Our names but left upon some carven stone
In Greece, still growing fainter day by day.
And this work wrought within the sunny bay,
Nor yet without the help of Gods, shall lie
A wonder to the wild beasts passing by,   60
While on her fallen masts the sedge-birds sing,
Unseen of men, a clean forgotten thing."

  So spake he, setting courage in their hearts
To try the unknown dark, and to their parts
All gat them swiftly, and they struck the mast,
And deftly steered, from out the sunlight passed
Into the cold, bat-haunted cavern low,
And thrusting out with poles, made shift to go
Against the stream, that with a hollow sound
Smote Argo's stem. Then Jason, looking round,   70
Trembled himself, for now, indeed, he thought,
Though to the toiling heroes he said nought:—
"What do we, if this cavern narrows now,
Or over falls these burrowing waters flow,
And drive us back again into the sun,
Cursing the day this quest was first begun,
Or somewhat traps us here, as well it may,
And ends us all, far from the light of day."

  Therewith he bade them light the torches up,
And to the mountain Gods to pour a cup,   80
And one unto the river Gods, and pray
That they might come into the light of day,

When they had pierced the mountain through and
    through.
So from the torches trains of sparkles flew,
And strangely flashed their arms in that dark place,
And white and haggard showed each anxious face
Against those dripping walls of unknown stone.
  But now in Jason's hand the cup outshone,
Full of red wine, pressed by the Grecian sea,
And lifting high his hand, he cried: "O ye,   90
Both Gods and nymphs who in this wild land dwell,
In hill or river, henceforth may ye tell
How through your midst have passed the Minyæ;
And if, ye helping, the cold northern sea
We safely reach, and our desired home,
Thither the fame and fear of you shall come,
And there a golden-pillared house shall stand,
Unto our helpers in this savage land.
Nor when we reach the other side of this
Grim cavern, due observance shall ye miss,   100
For whatso on the teeming plain we snare,
Slain with due rites shall smoke before you there."
  So spake he, and twice poured the fragrant wine;
But they, well-pleased to have the gift divine,
And noting well his promises, took heed
Unto his prayers, and gave the heroes speed.
Then Jason straightway bade more torches light,
And Argo pushed along, flared through the night
Of the dank cavern, and the dull place rang
With Grecian names, as loud the heroes sang,   110
For hope had come into their hearts at last.

                 o

So through the winding cave three days they passed.
But on the fourth day Lynceus gave a cry,
Smiting his palms together, who could spy,
Far off, a little white speck through the dark,
As when the 'lated traveller sees the **spark**
Of some fair-lighted homestead glitter **bright.**
But soon to all men's eyes the joyous sig**ht**
Showed clear, and with redoubled force they pushed
Swift Argo forth, who through the water rushed   120
As though she longed for daylight too and air.
And so within an hour they brought her there,
And on the outer world the sun shone high,
For it was noon; so mooring presently,
On the green earth they clean forgot their pain,
For joy to feel the sweet soft grass again,
And see the fair things of the world, and feel
The joyous sunlight that the sick can heal,
And soft tormenting of the western wind.

And there for joy about their heads they twined 130
The yellow autumn flowers of the field,
And of untimely sorrow were they healed
By godlike conquering wine; nor yet forgot
Their promise to the Gods, but on that spot,
Of turf and stones they built up altars twain,
And sent the hunters forth, and not in vain;
For Atalanta, swifter than a man,
Arcas, and mighty Theseus, overran
A white high-crested bull, and tough cords threw
About his horns, and so by main force drew   140
The great beast to the altars, where the knife

Of wise Asclepius ended his hot life.
And there they feasted far into the night.

But when their toil the next returning light
Brought back to them, they gat unto the oar,
While Jason anxiously scanned either shore;
For now the stream was narrowing apace,
And little more than just enough of space
Was left the oars; but deep it ran and slow,
And through a like flat grassy plain did go   150
As that which ere its burrowing it had cleft;
But lower were the hills, and on the left
So low they grew, they melted quite away
To woody swells before the end of day.

Full many a league upon that day they made,
And the next day the long oars down they laid,
For at their back the steady south-west blew,
And low anigh their heads the rain-clouds flew;
Therefore they hoisted up their sail to it,
And idle by the useless oars did sit,   160
Watching the long wave from their swift sea-plough
Sweep up the low green bank, for soothly now,
A pebble ill-thrown by a stripling's hand
From Argo's deck, had lighted on the land;
And yet far inland still they seemed to be,
Nor noted ought to tell them of the sea.

So on that night, for thought of many things,
Full little sleep fell on the troubled kings;
But Argus slept, and at the dawn he dreamed,
Not wholly sleeping, and to him it seemed   170

That one said to him: "Where is now become
The cunning that thou learnedst in thine home,
O wise artificer? What dost thou here,
While in thy fellows' hearts is gathering fear?
Now from the north thou seest this river flow,
Why doubtest thou to find another go
Into the cold green icy northern sea?
Lo! if thou willest well to trust in me,
About the noontide of this very day,
At the wood's end I bid thee Argo stay,   180
And from her straightway let the Minyæ land
And take the adze and wood-axe in the hand,
And let them labour hard, with thee to guide,
Until on wheels thy well-built keel shall glide;
And this being done as pleases thy wise mind,
Doubt not a northern-flowing stream to find,
For certainly some God shall show it thee.
And if thou wishest now to ask of me,
No dream I am, but lovely and divine,
Whereof let this be unto thee a sign,   190
That when thou wak'st the many-coloured bow
Across the world the morning sun shall throw,
But me indeed thine eyes shall not behold."

  Then he, awaking in the morning cold,
A sprinkle of fine rain felt on his face,
And leaping to his feet, in that wild place,
Looked round and saw the morning sunlight throw
Across the world the many-coloured bow,
And trembling knew that the high Gods indeed

Had sent the Messenger unto their need. 200
And when the Minyæ, running out the oars
That windless morning, found them touch the shores
On either side, then ere one said a word,
He cried, and said: "O Jason, chief and lord,
And ye, fair fellows, to no bitter end
Our quest is come; but this sharp keel shall send
A glittering foam-heap up in the wide sea,
If ye will hear my words and trust in me."

   Therewith he told them of that dream divine,
And of the many-coloured arched sign, 210
And gladdened all their hearts, for well they knew
That some God helped them, and straightway they
     threw
Hawsers ashore, wherewith their keel to tow,
And swiftly through the water made her go,
Until they reached the ending of the wood,
Just at the noonday, and there thought it good
To rest till morning: but at dawn of day
Gat forth, and mighty blows began to lay
On many a tree, making the tall trunks reel,
That ne'er before had felt the woodman's steel. 220

   So many days they laboured, cutting down
The smooth grey beeches, and the pine-trees brown,
And cleft them into planks and beams foursquare.
And so, with Argus guiding all things there,
A stage with broad wheels nigh the stream they made,
And then from out the water Argo weighed
Little by little, dealing cunningly,
Till on the stage the great black ship did lie,

And all things waited for the setting forth
Unto some river flowing toward the north. 230
  But midst all this, as painfully they wrought,
Passed twenty days, and on their heads was brought
The first beginning of the winter cold;
For now the wind-beat twigs had lost their hold
Of the faint yellow leaves, and thin and light
The forest grew, and colder night by night,
Or soaked with rain, and swept with bitter wind,
Or with white creeping mist made deaf and blind.
  Meanwhile for long there came no sign at all,
Nor yet did sight of man to them befall, 240
To guide them on their way, though through the trees,
Singly at times, at times in twos and threes,
Both for their daily flesh they hunted oft,
And also fain of fells to clad them soft,
And guard their bodies from the coming cold;
Yet never any man did they behold,
Though underneath the shaft and hunting-spear,
Fell many a stag, and shuffling crafty bear,
And strange the Minyæ showed in shaggy spoil.
  But now, at ending of their woodwright's toil, 250
It chanced Argus' self alone to go,
One bitter day, when the first dusty snow
Was driven through the bare boughs from the east,
In hot chase of the honey-loving beast
Far from his fellows: him he brought to bay
Nigh to the dusk of that quick-darkening day,
Deep in the forest 'mid a clump of yews,
And ere the red-eyed beast again could choose

To fight or flee, ran in, and thrust his spear
Into his heart; then fell the shaggy bear, 260
As falls a landslip by the mining sea,
With grass and bracken, and wind-bitten tree,
And Argus, drawing out his two-edged knife,
Let out the last spark of his savage life;
But as he arose, he heard a voice that said:—
"Good luck, O huntsman, to thine hardihead,
Well met thou art to me, who wander far
On this first winter night that shows no star."

 Then looking up, he saw a maid draw nigh,
Like those who by Thermodon live and die; 270
Her legs and arms with brazen scales were clad,
Well-plated shoes upon her feet she had,
And fur-lined, gold-wrought raiment to the knee,
And on her head a helm wrought royally;
In her slim hand a mighty bow she bore,
And at her back well-feathered shafts good store,
And in her belt a two-edged cutting sword.
Then straightly answered Argus to her word:—
"Lady, not far hence are my fellows stayed,
But on hard earth this night will they be laid, 280
And eat the flesh of beasts their hands have slain.
For from the sea we come, to meet again
The ocean that the round world rings about,
Still wandering on, in trouble and in doubt."
 "Nay," said she, "let us set on through the wood,
For food and fire alone to me are good,
And guarded sleep among such folk as thee,
For being alone, I fear the enemy,

The savage men our bands are wont to chase
Through these wild woods, from tangled place to
    place."

  Then Argus swiftly flayed off the bear's hide,
And through the wood went with her side by side;
But long ere they could reach the skirts of it,
Across the world the wings of night 'gan flit;
Then blindly had he stumbled through the place,
But still the damsel went before a pace,
Leading him on; and as she went, she shed
A faint light round, but no word Argus said,
Because he deemed she was a thing divine,
And in his heart still thought upon the sign.

  So went the twain till nigh the woods were past,
And the new-risen moon slim shadows cast
Upon the thin snow, and the windless sky
Was cleared, and all the stars shone frostily.
Therewith she stopped, and turned about on him,
And with the sight his dazzled eyes did swim,
So was she changed, for from her raiment light
Her rosy limbs showed 'gainst the wintry white,
Not shrinking from the snow; her arms were bare,
Her head unarmed set round with yellow hair,
And starred with unnamed dainty glimmering things;
From her two shoulders many-coloured wings
Rose up, and fanning in the frosty night,
Shone as they moved with sparkles of strange light;
And on an ivory rod within her hand
A letter bound round by a golden band
He saw. Then to the dazed man she said:—

"Argus, be glad, and lifting up thine head,
Look through these few last trees upon the plain,
Smooth and unseamed, though never crossed by
    wain,   320
And thank the Gods that led you here at last,
For in no long time shall the leagues be passed
'Twixt you and a swift river running north.
But now next morn at daybreak get ye forth,
And labour all ye may, for see the sky
How clear it is—the few light clouds are high,
And from the east light blows the frosty wind;
Firm will the way be now, nor ill to find,
But surely in few days will come the snow,
And all the plain, so smooth and even now,   330
Shall be swept into drifts impassable.
And now I bid thee heed the great downs well
Thou seest bar the northern way to thee;
Left of the moon a wide pass thou mayst see;
Look—where the yew-trees o'er the whitened grass
Mix with the dark sky: make ye for that pass,
While yet endures the east wind and the frost,
And in your journey shall ten days be lost,
If that ye labour hard: but coming there,
Shall ye behold a clear green river fair,   340
Unfrozen yet, swift-running, that will hold
Great Argo well: now at my word be bold,
And set her therein, and the black ship tow
Adown the stream, though not far shall ye go,
But, reaching a great forest, bide ye there,
And there the coming unknown winter bear.

The days shall darken, the north-wind shall blow,
And all about shall swirl the drifting snow,
And your astonished eyes shall soon behold
Firm earth and river one with binding cold,   350
And in mid-winter then shall ye be shut;
But ere that haps shall ye build many an hut,
And dwell there as ye may, until the spring
Unchains the streams, and quickens everything.
Then get ye down the river to the sea.

"Nor doubt thou aught since thou beholdest me,
For I indeed am Iris; but farewell,
For of my finished message must I tell
To her that sent me to this dreary place."

Thus spake she, and straightway before his face 360
She spread her fair wings wide, and from the earth
Rose upwards toward the place that gave her birth,
Still growing faint and fainter 'neath the moon,
Till from his wondering eyes she vanished soon.
But she being gone, he gat him straight away
Unto his fellows, bidding them 'gainst day
Be ready to set forth, and told his tale.
And they, not fearing that his word should fail,
Gat them to sleep, and ere the late dawn came,
By the faint starlight and the flickering flame   370
Of their own watch-fires were upon the way.

So at the cables toiled all men that day
In bands of twenty, and strong shoulders bore
The unused yoke, and laboured very sore,
And yet with all their toil few miles they made,
Though 'gainst that bitter labour sweet hope, weighed,

Was found the heavier, and their hearts were cheered
With wine and food ere the noontide they neared;
Nor as they laboured did the Thracian spare
To cast his music on the frosty air, 380
That therewith ringing, gladdened every heart.
So till the evening did each man his part,
When all that night they slept, and at daybreak
The twisted cables in strong hands did take
And laboured on, not earning warriors' meed,
But like some carl's unkempt and rugged steed,
That to the town drags his corn-laden wain.

But neither was the heavenly word in vain,
For as the yew-clad hill they drew anear
The grey-eyed keen Messenian could see clear, 390
From the bare top of a great ashen-tree,
The river running to the northern sea,
Showing all dull and heavy 'gainst the snow,
And when the joyful tidings they did know,
Light grew their hearts indeed, and scarcely less
They joyed than he who, lying all helpless
In dreary prison, sees his door ope wide,
And half-forgotten friends stand by his side.
So on the tenth day through the pass they drew
Their strange ship-laden wain, and came unto 400
A deep dark river, their long promised road;
Then from the car they slipped its heavy load,
And when safe in the stream the keel had slid,
They with strong axes their own work undid,
And to the Goddess a great altar made

Of planks and beams, foursquare, and thereon laid
A white wild bull, and barley cakes, and spice,
Not sparing gold and goodly things of price;
And fire being set thereto, and all things done
That they should do, by a faint mid-day sun,   410
Seaward they turned, and some along the shore,
With lightened hearts the hempen tow-ropes bore,
And some on Argo's deck abode their turn.

But now did Jason's heart within him burn
To show his deeds to other men than these,
Nor did he quite forget the palaces
Of golden Æa, long left, as a dream,
Or Æson's beauteous house, whose oaken beam
Cleft the dark wintry river, as they went
With longing eyes and hearts still northward bent, 420
And fain he was to see his dainty bride,
That wrapt in muffling furs sat by his side,
Sit 'neath some heavy rustling summer tree,
Thin clad, to drink the breezes from the sea.

Now the next day the great oak-wood they reached,
And as the Goddess bade them, there they beached
Their sea-beat ship, on which from side to side
They built a roof against the snowy tide,
And round about her, huts wherein to dwell,
When on their heads the full midwinter fell,   430
And round the camp a wooden wall they made,
That by no men or beasts they might be frayed.
Meanwhile, the frost increased, and the thin snow
From off the iron ground the wind did blow,
And in the cold, dark stream, from either bank

The ice stretched forth; at last, ere the sun sank,
One bitter day, low grew the clouds and dun
A little northward of the setting sun,
Wherefrom, at nightfall, sprung a furious blast,
That, ere the middle of the night was past,   440
Brought up the snow from some untrodden land,
Joyless and sunless, where in twilight stand,
Amid the fleecy drift with faces wan,
Giants immoveable by God or man.

  So 'mid the many changes of the night,
The silent snow fell till the world was white,
And to those southland folk entrapped, forlorn
The waking was upon the morrow morn,
And few were light of foot enough to go
Henceforth about the woods their darts to throw   450
At bird or beast, though, as the wild-fowl passed
South o'er their camp, yet flew they not so fast
As Arcas' arrows, and the elk at bay
Deep in the forest, seldom found a way
To 'scape from Jason's mighty well-steeled spear,
And Atalanta's feet outran the deer
And slew him, tangled in the wreathed drift.

  Nor for the rest, did they yet lack the gift
Of sunny Bacchus, but by night and day,
By firelight passed the snowy time away,   460
Forgetting not their fathers, or the time
When all the world still dwelt in equal clime,
But each to each amid the wine-cups told
Unwritten, half-forgotten tales of old.

BOOK XII.

The heroes reach the northern sea: and pass unknown lands, and seas without land, till they come at last to the Pillars of Hercules.

MOST pitiless and stark the winter grew
   Meanwhile, beneath a sky of cloudless blue,
And sun that warmed not, till they nigh forgot
The green lush spring, the summer rich and hot,
The autumn fragrant with slow-ripening fruit;
Till each grew listless, dull to the heart's root;
For day passed day, and yet no change they saw
In the white sparkling plain without a flaw,
No cloud, no change within the sunny sky,
Or in the wind, that rose at noon, to die   10
Before the sunset, and no change at all
In the drear silence of the dead nightfall.
  Ten weeks they bode there, longing for the spring,
And to the hearts of some the thought would cling
That thus they should be till their lives were past,
And into hopeless bonds that land was cast;
But on a day the wind, that rose at noon,
Died not at night, and the white, sharp-edged moon,
Just as the west had given it to sight,
Was hidden from the watchers of the night   20
By fleecy clouds, and the next dawn of day
Broke o'er the Minyæ colourless and grey,

With gusts of fitful wind 'twixt south and east,
That with the day grew steadier and increased,
Until a south-west gale blew o'er the snow,
And northward drove the steel-blue clouds and low.
And on that night the pattering of the rain
Roused them from sleep, and next they saw the plain
Made grey and ugly with quick-coming thaw,
And all the sky beset with fowl they saw, 30
Who sniffed the wind and hastened from the sea
Unto the floods now coming certainly.

For from their camp the Minyæ beheld
How the swift river from the high ground swelled,
And still tormented by the wind and rain,
Burst from the ice and covered all the plain
With breadth of turbid waters, while around
Their high-raised camp again they saw the ground
Freed from the swathing snow; nor was it long
Ere in the woods the birds began their song, 40
For March was come and life to everything,
Nor did the buds fear much the doubtful spring.

Now in few days the sun shone out again,
The waters drew from off the flooded plain,
And all was bright and soft as it might be,
Though bank-high rolled the river to the sea,
Made perilous with trees and heavy drift;
Natheless on rollers Argo did they lift,
And drew her toward the stream in spite of all
The ills they saw, and chances that might fall; 50
And there they launched her, being now most fain
Once more to try the green and shifting plain,

And for the praise of other men they yearned
And all the goods of life so dearly earned,
Nor failed desire and longing love to come
That spring-tide to those rovers far from home.
   Therefore with joy they shouted, when once more
They felt great Argo move, and saw the shore
Keep changing as they swept on toward the sea,
With cheerful hearts still rowing steadily;   60
For now the ashen oars could they thrust forth
Into the widened stream, that toward the north
Ran swiftly, and thenceforward day by day
Toiling, they made full many a league of way.
Nor did they see great hills on either hand,
When they had fairly passed the woody land
Where they abode the winter; neither heard
The sound of falls to make their hearts afeared,
But through great woods the gentle river ran,
And plains where fed the herds unowned of man; 70
Though sometimes in the night-time did they hear
Men's voices calling out, far-off and near,
But in some tongue not one among them knew,
No, not the Queen: but Lynceus, passing through
The woods with Idas, following up a bear,
A sudden clamour of men's tongues did hear,
And in a cleared space came upon a throng
Of naked men and women, fair and strong,
About a fire, just at point to eat,
But at the flash of arms they to their feet   80
Rose suddenly, and swiftly gat away,
Nor durst the twain give chase to them that day,

But coming to that fire, laid their hands
On a brass cauldron, and three woollen bands,
That seemed like belts or fillets for their heads,
Set thick with silver knots and amber beads.
Now round the brazen cauldron, graven well,
Were uncouth letters, that some tale might tell,
If any them could read; so when the fleece
Was offered up unto the Gods of Greece, 90
This thing in fair Messene Idas hung
In the white fane where deeds of war are sung.

But through all this the wearied Minyæ
Were drawing nigh unto the northern sea,
And marshier grew the plain as on they went,
And eastward the still-widening river bent,
Until one day at eve, with chilling rain,
The north-wind blew across the marshy plain
Most cold and bitter, but to them as sweet
As the rose-scented zephyr those do meet 100
Who near the happy islands of the blest;
For as upon their eager brows it pressed,
They sniffed withal the odour of the sea,
And going on a mile, they seemed to be
Within some eddy rippling languidly,
And when the stream they tasted that went by
Their shielded bulwark, better was the draught
Than any wine o'er which a king has laughed,
For still it savoured of the bitter sea.

So fell the night, and next day joyously 110
They met the full flood, whose first toppling wave
Against the sturdy prow of Argo drave,

And with good heart, as 'midst the sweeping oars
It tossed and foamed, and swept the muddy shores,
They toiled, and felt no weariness that day.
But though right well they gat them on their way
They failed ere dark the open sea to reach;
But in the night the murmur of the beach,
Tormented by the changeful dashing seas,
Came to their ears upon the fitful breeze.   120
Then sore they longed for dawn, and when it broke
Again the waters foamed beneath their stroke,
Till they had gained that river's utmost reach,
Which from the sea by a low sandy beach
Was guarded well, all but a little space,
Through which now rushed in headlong, foaming race,
The huddled waters of the flowing tide.
So there the Minyæ thought it good to bide
And wait the ebb, dreading some hidden bank;
And while they waited to good hap they drank,   130
And poured out wine unto the deity
Who dwelt between the river and the sea,
Forgetting not the great Earth-shaking One,
Nor Her by whose help thus far they had run
Their happy course unto that river's mouth.
And now the wind had changed, and from the south
Blew softly, and the hot sun shining forth,
Made lovely land of that once bitter north,
And filled their hearts with longing thoughts of love,
And worship of the sea-born seed of Jove.   140

But as they waited thus, with hearts that burned
To try the sea, the tide grew high and turned,

And seaward through the deepened channel ran
In gentle ripple 'gainst the breakers wan.
Then thither gat the joyous Minyæ,
And shouting, drave out Argo to the sea.

But when the first green ridge swept up her bow,
Then Jason cried: "And who shall stop us now?
And who shall drive us unto other end,
Than that we will? Let whoso be our friend, 150
Whoso our foe, henceforth, until the earth
Forgets of changeful men the death and birth,
We shall not be forgotten anywhere,
But our deeds told shall free sad folk from care."
So spake he, and his love beholding him,
Trembled for joy and love in every limb,
And inwardly she saw an ivory throne,
And Jason sitting with her there alone,
High o'er wise men and warriors worshipping.
For they were young, nor yet had felt the sting 160
Of poisonous fear, nor thought of coming age
And bitter death, the turning of the page
By those who quite forget what they have read,
Taking no heed of living folk or dead.

Now hoisting sail, and labouring with the oar,
They passed along the amber-bearing shore,
A low coast, backed by pine-woods: none the less
Some days they needs must pass in idleness,
And lie-to, 'midst white rolling mist and blind,
Lest Argo on some shallow death should find; 170

Yet holpen by the steersman's mighty sire,
Safely they sailed until the land rose higher,
And through a narrow strait at last they went,
Brushing the unknown coast, where, with bows bent,
They saw a skin-clad folk awaiting them,
Who stood to watch the well-built Argo stem
The rushing tide upon the shingly beach,
And thence, as knowing that they could not reach
The heroes with their arrows, shook their spears,
And shouted unknown threats to careless ears. 180

But when against the midst of them they came,
Forth strode a huge man, with red hair like flame,
And his huge bow against them strongly drew,
Wherefrom a swift shaft straight to Argo flew,
And whistling over Jason's head, stuck fast
Over the barb-points in the gleaming mast.
Then all men praised that archer; but the man
Who in Arcadian woods all beasts outran,
Straight drew his bow unto the arrow-head,
And no man doubted that wild king was dead: 190
Natheless, unmoved they saw the archer stand,
And toward the Arcadian arrow stretch his hand,
That midmost of his skin-clad body smote,
But bounded back as from an iron coat.
Then loud his people shouted, and all drew
Their feeble bows, but short their arrows flew,
And through the straits the wondering Minyæ
Passed out unscathed into the open sea,
While still of wizardry and charms they spoke.

But Jason from the mast the arrow broke, 200

That erewhile had so scantly missed his life,
And found it scored as by a sharp-edged knife,
From barb to notch, with what seemed written words,
In tongue unknown to aught but beasts and birds.
So when Medea saw it, straight she said:
  "Fair love, now praise some God thou art not dead,
For from the Cimbrian folk this arrow came,
And its sharp barbs within a wizard's flame
Were forged with peril, and the shaft of it
Was carved by one who in great fear did sit   210
Within the haunted places of the wood,
And tears are on its feathers, and red blood:
Nor ask me now the name of her who taught
This wisdom to me: but two arrows brought
From this same folk to Æa have I seen,
By one whose wounds will evermore be green
While on the earth he dwells." So spoke the maid,
But Jason, wondering at the words she said,
Gazed on her fair face, smiling lovingly,
Nor cared to think that he must one day die.   220

  Now rose a south-east gale, and Argo lost
All sight of land, and the vexed Minyæ, tost
From sea to sea, began to feel a fear
They yet might pass into some ocean drear,
Beyond the circling sea that rings the world,
And down a bottomless abyss be hurled,
To fall for ever: then the winged twain,
That erst had been the loathly harpies' bane,
Came forth, and on the prow with wings spread wide,

Half stood, half floated, while aloud they cried :— 230
"What dost thou, Father? art thou sleeping then,
And does it not suffice that trading men
Float up and down, dead corpses on the sea,
While all their wealth is lying wretchedly
On Nereus' pavement; but must we too drive
Before this south wind, hopeless though alive,
Until the furthest gulfs shall suck us down,
And land our battered keel at Pluto's town?"

So spake they; but still blew the south the same
Until the starless night upon them came, 240
But then a little did its fury lull,
And when the rain-beat night was at its full,
Fell to a light breeze, though still many a sea
Swept Argo's deck, and still the Minyæ
Had dread of some returning hideous blast.
But when the doubtful night from them had past,
Barefoot upon the prow Medea stood,
And burning in a censer hallowed wood,
With muttered words she swung it, nor took heed
Of how the wind was dealing with her weed. 250
Nor with firm-planted feet one whit did reck
Of washing of the brine about the deck,
But swung her censer till a bright red flame
From out the piercings of its cover came;
Then round she turned and said: "O Minyæ,
Fear not to die within the northern sea,
For on my head hither the north wind comes,
And ye some day shall surely see your homes.
But since upon us yet lies heavily

My brother's death, forget not we must see 260
My father's godlike sister, who one day
With all due rites that blood shall wash away.

"And now, behold the sun shines through the clouds,
And ye may hear across the well-strained shrouds
The longed-for wind, therefore make no delay,
For time it is that we were on our way,
So let Erginus to the south-west steer;—

"But sleep to me of all things now is dear,
For with two mighty ones but for your sake
Have I contended. He who still doth shake 270
The firm-set earth, and She who draws the sea
This way and that, the while in majesty
She sits, regarding little but her will;—
The fear of these my heavy heart doth fill."

So said she, and with pale and languid face
And half-shut eyes, unto the guarded place,
Where was her golden bed, the maiden came.
And in her dreams at first saw blood and flame
O'er all the world, and nothing green or fair;
Then in a snowy land, with body bare, 280
Went wandering long, be-mocked of uncouth things;
Then stood before the judgment-seat of kings,
Knowing no crime that she was charged withal,
Until at last deep sleep on her did fall
Like death itself, wherein the troublous past
And fearsome future in one tomb are cast.

Meanwhile the Minyæ, joyful at her tale,
Ran out the oars and hoisted up the sail,

And toward the south with good hearts 'gan to go,
While still they felt the favouring north wind blow,　290
And the third day again they saw the land,
That in white cliffs rose up on the right hand,
Coasting whereby, they came into a strait,
Or so they deemed, for as the day grew late,
Beneath a frosty light-blue sky and cold
Another country could they now behold
Dim o'er the glittering sea; but in the night
They by the moon past the high cliff and white
Ceased not to sail, and lost the other shore
When the day broke, nor saw it any more,　　300
As the first land they coasted, that changed oft
From those high cliffs to meadows green and soft,
And then to other cliffs, some red, some grey,
Till all the land at noon of the fourth day
They left astern, sailing where fate might lead,
Of sun or stars scarce taking any heed,—
Such courage in their hearts the White-armed **set**,
Since, clad in gold, was Pelias living yet.

　But to the Gods now did they sacrifice
As seafarers may do, and things of price　　310
Gave to the tumbling billows of the sea,
That for their lives still cried out hungrily,
And though for many days they saw no shore,
Yet fainted not their hearts as heretofore,
For as along the pathless plain they went,
The white-foot messenger the Goddess sent,
Who, unseen, whispered in the helmsman's ear,
And taught him how the goodly ship to steer;

And on a time it chanced as the day broke,
And to their life the longing Minyæ woke,   320
Across the risen sun the west wind blew
A thin light rain, which He, just shining through,
Showed to them all the many-coloured sign;
Then to the Goddess did they pour out wine,
Right glad at heart; but she the live-long day
By Argo's prow flew o'er the shifting way
Unseen of all, and turned them still to land;
And as they went the Thracian's cunning hand
Stole o'er the harp-strings till Arion's steeds
Gat them from 'twixt the tangled water-weeds,   330
And lifted listening heads above the sea,
And sea-birds, pensive with the harmony,
About the mast, above the singer hung,
With quivering wings, as from full heart he sung:—

   "O death, that maketh life so sweet,
   O fear, with mirth before thy feet,
   What have ye yet in store for us,
   The conquerors, the glorious?
   "Men say: 'For fear that thou shouldst die
   To-morrow, let to-day pass by   340
   Flower-crowned and singing;' yet have we
   Passed our to-day upon the sea,
   Or in a poisonous unknown land,
   With fear and death on either hand,
   And listless when the day was done
   Have scarcely hoped to see the sun
   Dawn on the morrow of the earth,

Nor in our hearts have thought of mirth.
And while the world lasts, scarce again
Shall any sons of men bear pain   350
Like we have borne, yet be alive.

"So surely not in vain we strive
Like other men for our reward;
Sweet peace and deep, the chequered **sward**
Beneath the ancient mulberry-trees,
The smooth-paved gilded palaces,
Where the shy thin-clad damsels sweet
Make music with their gold-ringed feet.
The fountain court amidst of it,
Where the short-haired slave maidens sit,   360
While on the veined pavement lie
The honied things and spicery
Their arms have borne from out the town.

"The dancers on the thymy **down**
In summer twilight, when the earth
Is still of all things but their mirth,
And echoes borne upon the wind
Of others in like way entwined.

"The merchant towns' fair market-place,
Where over many a changing face   370
The pigeons of the temple flit,
And still the outland merchants sit
Like kings above their merchandise,
Lying to foolish men and wise.

"Ah! if they heard that we were come
Into the bay, and bringing home
That which all men have talked about,

Some men with rage, and some with doubt,
Some with desire, and some with praise,
Then would the people throng the ways, 380
Nor heed the outland merchandise,
Nor any talk, from fools or wise,
But tales of our accomplished quest.

"What soul within the house shall rest
When we come home? The wily king
Shall leave his throne to see the thing;
No man shall keep the landward gate,
The hurried traveller shall wait
Until our bulwarks graze the quay,
Unslain the milk-white bull shall be 390
Beside the quivering altar-flame;
Scarce shall the maiden clasp for shame
Over her breast the raiment thin
The morn that Argo cometh in.

"Then cometh happy life again
That payeth well our toil and pain
In that sweet hour, when all our woe
But as a pensive tale we know,
Nor yet remember deadly fear;
For surely now if death be near, 400
Unthought-of is it, and unseen
When sweet is, that hath bitter been."

Thus sung the Thracian, and the rowing-folk
Sent Argo quivering with the well-timed stroke
Over the green hills, through great clouds of spray,
And as they went upon their happy way

About the deck the longing men would stand
With wistful eyes still gazing for the land;
Which yet they saw not, till the cool fresh night
Had come upon them, with no lack of light,   410
For moon and stars shone brightly overhead,
Nor through the night did Iris fail to lead
The wave-tossed Argo o'er the glittering sea.

  So as the moon set, did there seem to be
Upon their larboard, banks of high-piled cloud,
Which from their sight the last dark hour did shroud,
Then came the twilight, and those watchers fain
Against the eastern light beheld again
The clouds unchanged, and as the daylight grew,
Lynceus cried out: "Some land we draw unto!   420
Look forth, Erginus, on these mountains grey,
If thou, perchance, hast seen them ere to-day."

  Therewith all turned about, and some men ran
To hear what words the God-begotten man
Would say, who answered: "Lynceus, and all ye,
The man we left erewhile across the sea
Might tell us this, the godlike Hercules;
Yet I myself think that the landless seas
No more shall vex us now, but that we come
Unto the gates that look into our home: 430
So trim the sails, for thither will I steer,
Seeking what lies beyond with little fear,
Since surely now I see the Iberian land
That 'gainst the shore of Africa doth stand,
To break these mighty billows, ever pressed
Each against each from out the landless west."

So with glad hearts all men his bidding did,
And swiftly through the water Argo slid,
Till as the sun rose were they near the strait,
At whose mouth but a little did they wait   440
Till they had eaten, pouring honied wine
Unto the Gods, then biding no new sign,
They cried aloud, and running out the oars,
They swept great Argo midmost 'twixt the shores
Of either land, and as her gilded prow
Cleft the new waters, clean forgotten now
Grew all the wasteful washing of the main,
And clean forgotten the dull hopeless pain,
In the great swirling river left so long,
And in all hearts the memory was strong   450
Of the bright Grecian headlands and the bay
They left astern upon a glorious day.

BOOK XIII.

Medea sees Circe, and has good counsel from her.

BUT as along the shore they sailed next day,
Full many a headland on their lucky way
Erginus knew, but said no towns there were
Within that land, but that from year to year
Well-nigh untilled the earth her produce gave,
And many a herd the houseless people drave,
And using neither roof nor sheltering wall,
Dwelt but in tents, and had no want at all.

With that he bade them trim the bellying sail,
For from the land now blew a gentle gale,   10
Spice-laden, warm, that made their full hearts yearn
For unseen things, but soon they left astern
That fruitful place, the lion-haunted land,
Nor saw but tumbling seas on either hand.

Three days they sailed, and passed on the third day
A rock-bound coast upon their left that lay,
But on the morrow eve made land again,
Stretched right ahead across the watery plain,
Whereto ere nightfall did they draw anear,
And so lay-to till dawn with little fear;   20
For from the shore a light, soft land-wind blew.

But as the dead night round about them **drew**,
The ceaseless roar of savage beasts they heard,
Mingled with sounds like cries of men afeared,
And blare of horns, and clank of heavy chains,
And noise of bells, such as in moonlit lanes
Rings from the grey team on the **market-night**.

And with these noises did they see **a light**,
That seemed to light some crown of palaces,
Shining from out a grove of thickset trees.   30
Then did the Minyæ doubt if they were come
Unto some great king's well-adorned home,
Or if some temple of a God were there,
Or if, indeed, the spirits of the air
Haunted that place: so slowly passed away
The sleepless night, and at the dawn of day
Their longing eyes beheld a lovely land,
Green meadows rising o'er a yellow strand,

Well-set with fair fruit-bearing trees, and groves
Of thick-leaved elms, all populous of doves,   40
And watered by a wandering clear green stream;
And through the trees they saw a palace gleam
Of polished marble, fair beyond man's thought.
  There as they lay, the sweetest scents were brought
By sighing winds across the bitter sea,
And languid music breathed melodiously,
Steeping their souls in such unmixed delight,
Their hearts were melted, and all dim of sight
They grew, and scarce their hands could grip the oar,
And as they slowly neared the happy shore,   50
The young men well-nigh wept, and e'en the wise
Thought they had reached the gate of Paradise.
  But 'midst them all Medea thoughtfully
Gazed landward o'er the ripple of the sea,
And said no word, till from her precious things
She drew a casket full of chains and rings,
And took therefrom a chaplet brown and sere,
And set it on her head: and now being near
The yellow strand, high on the poop she stood,
And said: "O heroes, what has chilled your blood,   60
That in such wise ye gaze upon this land
With tearful eye, and nerveless, languid hand,
And heaving breast, and measureless desire?
Be wise, for here the never-dying fire,
The God-begotten wonder, Circe, lights,
The wise of women, framer of delights
That being of man once felt, he ne'er shall cease
To long for vainly, as the years increase

On his dulled soul, shut in some bestial form.

"And good it had been that some bitter storm 70
Were tossing Argo's planks from sea to sea,
Than ye had reached this fair land, but for me,
Who amid tears and prayers, and nameless pain,
Some little wisdom have made shift to gain:
Look forth upon the green shore, and behold
Those many beasts, all collared with fine gold,
Lions and pards, and small-eyed restless bears,
And tusked boars, who from uneasy lairs
Are just come forth; nor is there 'mongst them one
But once walked upright underneath the sun, 80
And had the name of man: such shall ye be,
If from the ship ye wander heedlessly,
But safely I my kinswoman may meet,
And learn from her the bitter and the sweet
That waits us ere ye come to Greece again,
And see the wind-swept green Thessalian plain.

" Meanwhile, let nothing tempt you to the land,
Nor unto anything stretch forth the hand
That comes from shore, for all ye may see there
Are but lost men and their undoers fair." 90

But with that word they furrowed the wet sand,
And straight they ran the gangway out to land,
O'er which, with girded raiment, passed the queen;
But now another marvel was there seen,
For to the shore, from many a glade and lawn,
The golden-collared sad-eyed beasts were drawn
In close-set ranks above the sea-beat shore,
And open-mouthed, with varying moan and roar,

White-foot Medea did they seem to threat;
Whereat the Minyæ on their bow-strings set
The notches of their arrows, but the maid
Turned round about, with calm face unafraid,
And said: "O Minyæ, lay your weapons down,
Nor fear for me; behold this chaplet brown,
Whose withered leaves rest lightly on my head,
This is the herb that Gods and mortals dread,
The Pontic Moly, the unchanging charm."

Then up the beach she passed, and her white arm
This way and that the leopards thrust aside,
And 'mid the grisly swine her limbs did glide,
And on a lion's mane her hand she laid;
But still with moans they thronged about the maid,
As she passed onward to the palace white,
Until the elm-groves hid her from the sight.

Then they with fearful hearts did sacrifice
Unto the Gods in their seafaring wise,
But of the lovely land were they so fain
That their return they scarcely counted gain,
Unto the green plain dotted o'er with folds
And that fair bay that Pelion beholds.

Meanwhile Medea through the thick-leaved grove
Passed underneath the moaning of the dove,
Not left by those strange beasts; until at last
Her feet from off the sparse long grasses passed
Unto a sunny space of daisied sward,
From which a strange-wrought silver grate did guard
A lovely pleasance, set with flowers, foursquare,

Q

On three sides ending in a cloister fair
That hid the fair feet of a marble house,
Carved thick with flowers and stories amorous.   130
And midmost of the slender garden trees
A gilded shrine stood, set with images,
Wherefrom the never-dying fire rose up
Into the sky, and a great jewelled cup
Ran over ever from a runlet red
Of fragrant wine, that 'mid the flowers shed
Strange scent that grapes yield not to any man,
While round about the shrine four streamlets ran
From golden founts to freshen that green place.

  So there Medea stayed a little space,   140
Gazing in wonder through the silver rail
That fenced that garden from the wooded vale;
For damsels wandered there in languid wise
As though they wearied of that Paradise,
Their jewelled raiment dragging from its stalk
The harmless daisy in their listless walk.
But though from rosy heel to golden head
Most fair they were and wrought with white and red,
Like to the casket-bearer who beguiled
The hapless one, and though their lips still smiled,   150
Yet to the Colchian, heavy-eyed they seemed,
And each at other gazed as though she dreamed;
Not noting aught of all the glorious show
She joined herself, nor seeming more to know
What words she spoke nor what her fellows sung,
Nor feeling arms that haply round her clung.

  For here and there the Colchian maid could see

Some browned seafarer kissing eagerly
White feet or half-bared bosom, and could hear
A rough voice stammering 'twixt love and fear   160
Amid the dreamy murmur of the place,
As on his knees, with eager upturned face,
Some man would pour forth many a fruitless word,
That did but sound like song of a wild bird
Unto his love ; while she for all reply,
Still gazing on his flushed face wearily,
Would undo clasp and belt, and show to him
Undreamed-of loveliness of side or limb.

  And in such guise of half-stripped jewelled weed,
The men entrapped, Medea saw them lead   170
Into the dark cool cloister, whence again
They came not forth, but four-foot, rough of mane,
Uncouth with spots and dangerous of claw.

  But when the sad-eyed beasts about her saw
These draw towards them and beheld the gate
Open and shut, and fellows to that state
New come, they whined, and brushing round her feet
Prayed for return unto that garden sweet,
Their own undoing once, that yet shall be
Death unto many a toiler of the sea,   180
Because all these outside the silver grate
Were men indeed though inarticulate,
And, spite of seeming, in none otherwise,
Did longing torture them, than when in guise
Of men they stood before that garden green,
And first their eyes the baneful place had seen.

  But now the queen grew wrath, for in her way,

Before the gate a yellow lion lay,
A tiger-cat her raiment brushed aside,
And o'er her feet she felt a serpent glide,   190
The swine screamed loud about her, and a pard
Her shining shoulder of her raiment bared
With light swift clutch; then she from off her head
Took the sere moly wreath, and therewith said:—
"What do ye, wretches, know ye not this sign,
That whoso wears is as a thing divine?
Get from this place, for never more can ye
Become partakers of the majesty
That from man's soul looks through his eager eyes.
Go—wail that ever ye were made so wise   200
As men are made; who chase through smooth and
    rough
Their own undoing, nor can have enough
Of bitter trouble and entangling woe."

 Then slowly from her did those monsters go,
In varied voices mourning for their lot
And that sweet poison ne'er to be forgot.

 But straight with serious face the Colchian maid
Her slender fingers on the latchet laid
That held the silver gate, and entered in;
Nor did those weary images of sin   210
Take any heed of her as she passed by,
But, if they met her eyes, stared listlessly,
Like those who walk in sleep, and as they dream
Turn empty faces to the lightning's gleam,
And murmur softly while the thunder rolls.

Swiftly she passed those bodies void of souls,
And through the darkling corridor she passed,
And reached a huge adorned hall at last,
Where sat alone the deathless sorceress,
Upon whose knees an open book did press, 220
Wherein strange things the Gods knew not, she read;
A golden vine-bough wreathed her golden head,
And her fair body a thin robe did touch
With silken folds, but hid it not so much
As the cool ripple hides Diana's feet,
When through the brook the roe-deer, slim and fleet,
She follows at the dawning of the day.

 Smiling, she put the wondrous book away
As the light footsteps fell upon her ear,
She raised her head, and when the queen drew near, 230
She said: "O wanderer from dark sea to sea,
I greet thee well, and dear thou art to me;
Though verily if I could wish for aught,
I could have wished thou hadst been hither brought
Ere that had happed to thee that haps to all,
Into the troublous sea of love to fall,
Then like unto the gods shouldst thou have been,
Nor ever died, but sitting here have seen
The fashion of the foolish world go by,
And drunk the cup of power and majesty. 240

 "But now it may not be, and thou must come
With him thou boughtedst, to a troublous home;
But since indeed the fates will have it so,
Take heed thou dost the things I bid thee do.
And, first, since thou wouldst have me purify

Your hands of his blood that thou sawest die
'Twixt yellow Phasis and the green-ridged sea,
Behold, this is not possible to me,
Nor ever must another altar stand
In this green nook of the Italian land,   250
To aught but me, no, not unto my Sire;
But unto him shall ye light ruddy fire,
When, drawing nigh to your desired home,
Unto the headland of Malea ye come;
And then, indeed, I bid you not to spare
Spices and golden things and raiment fair,
But to the country folk give things of price,
And from them take wherewith to sacrifice,
A hundred milkwhite bulls, a hundred kine,
And many a jar of unmixed honied wine,   260
And, crowned with olive, round the altars sing
Unto **the** God who gladdens everything,
Thy father's father, the all-seeing Sun.
And then the deed thy Jason's spear has done
Mayst thou forget, it shall not visit thee.
Moreover, sailing hence across the sea,
A waste of yellow sand shall ye pass by
'Neath the Trinacrian cliffs, whereon shall lie
Fair women, fairer than thine eyes have seen.
And if thou still wouldst be a Grecian queen,   270
When to that deadly place ye draw anear,
And sweetest music ye begin to hear,
Bid your bold love steer Argo from the land,
While Thracian Orpheus takes his harp in hand,
And sings thereto some God-delighting strain.

And surely else shall all your toil be vain,
For deadlier than my gardens are those sands;
And when the mariner's toil-hardened hands
Reach out unto those bodies fair and white,
They clasp but death instead of their delight.   280

  "But, doing as I bid, Malea reach,
And after, nigh Iolchos Argo beach,
Yet at the city haste ye not to land,
For still the sceptre presses Pelias' hand,
And Æson is at rest for evermore;
Bid then thy folk lurk by some wooded shore,
And to the white-walled city straightly wend
Thyself alone, and safely there make end
Of the King's life; nor need I teach thee how,
For deep unfailing wiles thy soul doth know.   290

  "What more? what more? I see thy grey eyes ask,
What course, what ending to the tangled task
The Gods have set before me, ere I die?
O child, I know all things, indeed, but why
Shouldst thou know all, nor yet be wise therefore,
Me knowledge grieves not, thee should it grieve
        sore,
Nor knowing, shouldst thou cease to hope or fear.
What! do men think of death ere it draws near?
Not so, else surely would they stint their strife,
For lengthening out their little span of life,   300
But where each found himself there should he sit,
Not moving hand or foot for thought of it.
Wherefore the Gods, wishing the earth to teem
With living wills like theirs, nor as a dream

To hold but beauty and the lives of beasts,
That **they** may have fair stories for their feasts,
Have given them forgetfulness of death,
Longings and hopes, and joy in drawing breath,
And they live happy, knowing nought at all,
Nor what death is, where that shall chance to fall. 310
For while he lives, few minutes certainly
Does any man believe that he shall die.
Ah, what? thou hang'st thine head, and **on** thy feet
Down rain the tears from thy grey eyes and sweet;
Weep not, nor pity thine own life too much:
Not painless shall it be, indeed, or such
As the Gods live in their unchanged abode,
And yet not joyless; no unmeasured load
Of sorrows shall thy dull soul learn to bear,
With nought to keep thee back from death but fear, 320
Of what thou know'st not, knowing nought but **pain**.

"**But** though full oft thou shalt lift hands in vain,
Crying to what thou know'st not in thy **need**,
And blind with agony, yet oft, indeed,
Shalt thou go nigh to think thyself **divine**,
For love of what thou deemest to be **thine**,
For joy of what thou dreamest cannot die.

"**Live then** thy life, nor ask for misery,
Most certain if thou knewest what must **be**,
And then, at least, this shall not hap to thee, 330
To be like those who people my sad groves,
Beneath the moaning of the grey-winged doves.
And midst all pain and joy, and wrong and **right**,

Thy name to all shall be a dear delight
While the world lasts, if this avail thee aught.

"Farewell, O child, whose feet alone have brought
An earthly damsel to my house of gold,
For surely those thou didst erewhile behold
These hands have made, and can unmake again,
Nor know they aught of love, or fear, or pain.   340
Go, loiter not, this place befits thee nought,
Thou knowest many things full dearly bought,
And well I love thee, being so wise and fair,
But what is knowledge in this deadly air,
That floats about thee, poisoning hearts of man.
Behold I see thy cheeks, that erst were wan,
Flaming with new desire, and in thine eyes
Shine out new thoughts that from thine heart arise;
Gird up thy raiment, nor run slower now
Than from the amorous bearer of the bow   350
Once Daphne ran; nor yet forget the word
That thou from deadly lips this day hast heard."

So said she, and thereat the Colchian maid
Turned from her fair face shuddering and afraid,
With beating heart, and flushed face like the rose
That in the garden of Damascus grows,
And catching up her raiment, hurried through
The mighty hall, where thick the pillars blue
Stood like a dream to hold the roof aloft;
But as she left it, musky odours soft   360
Were cast about her by the dallying breeze,
That through the heavy-fruited garden-trees

Blew o'er those golden heads and bodies white,
And limbs well made for manifold delight,
From 'twixt whose fingers and the strings, did flow
Sweet music such as Helicon might know.

  But dizzied, hurrying through the place she past,
Nor any look upon their beauty cast,
Nor any thought unto the music gave,
But set herself her own vext soul to save   370
From that dread place; beginning now to run
Like to a damsel of the lightfoot One,
Who oft from twilight unto twilight goes
Through still dark woods, where never rough wind
       blows.

  So, the grove passed, she made good speed to reach
The edges of the sea, the wind-swept beach;
But as she ran, afar the heroes saw
Her raiment fluttering, and made haste to draw
Their two-edged swords, and their strong bows to
       string,
Doubting that she was chased of some dread thing; 380
And Jason leapt ashore, and toward her ran,
And with him went the arrow-loving man,
The wise Arcadian, and the Minyæ
Got ready shielded Argo for the sea.

  But ere these met her, with uplifted hand,
She cried: "Turn back, nor deeper in this land
Thrust ye your souls; nought chases me but fear,
And all is well if on the sea we were;
Yea, if we once were free from fear and spell,
Then, truly, better were all things than well."   390

Thereat they stayed, but onward still she ran
Until she reached them, and the godlike man
Took by the arm, and hurrying him along,
Stayed not until their feet were set among
The last faint ripples of the gentle sea,
Wherefrom they boarded Argo speedily,
And Jason bid all men unto the oar.

With that they left the fair death-bearing shore,
Not gladlier than some fair young man may leave
His love, upon the odorous summer eve, 400
When she turns sighing to her father's house,
And leaves him there alone and amorous,
Heartsick with all that shame has let him see,
Grieved that no bolder he has dared to be.

BOOK XIV.

The Sirens—The Garden of the Hesperides—The heroes do sacrifice at Malea.

NOW o'er the open sea they took their way,
 For three days, and at dawning of the day,
Upon the fourth, saw the Trinacrian shore,
And there-along they coasted two days more.
Then first Medea warned them to take heed,
Lest they should end all memory of their deed
Where dwell the Sirens on the yellow sand,
And folk should think some tangled poisonous land

Had buried them, or some tumultous sea
O'er their white bones was tossing angrily;   10
Or that some muddy river, far from Greece,
Drove seaward o'er the ringlets of the fleece.

But when the Minyæ hearkened to this word,
With many a thought their wearied hearts were stirred,
And longing for the near-gained Grecian land,
Where in a little while their feet should stand;
Yet none the less like to a happy dream,
Now, when they neared it, did their own home seem,
And like a dream the glory of their quest,
And therewithal some thought of present rest   20
Stole over them, and well-nigh made them sigh
To hear the sighing restless wind go by.

But now, nigh even on the second day,
As o'er the gentle waves they took their way,
The orange-scented land-breeze seemed to bear
Some other sounds unto the listening ear
Than all day long they had been hearkening—
The land-born signs of many a well-known thing.
Thereat Medea trembled, for she knew
That nigh the dreadful sands at last they drew,   30
For certainly the Sirens' song she heard,
Though yet her ear could shape it to no word,
And by their faces could the queen behold
How sweet it was, although no tale it told,
To those worn toilers o'er the bitter sea.

Now, as they sped along, they presently,
Rounding a headland, reached a little bay,
Walled from the sea by splintered cliffs and grey,

Capped by the thymy hills' green wind-beat head,
Where 'mid the whin the burrowing rabbits fed.
And 'neath the cliff they saw a belt of sand,
'Twixt Nereus' pasture and the high scarped land,
Whereon, yet far off, could their eyes behold
White bodies moving, crowned and girt with gold,
Wherefrom it seemed that lovely music welled.
  So when all this the grey-eyed queen beheld,
She said: " O Jason, I have made thee wise
In this and other things; turn then thine eyes
Seaward, and note the ripple of the sea,
Where there is hope as well as fear for thee.
Nor look upon the death that lurketh there
'Neath the grey cliff, though sweet it seems and fair;
For thou art young upon this day to die.
Take then the helm, and gazing steadily
Upon the road to Greece, make strong thine hand,
And steer us toward the lion-haunted land:
And thou, O Thracian! if thou e'er hast moved
Men's hearts, with stories of the Gods who loved,
And men who suffered, move them on this day,
Taking the deadly love of death away,
That even now is stealing over them,
While still they gaze upon the ocean's hem,
Where their undoing is if they but knew."

  But while she spake, still nigher Argo drew
Unto the yellow edges of the shore,
And little help she had of ashen oar,
For as her shielded side rolled through the sea,

Silent with glittering eyes the Minyæ
Gazed o'er the surge, for they were nigh enow
To see the gusty wind of evening blow   70
Long locks of hair across those bodies white,
With golden spray hiding some dear delight;
Yea, nigh enow to see their red lips smile,
Wherefrom all song had ceased now for a while,
As though they deemed the prey was in the net,
And they no more had need a bait to set,
But their own bodies, fair beyond man's thought,
Under the grey cliff, hidden not of aught
But of such mist of tears as in the eyes
Of those seafaring men might chance to rise.   80

  A moment Jason gazed, then through the waist
Ran swiftly, and with trembling hands made haste
To trim the sail, then to the tiller ran,
And thrust aside the skilled Milesian man,
Who with half-open mouth, and dreamy eyes,
Stood steering Argo to that land of lies;
But as he staggered forward, Jason's hand
Hard on the tiller steered away from land,
And as her head a little now fell off
Unto the wide sea, did he shout this scoff   90
To Thracian Orpheus: "Minstrel, shall we die,
Because thou hast forgotten utterly
What things she taught thee that men call divine,
Or will thy measures but lead folk to wine,
And scented beds, and not to noble deeds?
Or will they fail as fail the shepherd's reeds
Before the trumpet, when these sea-witches

Pipe shrilly to the washing of the seas?
I am a man, and these but beasts, but thou
Giving these souls, that all were men ere now   100
Shall be a very God and not a man!"

  So spake he; but his fingers Orpheus ran
Over the strings, and sighing turned away
From that fair ending of the sunny bay;
But as his well-skilled hands were preluding
What his heart swelled with, they began to sing
With pleading voices from the yellow sands,
Clustered together, with appealing hands
Reached out to Argo as she turned away,
While o'er their white limbs flew the flakes of
    spray,   110
Since they spared not to set white feet among
The cold waves heedless of their honied song.

  Sweetly they sung, and still the answer came
Piercing and clear from him, as bursts the flame
From out the furnace in the moonless night;
Yet, as their words are no more known aright
Through lapse of many ages, and no man
Can any more across the waters wan
Behold those singing women of the sea,
Once more I pray you all to pardon me,   120
If with my feeble voice and harsh I sing
From what dim memories may chance to cling
About men's hearts, of lovely things once sung
Beside the sea, while yet the world was young.

The Sirens.

O happy seafarers are ye,
   And surely all your ills are past,
And toil upon the land and sea,
   Since ye are brought to us at last.

To you the fashion of the world,
   Wide lands laid waste, fair cities burned,   130
And plagues, and kings from kingdoms hurled,
   Are nought, since hither ye have turned.

For as upon this beach we stand,
   And o'er our heads the sea-fowl flit,
Our eyes behold a glorious land,
   And soon shall ye be kings of it.

Orpheus.

A little more, a little more,
   O carriers of the Golden Fleece,
A little labour with the oar,
   Before we reach the land of Greece.   140

E'en now perchance faint rumours reach
   Men's ears of this our victory,
And draw them down unto the beach
   To gaze across the empty sea.

But since the longed-for day is nigh,
   And scarce a God could stay us now,
Why do ye hang your heads and sigh,
   Hindering for nought our eager prow?

The Sirens.

Ah, had ye chanced to reach the home
　　Your fond desires were set upon,　　　　150
Into what troubles had ye come,
　　What barren victory had ye won.

But now, but now, when ye have lain
　　Asleep with us a little while
Beneath the washing of the main,
　　How calm shall be your waking smile!

For ye shall smile to think of life
　　That knows no troublous change or fear,
No unavailing bitter strife,
　　That ere its time brings trouble near.　　160

Orpheus.

Is there some murmur in your ears,
　　That all that we have done is nought,
And nothing ends our cares and fears,
　　Till the last fear on us is brought?

The Sirens.

Alas! and will ye stop your ears,
　　In vain desire to do aught,
And wish to live 'mid cares and fears,
　　Until the last fear makes you nought?

Orpheus.

Is not the May time now on earth,
　　When close against the city wall　　　　170
The folk are singing in their mirth,
　　While on their heads the May-flowers fall?

R

The Sirens.

Yes, May is come, and its sweet breath
    Shall well-nigh make you weep to-day,
And pensive with swift-coming death,
    Shall ye be satiate of the May.

Orpheus.

Shall not July bring fresh delight,
    As underneath green trees ye sit,
And o'er some damsel's body white
    The noontide shadows change and flit?   180

The Sirens.

No new delight July shall bring
    But ancient fear and fresh desire,
And, spite of every lovely thing,
    Of July surely shall ye tire.

Orpheus.

And now, when August comes on thee,
    And 'mid the golden sea of corn
The merry reapers thou mayst see,
    Wilt thou still think the earth forlorn?

The Sirens.

Set flowers on thy short-lived head,
    And in thine heart forgetfulness   190
Of man's hard toil, and scanty bread,
    And weary of those days no less.

Orpheus.

Or wilt thou climb the sunny hill,
   In the October afternoon,
To watch the purple earth's blood fill
   The grey vat to the maiden's tune?

The Sirens.

When thou beginnest to grow old,
   Bring back remembrance of thy bliss
With that the shining cup doth hold,
   And weary helplessly of this.   200

Orpheus.

Or pleasureless shall we pass by
   The long cold night and leaden day,
That song, and tale, and minstrelsy
   Shall make as merry as the May?

The Sirens.

List then, to-night, to some old tale
   Until the tears o'erflow thine eyes;
But what shall all these things avail,
   When sad to-morrow comes and dies?

Orpheus.

And when the world is born again,
   And with some fair love, side by side,   210
Thou wanderest 'twixt the sun and rain,
   In that fresh love-begetting tide;

Then, when the world is born again,
    And the sweet year before thee lies,
Shall thy heart think of coming pain,
    Or vex itself with memories?

The Sirens.

Ah! then the world is born again
    With burning love unsatisfied,
And new desires fond and vain,
    And weary days from tide to tide.   220

Ah! when the world is born again,
    A little day is soon gone by,
When thou, unmoved by sun or rain,
    Within a cold straight house shall lie.

Therewith they ceased awhile, as languidly
The head of Argo fell off toward the sea,
And through the water she began to go,
For from the land a fitful wind did blow,
That, dallying with the many-coloured sail,
Would sometimes swell it out and sometimes fail,   230
As nigh the east side of the bay they drew;
Then o'er the waves again the music flew.

The Sirens.

Think not of pleasure, short and vain,
Wherewith, 'mid days of toil and pain,
With sick and sinking hearts ye strive
To cheat yourselves that ye may live

With cold death ever close at hand,
Think rather of a peaceful land,
The changeless land where ye may be
Roofed over by the changeful sea.   240

ORPHEUS.

And is the fair town nothing then,
The coming of the wandering men
With that long talked of thing and strange,
And news of how the kingdoms change,
The pointed hands, and wondering
At doers of a desperate thing?
Push on, for surely this shall be
Across a narrow strip of sea.

THE SIRENS.

Alas! poor souls and timorous,
Will ye draw nigh to gaze at us   250
And see if we are fair indeed,
For such as we shall be your meed,
There, where our hearts would have you go.
And where can the earth-dwellers show
In any land such loveliness
As that wherewith your eyes we bless,
O wanderers of the Minyæ,
Worn toilers over land and sea?

ORPHEUS.

Fair as the lightning thwart the sky,
As sun-dyed snow upon the high   260

Untrodden heaps of threatening stone
The eagle looks upon alone,
O fair as the doomed victim's wreath,
O fair as deadly sleep and death,
What will ye with them, earthly men,
To mate your three-score years and ten?
Toil rather, suffer and be free,
Betwixt the green earth and the sea.

The Sirens.

If ye be bold with us to go,
Things such as happy dreams may show   270
Shall your once heavy eyes behold
About our palaces of gold;
Where waters 'neath the waters run,
And from o'erhead a harmless sun
Gleams through the woods of chrysolite.
There gardens fairer to the sight
Than those of the Phæacian king
Shall ye behold; and, wondering,
Gaze on the sea-born fruit and flowers,
And thornless and unchanging bowers,   280
Whereof the May-time knoweth nought.

So to the pillared house being brought,
Poor souls, ye shall not be alone,
For o'er the floors of pale blue stone
All day such feet as ours shall pass,
And, 'twixt the glimmering walls of glass,
Such bodies garlanded with gold,
So faint, so fair, shall ye behold,

And clean forget the treachery
Of changing earth and tumbling sea. 290

Orpheus.

O the sweet valley of deep grass,
Where through the summer stream doth pass,
In chain of shallow, and still pool,
From misty morn to evening cool;
Where the black ivy creeps and twines
O'er the dark-armed, red-trunked pines,
Whence clattering the pigeon flits,
Or, brooding o'er her thin eggs, sits,
And every hollow of the hills
With echoing song the mavis fills. 300
There by the stream, all unafraid,
Shall stand the happy shepherd maid,
Alone in first of sunlit hours;
Behind her, on the dewy flowers,
Her homespun woollen raiment lies,
And her white limbs and sweet grey eyes
Shine from the calm green pool and deep,
While round about the swallows sweep,
Not silent; and would God that we,
Like them, were landed from the sea. 310

The Sirens.

Shall we not rise with you at night,
Up through the shimmering green twilight,
That maketh there our changeless day,
Then going through the moonlight grey,

Shall we not sit upon these sands,
To think upon the troublous lands
Long left behind, where once ye were,
When every day brought change and fear?
There, with white arms about you twined,
And shuddering somewhat at the wind　　　320
That ye rejoiced erewhile to meet,
Be happy, while old stories sweet,
Half understood, float round your ears,
And fill your eyes with happy tears.

　Ah! while we sing unto you there,
As now we sing, with yellow hair
Blown round about these pearly limbs,
While underneath the grey sky swims
The light shell-sailor of the waves,
And to our song, from sea-filled caves　　　330
Booms out an echoing harmony,
Shall ye not love the peaceful sea?

Orpheus.

　Nigh the vine-covered hillocks green,
In days agone, have I not seen
The brown-clad maidens amorous,
Below the long rose-trellised house,
Dance to the querulous pipe and shrill,
When the grey shadow of the hill
Was lengthening at the end of day?
Not shadowy or pale were they,　　　340
But limbed like those who 'twixt the trees,
Follow the swift of Goddesses.

Sunburnt they are somewhat, indeed,
To where the rough brown woollen weed
Is drawn across their bosoms sweet,
Or cast from off their dancing feet;
But yet the stars, the moonlight grey,
The water wan, the dawn of day,
Can see their bodies fair and white
As Hers, who once, for man's delight,   350
Before the world grew hard and old,
Came o'er the bitter sea and cold;
And surely those that met me there,
Her handmaidens and subjects were;
And shame-faced, half-repressed desire
Had lit their glorious eyes with fire,
That maddens eager hearts of men.
O would that I were with them when
The risen moon is gathering light,
And yellow from the homestead white   360
The windows gleam; but verily
This waits us o'er a little sea.

The Sirens.

Come to the land where none grows old,
And none is rash or over-bold,
Nor any noise there is or war,
Or rumour from wild lands afar,
Or plagues, or birth and death of kings;
No vain desire of unknown things
Shall vex you there, no hope or fear
Of that which never draweth near;   370

But in that lovely land and still
Ye may remember what ye will,
And what ye will, forget for aye.
  So while the kingdoms pass away,
Ye sea-beat hardened toilers erst,
Unresting, for vain fame athirst,
Shall be at peace for evermore,
With hearts fulfilled of Godlike lore,
And calm, unwavering Godlike love,
No lapse of time can turn or move.   380
There, ages after your fair fleece
Is clean forgotten, yea, and Greece
Is no more counted glorious,
Alone with us, alone with us,
Alone with us, dwell happily,
Beneath our trembling roof of sea.

Orpheus.

  Ah! do ye weary of the strife
And long to change this eager life
For shadowy and dull hopelessness,
Thinking indeed to gain no less   390
Than far from this grey light to lie,
And there to die and not to die,
To be as if ye ne'er had been,
Yet keep your memory fresh and green,
To have no thought of good or ill,
Yet feed your fill of pleasure still?
O idle dream! Ah, verily
If it shall happen unto me

That I have thought of anything,
When o'er my bones the sea-fowl sing,
And I lie dead, how shall I pine
For those fresh joys that once were mine,
On this green fount of joy and mirth,
The ever young and glorious earth;
Then, helpless, shall I call to mind
Thoughts of the sweet flower-scented wind,
The dew, the gentle rain at night,
The wonder-working snow and white,
The song of birds, the water's fall,
The sun that maketh bliss of all;
Yea, this our toil and victory,
The tyrannous and conquered sea.

The Sirens.

Ah, will ye go, and whither then
   Will ye go from us, soon to die,
To fill your three-score years and ten,
   With many an unnamed misery?

And this the wretchedest of all,
   That when upon your lonely eyes
The last faint heaviness shall fall
   Ye shall bethink you of our cries,

Come back, nor grown old, seek in vain
   To hear us sing across the sea.
Come back, come back, come back again,
   Come back, O fearful Minyæ!

ORPHEUS.

Ah, once again, ah, once again,
  The black prow plunges through the sea,
Nor yet shall all your toil be vain,
  Nor ye forgot, O Minyæ.

In such wise sang the Thracian, in such wise
Out gushed the Sirens' deadly melodies; 430
But long before the mingled song was done,
Back to the oars the Minyæ, one by one,
Slunk silently; though many an one sighed sore,
As his strong fingers met the wood once more,
And from his breast the toilsome breathing came.
  But as they laboured, some for very shame
Hung down their heads, and yet amongst them some
Gazed at the place whence that sweet song had come;
But round the oars and Argo's shielded side
The sea grew white, and she began to glide 440
Swift through the waters of that deadly bay;
But when a long wake now behind her lay,
And still the whistle of the wind increased,
Past shroud and mast, and all the song had ceased,
Butes rose up, the fair Athenian man,
And with wild eyes betwixt the rowers ran
Unto the poop and leapt into the sea;
Then all men rested on their oars, but he
Rose to the top, and towards the shore swam fast;
While all eyes watched him, who had well-nigh
    past 450
The place where sand and water 'gan to meet

In wreaths and ripples round the ivory feet,
When sun-burnt swimmer, snow-white glancing limb,
And yellow sand unto their eyes grew dim,
Nor did they see their fellow any more.

But when they once again beheld the shore
The wind sung o'er the empty beach and bare,
And by the cliff uprose into the air
A delicate and glittering little cloud,
That seemed some many-coloured sun to shroud; 460
But as the rugged cliff it drew above
The wondering Minyæ beheld it move
Westward, toward Lilybæum and the sun.

Then once more was their seaward course begun,
And soon those deadly sands were far astern,
Nor ever after could the heroes learn
If Butes lived or died; but old tales tell
That while the tumbling waves he breasted well,
Venus beheld him, as unseen she drew
From sunny Cyprus to the headland blue 470
Of Lilybæum, where her temple is;
She, with a mind his sun-burnt brows to kiss,
E'en as his feet were dropping nigh the beach,
And ere his hand the deadly hands could reach,
Stooped, as the merlin stoops upon the dove,
And snatched him thence to be awhile her love,
Betwixt the golden pillars of her shrine,
That those who pass the Ægades see shine
From high-raised Lilybæum o'er the sea.

But far away the sea-beat Minyæ 480

Cast forth the foam, as through the growing night
They laboured ever, having small delight
In life all empty of that promised bliss,
In love that scarce can give a dying kiss,
In pleasure ending sweet songs with a wail,
In fame that little can dead men avail,
In vain toil struggling with the fateful stream,
In hope, the promise of a morning dream.

  Yet as night died, and the cold sea and grey
Seemed running with them toward the dawn of day,
Needs must they once again forget their death,   491
Needs must they, being alive and drawing breath,
As men who of no other life can know
In their own minds again immortal grow.

  But toward the south a little now they bent,
And for awhile o'er landless sea they went,
But on the third day made another land
At dawn of day, and thitherward did stand;
And since the wind blew lightly from the shore,
Somewhat abeam, they feared not with the oar   500
To push across the shallowing sea and green,
That washed a land the fairest they had seen,
Whose shell-strewn beach at highest of the tide
'Twixt sea and flowery shore was nowise wide,
And drawn a little backward from the sea
There stood a marble wall wrought cunningly,
Rosy and white, set thick with images,
And over-topped with heavy-fruited trees,
Which by the shore ran, as the bay did bend,
And to their eyes had neither gap nor end;   510

Nor any gate : and looking over this,
They saw a place not made for earthly bliss,
Or eyes of dying men, for growing there
The yellow apple and the painted pear,
And well-filled golden cups of oranges
Hung amid groves of pointed cyprus trees ;
On grassy slopes the twining vine-boughs grew,
And hoary olives 'twixt far mountains blue,
And many-coloured flowers, like as a cloud
The rugged southern cliffs did softly shroud ; 520
And many a green-necked bird sung to his mate
Within the slim-leaved, thorny pomegranate,
That flung its unstrung rubies on the grass,
And slowly o'er the place the wind did pass
Heavy with many odours that it bore
From thymy hills down to the sea-beat shore,
Because no flower there is, that all the year,
From spring to autumn, beareth otherwhere,
But there it flourished ; nor the fruit alone
From 'twixt the green leaves and the boughs outshone,
For there each tree was ever flowering. 531

 Nor was there lacking many a living thing
Changed of its nature, for the roe-deer there
Walked fearless with the tiger, and the bear
Rolled sleepily upon the fruit-strawn grass,
Letting the coneys o'er his rough hide pass,
With blinking eyes, that meant no treachery.
Careless the partridge passed the red fox by ;
Untouched the serpent left the thrushes brown,
And as a picture was the lion's frown. 540

But in the midst there was a grassy space,
Raised somewhat over all the flowery place,
On marble terrace-walls wrought like a dream;
And round about it ran a clear blue stream,
Bridged o'er with marble steps, and midmost there
Grew a green tree, whose smooth grey boughs did bear
Such fruit as never man elsewhere had seen,
For 'twixt the sunlight and the shadow green
Shone out fair apples of red gleaming gold.
Moreover round the tree, in many a fold,   550
Lay coiled a dragon, glittering little less
Than that which his eternal watchfulness
Was set to guard; nor yet was he alone,
For from the daisied grass about him shone
Gold raiment wrapping round two damsels fair,
And one upon the steps combed out her hair,
And with shut eyes sung low as in a dream;
And one stood naked in the cold blue stream,
While on the bank her golden raiment lay;
But on that noontide of the quivering day,   560
She only, hearing the seafarers' shout,
Her lovely golden head had turned about,
And seen their white sail flapping o'er the wall,
And as she turned had let her tresses fall,
Which the thin water rippling round her knee
Bore outward from her toward the restless sea.

  Not long she stood, but looking seaward yet,
From out the water made good haste to get,
And catching up her raiment hastily,
Ran up the marble stair, and 'gan to cry: 570

"Wake, O my sisters, wake, for now are come 570
The thieves of Æa to our peaceful home."

 Then at her voice they gat them to their feet,
And when her raiment all her body sweet
Once more had hidden, joining hand to hand,
About the sacred apples did they stand,
While coiled the dragon closer to the tree,
And raised his head above them threateningly.

 Meanwhile, from Argo many a sea-beat face
Gazed longingly upon that lovely place, 580
And some their eager hands already laid
Upon the gangway. Then Medea said:—
"Get back unto the oars, O Minyæ,
Nor loiter here, for what have such as we
To do herein, where, 'mid undying trees,
Undying watch the wise Hesperides,
And where the while they watch, scarce can a God
Set foot upon the fruit-besprinkled sod
That no snow ever covers? therefore haste,
Nor yet in wondering your fair lives waste; 590
For these are as the Gods, nor think of us,
Nor to their eyes can aught be glorious
That son of man can do; would God that I
Could see far off the misty headland lie,
Where we the guilt of blood shall wash away,
For I grow weary of the dashing spray,
And ceaseless roll of interwoven seas,
And fain were sitting 'neath the whispering trees
In homely places, where the children play,

Who change like me, grow old, and die some day." 600
   She ceased, and little soothly did they grieve,
For all its loveliness, that land to leave,
For now some God had chilled their hardihead,
And in their hearts had set a sacred dread,
They knew not why; but on their oars they hung,
A little longer as the sisters sung.

   " O ye, who to this place have strayed,
That never for man's eyes was made,
Depart in haste, as ye have come,
And bear back to your sea-beat home   610
This memory of the age of gold,
And for your eyes, grown over-bold,
Your hearts shall pay in sorrowing,
For want of many a half-seen thing.

   " Lo, such as is this garden green,
In days past, all the world has been,
And what we know all people knew,
But this, that unto worse all grew.
   " But since the golden age is gone,
This little place is left alone,   620
Unchanged, unchanging, watched of us,
The daughters of wise Hesperus.
   " Surely the heavenly Messenger
Full oft is fain to enter here,
And yet without must he abide,
Nor longeth less the dark king's bride
To set red lips unto that fruit

That erst made nought her mother's suit.
Here would Diana rest awhile,
Forgetful of her woodland guile,   630
Among these beasts that fear her nought.
Nor is it less in Pallas' thought,
Beneath our trees to ponder o'er
The wide, unfathomed sea of lore;
And oft-kissed Citheræa, no less
Weary of love, full fain would press
These flowers with unsandalled feet.

  "But unto us our rest is sweet,
Neither shall any man or God
Or lovely Goddess touch the sod   640
Where-under old times buried lie,
Before the world knew misery.
Nor will we have a slave or king,
Nor yet will we learn anything
But that we know, that makes us glad;
While oft the very Gods are sad
With knowing what the Fates shall do.
  "Neither from us shall wisdom go
To fill the hungering hearts of men,
Lest to them threescore years and ten   650
Come but to seem a little day,
Once given, taken soon away.
Nay, rather let them find their life
Bitter and sweet, fulfilled of strife,
Restless with hope, vain with regret,
Trembling with fear, most strangely set

'Twixt memory and forgetfulness;
So more shall joy be, troubles less,
And surely when all this is past,
They shall not want their rest at last.

"Let earth and heaven go their way,
While still we watch from day to day,
In this green place left all alone,
A remnant of the days long gone."

There in the wind they hung, as word by word
The clear-voiced singers silently they heard;
But when the air was barren of their song,
Anigh the shore they durst not linger long,
So northward turned forewearied Argo's head,
And dipping oars, from that fair country sped,
Fulfilled of new desires and pensive thought,
Which that day's life unto their hearts had brought.

Then hard they toiled upon the bitter sea,
And in two days they did not fail to be
In sight of land, a headland high and blue,
Which straight Milesian Erginus knew
To be the fateful place which now they sought,
Stormy Malea, so thitherward they brought
The groaning ship, and, casting anchor, lay
Beneath that headland's lee, within a bay,
Wherefrom the more part landed, and their feet
Once more the happy soil of Greece did meet.

Therewith they failed not to bring ashore
Rich robes of price and of fair arms good store,

And gold and silver, that they there might buy
What yet they lacked for their solemnity;
Then, while upon the highest point of land
Some built an altar, Jason, with a band
Of all the chiefest of the Minyæ,
Turned inland from the murmur of the sea. 690

  Not far they went ere by a little stream
Down in a valley they could see the gleam
Of brazen pillars and fair-gilded vanes,
And, dropping down by dank dark-wooded lanes
From off the hill-side, reached a house at last
Where in and out men-slaves and women passed,
And guests were streaming fast into the hall
Where now the oaken boards were laid for all.
With these the Minyæ went, and soon they were
Within a pillared hall both great and fair, 700
Where folk already sat beside the board,
And on the dais was an ancient lord.

  But when these saw the fearless Minyæ
Glittering in arms, they sprang up hastily,
And each man turned about unto the wall
To seize his spear or staff: then through the hall
Jason cried out: "Laconians, fear ye not,
Nor leave the flesh-meat while it yet is hot
For dread of us, for we are men as ye,
And I am Jason of the Minyæ, 710
And come from Æa to the land of Greece,
And in my ship bear back the Golden Fleece,
And a fair Colchian queen to fill my bed.
And now we pray to share your wine and bread,

And other things we need, and at our hands
That ye will take fair things of many lands."

"Sirs," said the ancient lord, " be welcome here,
Come up and sit by me, and make such cheer
As here ye can : glad am I that to me
The first of Grecian men from off the sea
Ye now are come." 720
      Therewith the great hall rang
With joyful shouts, and as, with clash and clang
Of well-wrought arms, up to the dais they went,
All eyes upon the Minyæ were bent,
Nor could they have enough of wondering
At this or that sea-tossed victorious king.

So with the strangers there they held high feast,
And afterwards the slaves drove many a beast
Down to the shore, and carried back again
Great store of precious things in pack and wain ; 730
Wrought gold and silver, gems, full many a bale
Of scarlet cloth, and fine silk, fit to veil
The perfect limbs of dreaded Goddesses ;
Spices fresh-gathered from the outland trees,
And arms well-wrought, and precious scarce-known
   wine,
And carven images well-nigh divine.

So when all folk with these were satisfied,
Back went the Minyæ to the water-side,
And with them that old lord, fain to behold
Victorious Argo and the Fleece of Gold. 740
And so aboard amid the oars he lay
Throughout the night, and at the dawn of day

Did all men land, nor spared that day to wear
The best of all they had of gold-wrought gear,
And every one, being crowned with olive grey,
Up to the headland did they take their way,
Where now already stood the crowned priests
About the altars by the gilt-horned beasts.
There as the fair sun rose, did Jason break
Over the altar the thin barley-cake,   750
And cast the salt abroad, and there were slain
The milk-white bulls, and there red wine did rain
On to the fire from out the ancient jar,
And high rose up the red flame, seen afar
From many another headland of that shore,
And through its fitful crackling and its roar,
From time to time in pleading song and prayer,
Swept by the wind about the summer air,
Clear rung the voices of the Minyæ
Unto the dashing of the conquered sea,   760
That far below thrust on by tide and wind
The crumbling bases of the headland mined.

BOOK XV.

Argo in ambush—Medea goes to Iolchos, and by her wiles brings Pelias to his death.

BUT on the morrow did the Minyæ
   Turn Argo's head once more to Thessaly,
And surely now the steersman knew his way,
As island after island every day
They coasted, with a soft land-wind abeam;
And now at last like to a troubled dream
Seemed all the strange things they had seen erewhile,
Now when they knew the very green sea's smile
Beneath the rising and the setting sun,
And their return they surely now had won   10
To those familiar things long left behind,
When on their sails hard drave the western wind.

  So past Eubœa did they run apace,
And swept with oars the perilous green race
Betwixt Cerinthus and the islands white;
But, when they now had doubled that dread height,
The shields that glittered upon Argo's side
They drew inboard, and made a shift to hide
Her golden eye and gleaming braveries,
And heaped the deck with bales of merchandize,   20
And on their yards sails patched and brown they bent,
And crawling slowly, with six oars they went,

Till Argo seemed like some Phœnician
Grown old and leaky, on the water wan.
  Now at the entering of their own green bay
There lies an island that men call to-day
Green Cicynethus, low, and covered o'er
With close-set trees, and distant from the shore
But some five furlongs, and a shallow sea
'Twixt main and island ripples languidly,   30
And on the shore there dwells not any man
For many a mile; so there Erginus ran
Argo disguised, and steering skilfully,
Cast anchor with the island on his lee;
Hid from the straits, and there struck sail and mast;
Then to the island shore the heroes past,
And with their wide war-axes 'gan to lop
Full many a sapling with green-waving top
And full-leaved boughs of spreading maple-trees,
And covered Argo's seaward side with these.   40
And then the shipmen did Medea bid
To hold a shallop ready, while she hid
Her lovely body in a rough grey gown
And heavy home-spun mantle coarse and brown,
And round about her a great wallet slung,
And to her neck an uncouth image hung
Of Tauric Artemis, the cruel maid.

  Then, all being ready, to the prince she said:—
"O well-beloved, amongst our foes I go
Alone and weak, nor do I surely know   50
If I shall live or die there; but do thou

Let one watch ever, who from off the prow
Shall look towards white Iolchos o'er the bay,
And watching, wait until the seventh day,
And if no sign thou hast from me by then,
Believe me slain at hands of wicked men,
Or shut in some dark prison at the least,
While o'er my head thy foe holds royal feast.

  "Then soothly if it lieth in thine heart
To leave this land untouched, do thou thy part;   60
Yet do I think thou wilt be man enow
Unto the white-walled town to turn thy prow,
And either die a man or live a king,
Honoured of all, nor lacking anything
But me thy love—whom thou wilt soon forget,
When with thy tears my lone tomb has been wet
A little space;—so be it, do thy will.
And of all good things mayst thou have thy fill
Before thou comest to the shadowy land
Where thou wilt strive once more to touch mine hand,
And have no power e'en to meet these eyes   71
That for thy love shall see such miseries."

  She ceased, nigh weeping, but he wept indeed,
Such tears as come to men in utmost need,
When all words fail them, and the world seems gone,
And with their love they fill the earth alone,
Careless of shame, and not remembering death.

  But she clung round about him, with her breath
Shortened with sobs, as she began to say:—
"Weep not, O love, for surely many a day   80
May we be merry and forget all ill,

Nor have I yet forgotten all my skill,
And ere the days are gone thou well mayst see
Thy deadly foe brought unto nought by me.
And if indeed the Gods give me the day,
Then shall thy wakeful watch see o'er the bay
Smoke in the day-time, red flame in the night
Rise o'er Iolchos' well-built walls and white;
Then linger not, but run out every oar,
And hasten toward the many-peopled shore   90
That is thine own thenceforth, as I am thine."

 Therewith from him she turned her face divine,
And reached the shallop over Argo's side,
That o'er the shallows soon began to glide,
Driven by arms of strong Eurydamas;
But when the keel dragged on the rank sea-grass,
She stepped ashore, and back the hero turned
Unto his fellows, who, with hearts that burned
Unto the quays to bring great Argo's stem,
And gain the glory that was waiting them,   100
Watched ever for the sign across the bay,
Till nigh the dawning of the seventh day.

 But from the shore unto a thick-leaved wood
Medea turned, drawing both cloak and hood
Right close about her, lest perchance some man,
Some hind, or fisher of the water wan,
Should wonder at her visage, that indeed
Seemed little worthy of that wretched weed.
 In that thick wood a little stream there was,
That here was well-nigh hidden of the grass,   110

And there swelled into pools both clear and deep,
Wherein the images of trees did sleep,
For it was noontide of the summer day.
To such a pool Medea took her way,
And reaching it, upon the grass laid down
Her rough grey homespun cloak and wallet brown;
And when her eyes had swept the space around,
Undid her tunic, that upon the ground
Fell huddled round her feet; nor did she spare
To strip the linen from her body fair, 120
And shoes from off her feet; then she drew near
The flowery edges of the streamlet clear,
And gazing down upon her image, stood,
Hearkening the drowsy murmur of the wood;
And since the wind was hushed that noon of day,
And moveless down her back the long locks lay,
Her very self an image seemed to be,
Wrought in some wondrous faint-hued ivory,
Carved by a master among cunning men.

So still she stood, that the quick water-hen 130
Noted her not, as through the blue mouse-ear
He made his way; the conies drew anear,
Nibbling the grass, and from an oak-twig nigh
A thrush poured forth his song unceasingly.

But in a while, sighing, she turned away,
And, going up to where the wallet lay,
She opened it, and thence a phial drew
That seemed to be well wrought of crystal blue,
Which when she had unstopped, therefrom she poured
Into the hollow of an Indian gourd, 140

A pale green liquor, wherefrom there arose
Such scent as o'er some poisonous valley blows,
Where nought but dull-scaled twining serpents dwell,
Nor any more now could the Colchian smell
The water-mint, the pine-trees, or the flower
Of the heaped-up sweet odorous virgin's bower.

   But shuddering, and with lips grown pale and wan,
She took the gourd, and with shut eyes began
Therefrom her body to anoint all o'er;
And this being done, she turned not any more   150
Unto the woodland brook, but hurrying,
Drew on her raiment, and made haste to sling
Her wallet round about her, nor forgot
The Tauric image, ere the lovely spot
She left unto the rabbit and the roe.

   And now straight toward Iolchos did she go,
But as she went, a hideous, fearful change
Had come on her; from sunken eyes and strange
She gazed around; white grew her golden hair,
And seventy years her body seemed to bear;   160
As though the world that coppice had passed by
For half an age, and caught her presently,
When from its borders once her foot had passed.

   Then she began to murmur, as she cast
From changed eyes glances on her wrinkled hands:
"O Jason! surely not for many lands,
Rich and gold-bearing lands, would I do this;
But yet with thee to gain good peace and bliss
Far greater things would I have done to-day."

So saying, she made haste upon her way,   170
Until at last, when it was well-nigh night,
She reached the city crowned with **towers white**,
And passing by the brazen gates of **it**,
Forewearied, by the fountain did she sit;
Where, as she waited, came an ancient crone,
Who, groaning, set her pitcher on the stone,
And seeing the Colchian, asked her what **she was**.

" Mother," Medea said, " I strive to pass
Unto fair Athens, where dwelt long ago
My fathers, if perchance folk yet may know   180
Where they lie buried, that on that same stone
I may lie down and die; a hapless one,
Whom folk once called Aglaia, once called **fair**;
For years, long years agone, my golden hair
Went down the wind, as carelessly I strayed
Along the wet sea-beach, of nought afraid,
And there my joy was ended suddenly,
For on me fell the rovers of the sea,
And bore me bound into the land **of** Thrace,
And thence to some unnamed, far northern place, 190
Where I, a rich man's daughter, learned to bear
Fetters and toil and scourging year by year;
Till it has happed unto me at the last,
Now that my strength for toil is overpast,
That I am free once more, if that is aught,
Whom in all wretched places death has sought,
And surely now will find—but wilt thou give
Some resting-place to me, that I may live
Until I come to Athens and my grave?

And certainly, though nought of gold I have, 200
In the far northland did I gather lore
Of this and that amid my labour sore;
And chiefly of this Goddess, rites I know,
Whose image round my neck thou seest now,
Well-shod Diana—and a whispered word
Within her inmost temple once I heard
Concerning this: how men may grow to be
E'en as the Gods, and gain eternity,
And how the work of years may be undone."

 When she had finished, the Thessalian crone, 210
Filling her jar with water, turned and said:—

 "Surely, Athenian, I am sore afraid,
Ere thou hast learned thy lesson utterly,
And gained that new life, thou thyself wilt die;
Nor will it profit me, who am a slave
Wishing for death, a wretched life to save:
But hearken now, if thou art wise and bold,
Then will I show thee how thou mayst earn gold
And thanks enow, by telling this thy tale
Unto rich folk, for them will it avail 220
To know thy secret; rise, and come with me,
And the king's daughters surely shalt thou see;
For on my road from nothing unto hell
His palace is the last lodge where I dwell,
And I am well aweary of it now,
And of my toil, thanked with hard word and blow."

 "I thank thee, mother," said the Colchian maid,
"Nor of king's daughters shall I be afraid,
Whose ears Latona's daughter erst have heard,

Nor trembled at the heavy dreadful word." 230
 Then on they passed, and as they went, the crone
Told her how Æson unto death was done,
And of the news that thither had been brought
Of those that o'er the sea that glory sought.
Namely, that when Æetes had been fain
To trap the Argo, all had been in vain,
Yet had he gone back well-nigh satisfied;
For in the night to him a voice had cried
Louder and clearer than a mortal can:—
"Go back to Æa, sun-begotten man, 240
And there forget thy daughter and thy fleece,
But yet be merry, for the thieves of Greece
Shall live no longer than a poor wretch may
Who lies unholpen on a lonely way
Wounded, possessing nought but many woes,—
Lo, thus it happeneth now unto thy foes!"
 This, said the crone, a Colchian had told
To Pelias, dweller in the house of gold,
And had large gifts from him; who when he knew
The certainty of this, old Æson slew 250
With all his house who at Iolchos were.
 "So," said she, "if, for quieting his fear
Of the sea-rover, such things he did give,
What would his gifts be if thou mad'st him live
His life again, with none of all his name
Alive, to give him fear of death or shame?"
With that they came unto the royal house
Where Pelias dwelt, grown old and timorous,
Oppressed with blood of those that he had slain,

Desiring wealth and longer life in vain. 260
  So there a court low-built the old crone sought,
And to her lodging the tired Colchian brought,
Where she might sleep, and gave her food and drink.
Then into sleep did wise Medea sink,
And dreamed that she herself, made ever young,
Gold-robed within some peaceful garden sung,
Like that where dwelt the wise Hesperides.
But as she walked between **the smooth-stemmed trees**
She saw the sea rise o'er the marble wall,
And rolling o'er, drown grass and flowers and all, 270
And draw on towards her, who no whit could move,
Though from the high land Jason, her own love,
Was shouting out to her, so then, at last,
She dreamed the waters over all had passed
And reached her feet, and o'er her coldly swept,
And still undrowned, beneath the waves she wept,
And still was Jason shouting to her there.
  Therewith she woke, and felt the morning air
Cold on her face, because the ancient crone
Over her couch the casement had undone. 280
And as she oped her eyes, she heard her say:—
"**Awake, O** guest, for yet another day
We twain must bear before we gain our rest.
But now indeed I think it to be best
That to my ladies I alone should show
That prayers, and rites, and wonders thou dost know,
Which thou wilt tell for gold; for sure I deem
That to **us** dying folk nought good doth seem,
But hoarding for the years we shall not see.

                                              T

So bide thou there, and I will come to thee
And bring thee word of what the queens may say."
   Then with these words she went upon her way,
While in her place alone Medea sat,
With eager heart, thinking of this and that,
And wishing that the glorious day were come,
When she should set her love within his home,
A king once more. So 'mid these thoughts, there came
Back to the place the wise Thessalian dame,
Who bade her rise and after her to go,
That she those marvels to the queens might show.
   Therewith she brought her to a chamber where
Abode the royal maidens slim and fair,
All doing well-remembered works; of whom
White-armed Alcestis sat before the loom,
Casting the shuttle swift from hand to hand.
The while Eradne's part it was to stand
Amongst the maids who carded out the wool
And filled the gleaming ivory shuttles full.
Amphinome, meantime, her golden head
Bent o'er the spinners of the milk-white thread,
And by the growing web still set aside
The many-coloured bundles newly dyed,
Blood-red, and heavenly blue, and grassy green,
Yea, and more colours than man yet has seen
In flowery meadows midmost of the May.
   Then to the royal maids the crone 'gan say :—
" Behold the woman, O my mistresses,
Who 'midst the close-set gloomy northern trees

Has late learned that I told you of; and ye
Who in this royal house live happily, 320
May well desire such life for evermore,
Which unto me were but a burden sore."

Therewith she left them, but folk say, indeed,
That she who spoke was nought but Saturn's seed,
In very likeness of that woman old,
Whose body soon folk came on, dead and cold,
Within the place where she was wont to dwell.
Now how these things may be, I cannot tell,
But certainly Queen Juno's will was good
To finish that which, in the oaken wood 330
Anigh the Centaur's cave, she first began,
Giving good heart to the strange-nurtured man.

But, she being gone, fair-limbed Amphinome
Said: "Reverend mother, welcome here ye be,
And in return for thy so hard-earned lore
That thou wilt teach us, surely never-more
Shalt thou do labour whilst thou dwellest here,
But unto us shalt thou be lief and dear
As though thou wert the best of all our blood."

But, pondering awhile, Medea stood, 340
Then answered: "Lady, I am now grown old,
And but small gifts to me were heaps of gold,
Or rest itself, for that the tomb shall give;
I say all things are nought, unless I live
So long henceforward, that I need not think
When into nothing I at last must sink;
But take me now unto the mighty king

That rules this land, and there by everything
That he holds sacred, let him swear to me
That I shall live in peace and liberty 350
Till quiet death upon my head is brought;
But this great oath being made, things shall be
By me, that never can be paid with gold; [wrought
For I will make that young which has grown old,
And that alive that ye have seen lie dead."

   Then much they wondered at the words she said,
And from the loom did fair Alcestis rise,
And tall Amphinome withdrew her eyes
From the fair spinners, and Eradne left
The carding of the fine wool for the weft. 360
Then said Eradne: "Mother, fear not thou,
Surely our father is good man enow,
And will not harm thee: natheless, he will swear
By whatsoever thing he holdeth dear,
Nor needst thou have a doubt of him at all.
Come, for he sitteth now within the hall."
With that, she took her shoes from off the ground,
And round her feet the golden strings she bound,
As did her sisters, and fair cloaks they threw
About them, and their royal raiment drew 370
Through golden girdles, gemmed and richly wrought,
And forth with them the Colchian maid they brought.
But as unto the royal hall they turned,
Within their hearts such hot desire burned
For lengthening out the life they knew so sweet,
That scarce they felt the ground beneath their feet,
And through the marble court long seemed the way.

But when they reached the place, glittering and gay
With all the slain man's goods, and saw the king
Wearing his royal crown and mystic ring,   380
And clad in purple, and his wearied face,
Anxious and cruel, gaze from Æson's place,
A little thing it seemed to slay him there,
As one might slay the lion in his lair,
Bestrewn with bones of beast, and man, and maid.

Then as he turned to them, Alcestis said:—
"O lord and father, here we bring to thee
A wise old woman, come from over sea,
Who 'mid the gloomy, close-set northern trees
Has heard the words of reverend Goddesses   390
I dare not name aloud; therefore she knows
Why this thing perishes, and that thing grows,
And what to unborn creatures must befall,
And this, the very chiefest thing of all,
To make the old man live his life again,
And all the lapse of years but nought and vain;
But we, when these strange things of her we heard,
Trembled before her, and were sore afeard,
In 'midst of all our measureless desire
Within thy veins and ours to set new fire,   400
And with thee live for many a happy day,
Whilst all about us passes soon away."

Now paler grew the king's face at this word,
And 'mid strange hopes he, too, grew sore afeard,
As sighing, he began to think of days
Now long gone by, when he was winning praise,
And thought: "If so be I should never die,

Then would I lay aside all treachery,
And here should all folk live without alarm,
For to no man would I do any harm, 410
Whatso might hap, but I would bring again
The golden age, free from all fear and pain."

But through his heart there shot a pang of fear,
As to the queen he said: "Why art thou here,
Since thou hast mastered this all-saving art,
Keeping but vagrant life for thine own part
Of what thou boastest with the Gods to share?
Thou, but a dying woman, nowise fair."

"Pelias," she said, "far from the north I come,
But in Erectheus' city was my home, 420
Where being alone, upon a luckless day,
By the sea-rovers was I snatched away,
And in their long-ship, with bound, helpless hands,
Was brought to Thrace, and thence to northern lands,
Of one of which I scarcely know the name,
Nor could your tongue the uncouth letters frame.
There had I savage masters, and must learn
With aching back to bend above the quern;
There must I learn how the poor craftsman weaves,
Nor earn his wages; and the barley-sheaves 430
Must bind in August; and across the snow,
Unto the frozen river must I go,
When the white winter lay upon the land,
And therewithal must I dread many a hand,
And writhe beneath the whistle of the whip.

"'Mid toils like these my youth from me did slip,
Uncomforted, through lapse of wretched years,

Till I forgot the use of sobs and tears,
And like a corpse about my labour went,
Grown old before my time, and worn and bent.   440
And then at last this good to me betid,
That my wise mistress strove to know things hid
From mortal men, and doubted all the rest,
Babblers and young, who in our fox's nest
Dwelt through the hideous changes of the year:
Then me she used to help her, and so dear
I grew, that when upon her tasks she went,
Into all dangerous service was I sent;
And many a time, within the woods alone,
Have I sat watching o'er the heaps of stone   450
Where dwell the giants dead; and many a time
Have my pale lips uttered the impious rhyme
That calls the dead from their unchanged abode;
Till on my soul there lay a heavy load
Of knowledge, not without reward, for I
No longer went in rags and misery,
But in such bravery as there they had
My toil-worn body now was fairly clad,
And feared by man and maid did I become,
And mistress of my mistress' dreary home.   460

"Moreover, whether that, being dead to fear,
All things I noted, or that somewhat dear
I now was grown to those dread Goddesses,
I know not, yet amidst the haunted trees
More things I learned than my old mistress did,
Yea, some things surely from all folk else hid,
Whose names once spoken would unroof this hall,

And lay Iolchos underneath a pall
Of quick destruction; and when these were learned,
At last my mistress all her wage had earned, 470
And to the world was dead for evermore.

"But me indeed the whole house hated sore,
First for my knowledge, next that, sooth to say,
I, when I well had passed my evil day,
And came to rule, spared not my fellows aught;
Whereby this fate upon my head was brought,
That flee I must lest worse should hap to me;
So on my way unto the Grecian sea
With weary heart and manifold distress,
My feet at last thy royal pavement press. 480
My lips beseech thy help, O mighty King!
Help me, that I myself may do the thing
I most desire, and this great gift may give
To thee and thine, from this time forth to live
In youth and beauty while the world goes by
With all its vain desires and misery.

"And if thou doubtest still, then hear me say
The words thou spakst upon a long-past day,
When thou wert fearful, and the half-shod man
Had come upon thee through the water wan." 490

She ceased awhile, and therewith Pelias,
With open mouth and eyes as fixed as glass,
Stared at her, wondering. Then again she said:—
"Awhile ago, when he thou knowest dead,
And he thou thinkest dead, were by thy side,
A crafty wile thou forgedst; at that tide

Telling the tale of Theban Athamas,
And how that Phryxus dead at Æa was.
Thinking (and not in vain) to light the fire
Of glorious deeds, and measureless desire   500
Of fame within the hearts of men o'erbold.

  "For thus thou saidst: 'So is the story told
Of things that happened forty years agone,
Nor of the Greeks has there been any one
To set the bones of Phryxus in a tomb,
Or mete out to the Colchian his due doom.'

  "So saidst thou then, and by such words didst drive
Thy nephew in a hopeless game to strive,
Wherefore thou deemest wisely he is dead,
And all the words that he can say are said."   510

  She ceased again, while pale and shuddering,
Across his eyes the crafty, fearful king
Drew trembling hands. But yet again she spoke:—
"What if the Gods by me the strong chain broke
Of thy past deeds, ill deeds wrought not in vain,
And thou with new desires lived again?
Durst I still trust thee with my new-gained life?
Who for the rest am not thy brother's wife,
Thy nephew, or thy brother. Be it so.
Yet since the foolish hearts of men I know,   520
Swear on this image of great Artemis
That unto me thy purpose harmless is,
Nor wilt thou do me hurt, or more or less.
Then while thy lips the ivory image press,
Will I call down all terrors that I know
Upon thine head if thou shouldst break thy vow.

"Yet for thyself dost thou trust what I say,
Or wilt thou still be **dying day by day** ?"

"**Yea**," said the king, " yea, whosoe'er thou art,
Needs must I trust thee, in such wise my heart   530
Desires life again when this is done.
Give me the image, O thou fearful one,
Who knowest **all my** life, who in the breath
Wherein **thou** prayest help still threatenest **death**."
   Then **on** the image **did** she swear the king,
But while he spoke was she still muttering,
With glittering eyes fixed on him ; but at last,
When from his lips the dreadful word had passed,
She said : "**O** King, pray **that** thou mayst not **die**
Before the fifth day's sun has risen high ;   540
Yet on to-morrow morn shalt thou behold
This hair of mine all glittering bright as gold,
My tottering feet firm planted on the ground,
My grey and shrivelled arms grown **white and round**,
As once, when by Ilissus' side I trod,
A snare of beauty to a very God,
To young men's eyes a fierce consuming fire."
   So saying, did she kindle fresh **desire**
In the king's fainting heart, until he thought—
"**Nay, if** new life hereby to me is brought,   550
Withal there may be brought a lovely mate
To share my happy days and scorn of fate."
Then did he bid his daughters straight to go
With that wise woman, nor spare aught to do
That she might bid them, and they wondering,

But in their hearts yet fearful of the thing,
Unto the women's chamber led her back,
And bade her say what matters she might lack.
 Then little did she ask unto her need,
But fair cold water, and some fitting weed,   560
And in a close-shut place to be alone,
Because no eye must see the wonder done.
 And "Oh," she said, "fair women, haste ye now,
For surely weaker every hour I grow,
And fear to die ere I can live again."
Then through the house they hastened, and with pain
A brazen caldron their fair hands bore up,
As well wrought over as a king's gold cup.
Which in a well-hung chamber did they set,
And filled with clear cold water, adding yet   570
New raiment wrought about with ruddy gold,
And snowy linen wrapped in many a fold.
 Then did Medea turn unto the three,
And said: "Farewell, for no more shall ye see
These limbs alive, or hear this feeble voice,
For either shall my changed lips rejoice
In my new beauty, or else stark and cold
This wretched body shall your eyes behold.
Wait now until six hours are over-passed,
And if ye still shall find the door shut fast,   580
Then let the men bring hammers, neither doubt
That thence my corpse alone shall they bear out.
But if the door is open or ajar,
Draw nigh and see how great my helpers are,
And greet what there ye see with little fear,

For whatsoever may have touched me here,
By then, at least, shall no one be with me,
And nought but this old sorceress shall ye see
Grown young again; alas! grown young again!
Would God that I were past the fear and pain!" 590

  So said the Colchian; but their fearful eyes
Turned hastily from such hid mysteries
As there might lurk; and to their bower they gat,
And well-nigh silent o'er the weaving sat,
And did **what** things they needs must do that day,
Until that six hours' space had passed away.

  Then had the sun set, and the whitening moon
Shone o'er the gardens where the brown bird's tune
Was quivering through the roses red and white,
And sweeter smelt the sweet flowers with the night; 600
But to the chamber where there lay alone
The wise Medea, up the faint grey stone
Two rose-trees climbed, along a trellis led,
And with their wealth of blossoms white and red
Another garden of the window made.

  So now the royal sisters, **sore afraid,**
Each with a taper in her trembling hand,
Before the fateful chamber-door did stand
And heard no noise; whereon Amphinome
Pushed at the door, that yielded, and the three 610
Passing with beating hearts the oaken door,
Pressed noiseless **feet** upon the polished floor,
Reddening the moonshine with their tapers' light.

  There they beheld the caldron gleaming bright,

And on the floor the heap of raiment rent
That erst had hid the body old and bent;
And there a crystal phial they beheld
Empty, that once some wondrous liquor held;
And by the window-side asleep they saw
The Colchian woman, white without a flaw   620
From head to heel; her round arms by her side,
Her fair face flushed with sweet thoughts, as a bride
Who waits the coming of some well-loved man.
Softly she breathed, the while the moonlight ran
In silver ripples o'er her hair of gold.

But when that loveliness they did behold,
They cried aloud for wonder, though not yet
Her happy dreaming thoughts would she forget,
But into spoken words her murmuring grew,
Though of their purport nought the sisters knew,   630
Since in the outland Colchian tongue she spoke;
Then, while they waited, slowly she awoke,
And looking round her, still with half-shut eyes,
She said: "O damsels, fain would I arise,
I hear the morning murmur of the birds
And lowing of released and hungry herds
Across the meadows, sweet with vetch and bean,
And the faint ripple of the Phasis green."

But with that last word did she start upright,
Shading her grey eyes from the tapers' light,   640
And said: "O queens, and are ye come to me
This eve, my triumph over time to see?
And is my boast for nought? behold me made

Like the fair casket-bearer who betrayed
The luckless man while yet the world was young."
So saying did she speak as one who sung,
So sweet her voice was; then she stepped adown
From off the silken couch, and rough and brown
They seemed beside her, fair maids though they were.

But silently they stood, and wondered there, 650
And from their hearts had flown all thoughts at last
But that of living while the world went past.

Then at her feet Alcestis knelt and prayed:—
" O, who can see thee, Goddess, unafraid,
Yet thou thyself hast promised life to us,
More than man's feeble life, and perilous,
And if thy promise now thou makest vain,
How can we live our thoughtless life again?
Then, would thou ne'er hadst left thine heavenly home,
And o'er the green Thessalian meadows come!" 660

Then spoke Medea: " Young as ye see me
The king, your father, in few days shall be,
And when that he has gained his just reward,
Your lives from death and danger will I guard,
Natheless no Goddess am I, but no more
Than a poor wanderer from shore to shore,
Though loved by her the swift of Goddesses,
Who now is glancing 'twixt the dark grey trees,
E'en while we speak. Now leave me to my rest,
For this new-changed body is oppressed 670
By all the thoughts that round my heart will throng
Of ancient days, and hopes forgotten long;
Go, therefore, but come hither with the sun

To do my bidding; then shall there be done
Another marvel ere the morn comes round,
If yet ye three are dwelling above ground."

  Then, trembling, they unto their chamber passed,
But, they being gone, she made the strong door fast,
And soon in deep sleep on the couch she lay
Until the golden sun brought back the day;   680
Nor could she fail arising to be glad
That once again her own fair form she had,
And as the fresh air met her pleasantly,
She smiled, her image in the bath to see
That had been lost since at the noon she stood
Beside the still pool in the lonely wood,
And she rejoiced her combed-out hair to bind,
And feel the linen in the morning wind
Fluttering about, in kissing side and limb,
And it was sweet about her ankles slim   690
To make the gemmed thongs of the sandals meet,
With rosy fingers touching her soft feet.

  But she being clad, there came the ladies three,
Who seemed by her but handmaidens to be,
And such indeed they were, as dumb with awe
In the fresh morn that loveliness they saw.

  Then said Medea: " Fair queens well be ye!
Surely in happy hour ye come to me,
Who, if I might, would do the whole world good.
But now take heed; is there some close dark wood 700
Anigh the town?—thither will we to-night,
And in that place, hidden from all men's sight,

Shall ye see wonders passing human thought.
But thither, by your hands there must be brought
Some ancient beast at very point to die,
That ye may see how loved an one am I
By dreadful Gods; there, too, must ye convey
A brazen caldron ere the end of day,
And nigh the place there must not fail to be
Some running stream to help our mystery.   710
Yet more; take heed that She who helpeth me,
Whose name I name not, willeth not to see
The robes of kings and queens upon her slaves;
Therefore, if ye would please the one who saves,
This night must ye be clad in smocks of black,
And all adornment must your bodies lack,
Nor must there be a fillet on your hair,
And the hard road must feel your feet all bare."

  "Lady," Eradne said, "all shall be done,
Nor wilt thou yet have had beneath the sun   720
More faithful servants than we are to thee;
But wilt thou not the king my father see,
And gladden him, that he may give thee things
Such as the heart desires—the spoil of kings?"

  "Nay," said Medea, "much have I to think
Ere the hot sun beneath the sea shall sink,
And much to call to mind, and for your sake
Unto my Helper many a prayer to make."

  With that they went, and she, being left alone,
Took up the image of the swift-foot one,   730
Which for a hidden casket served her well,
And wherein things were laid right strange to tell.

So this and that she looked at, and the while
She muttered charms learned in the river isle.

  But at the noontide did they bring her food,
Saying that all was ready in the wood,
And that the night alone they waited now,
Ere unto them those marvels she might show.
Therefore Medea bade them come again
When all the house of peaceful sleep was fain,   740
And nought was stirring: so at dead of night
They came to her in black apparel dight,
Bearing like raiment for the Colchian,
Who did it on before their faces wan
And troubled eyes; then out of gates they stole,
Setting their faces to the wished-for goal.

  Now nigh Anaurus a blind pathway leads
Betwixt the yellow corn and whispering reeds,
The home of many a shy, quick-diving bird;
Thereby they passed, and as they went they heard 750
Splashing of fish, and ripple of the stream;
And once they saw across the water's gleam
The black boat of some fisher of the night,
And from the stream had drawn back in affright,
But that the Colchian whispered: "Wise be ye,
Thessalian sisters, yet with certainty
Make onward to the wood, for who indeed,
Beholding our pale faces and black weed,
Would come the nigher to us? Would not he
Think that some dread things we must surely be, 760
And tremble till we passed? Haste, for the night

U

Is waning now, and danger comes with light."
Then on they passed, and soon they reached the wood,
And straight made for the midst of it, where stood
An old horned ram bound fast unto a tree,
Which the torch-bearer, tall Amphinome,
Showed to Medea, and not far therefrom
Unto a brazen caldron did they come,
Hidden with green boughs; then Medea bade
That by their hands a high pile should be made   770
Of fallen wood, and all else fit to burn;
Which done, unto the caldron did they turn
And bore it to the river, and did strain
Their fair round arms to bear it back again
When it was filled, and raised it on the pile.
And then with hands unused to service vile
Lit up the fire, while Medea took
Dried herbs from out her wallet, which she shook
Into the caldron; till at last a cloud
Rose up therefrom and the dark trees did shroud.   780

  Then did she bid them the old ram to lead
Up to the caldron's side, and with good heed
To quench his just departing feeble life;
So in his throat Eradne thrust the knife,
While in the white arms of Amphinome
And fair Alcestis, bleating piteously,
Feebly he struggled; so being slain at last,
Piecemeal his members did the sisters cast
Into the seething water: then drew back
And hid their faces in their raiment black,   790
The while Medea midst the flickering light

Still sprinkled herbs from out her fingers white,
And in a steady voice at last did say:—
  "O thou that turnest night into the day,
O thou the quencher of unhallowed fire,
The scourge of hot, inordinate desire,
Hast thou a mind to help me on this night,
That wrong may still be wrong, and right be right
In all men's eyes? A little thing I ask
Before I put an ending to my task."   800

  Scarce had she finished, ere a low black cloud
Seemed closing o'er the forest, and aloud
Medea cried: "Oh, strong and terrible!
I fear thee not, do what may please thee well."
Then as the pale Thessalians with affright
Crouched on the earth, forth leapt the lightning white
Over their shrinking heads, and therewithal
The thunder crashed, and down the rain did fall,
As though some angry deity were fain
To make a pool of the Thessalian plain.   810

  Till in a while it ceased, and all was stilled
Except the murmur of some brook new-filled,
And dripping of the thick-leafed forest trees
As they moved gently in the following breeze.
Yet still King Pelias' daughters feared to rise,
And with wet raiment still they hid their eyes,
And trembled, and white-armed Amphinome
Had dropped the long torch of the resin-tree,
That lay half-charred among the tall wet grass.
But unto them did wise Medea pass,   820
And said: "O, daughters of the sea-born man,

Rise up, for now the stars are growing wan,
And the grey dawn is drawing near apace;
Nor need ye fear to see another face
Than this of mine, and all our work is done
We came to do."

      Then slowly, one by one,
The sisters rose, and, fearful, drew anigh
The place where they had seen the old ram die;
And there beheld, by glimmering twilight grey,
Where on its side the brazen caldron lay,   830
And on the grass and flowers that hid the ground,
Half-charred extinguished brands lay all around,
But yet no token of the beast was there;
But 'mid the brands a lamb lay, white and fair,
That now would raise his new-born head and bleat,
And now would lick the Colchian's naked feet,
As close he nestled to her: then the three
Drew nigh unto that marvel timidly,
And gazed at him with wide eyes wondering.

 Thereat Medea raised the new-changed thing   840
In her white arms, and smiled triumphantly,
And said: "What things the Gods will do for me
Ye now behold; take, then, this new-born beast,
And hope to sit long ages at the feast,
And this your youth and loveliness to keep
When all that ye have known are laid asleep.
Yet steel your hearts to do a fearful thing,
Ere this can happen, for unto the king
Must your hands do what they have done to-night
To this same beast. And now, to work aright   850

What yet is needful to this mystery,
Will be four days' full bitter toil for me.
Take heed that silence, too, on this ye keep,
Or else a bitter harvest shall ye reap."

So said she, willing well indeed to know,
Before the promised sign she dared to show,
What honour Pelias in Iolchos had,
And if his death should make his people sad.

But now they turned back on their homeward way,
Fleeing before the coming of the day;   860
Nor yet the flinty way their feet did feel,
Nor their wet limbs the wind, that 'gan to steal
From out the north-west ere the sun did rise.
And swiftly though they went, yet did their eyes
Behold no more than eyes of those that dream
The crumbling edges of the swirling stream
Or fallen tree-trunks or the fallow rough.
But Juno sent them feeling just enough
By the lone ways to come unto the town
And fair-walled palace, and to lay them down 870
Upon their fragrant beds, that stood forlorn
Of their white bodies, waiting for the morn
In chambers close-shut from the dying night.

But since Medea fain would know aright
What the folk willed to Pelias in the town,
Early next day she did on her the brown
And ragged raiment, and the sisters told
That she must find the place where herbs were sold,
And there buy this and that; therewith she went

About the town, seeming crook-backed and bent; 880
And, hidden in her mantle and great hood,
Within the crowded market-place she stood,
And marked the talk of all the busy folk,
And ever found that under Pelias' yoke
All people groaned: and therefore with good heart
She set herself to work out all her part.

  For, going back, till the fifth day was gone
She dwelt within her chamber all alone,
Except that now and then the sisters came
To bring her food; and whiles they saw a flame, 890
Strange-coloured, burning on the hearth, while she
Was bending o'er it, muttering wearily,
And whiles they saw her bent o'er parchment strange,
And letters that they knew not; but no change
They ever saw upon her lovely face.

  But at the last, she, mindful of the place
Where lay fair Argo's glorious battered keel,
And that dread hidden forest of bright steel,
Said to Eradne, when her food she brought
Upon the sixth morn: "Sister, I have thought 900
How best to carry out the mystery
That is so dear at heart to thee and me,
And find that this night must the thing be done,
So seek a place where we may be alone,
High up, and looking southward o'er the bay;
Thither ere midnight must ye steal away,
And under a huge caldron set dry brands.
And that being done, take sharp swords in your hands,
And while I watch the sea, and earth, and air,

Go ye to Pelias' well-hung chamber fair; 910
There what ye will ye may most surely do,
If ye will work the way I counsel you.
Therewith a phial in her hand she set,
And said: "Who tasteth this will soon forget
Both life and death, and for no noise will wake
In two days' space; therefore this phial take,
And with the king's drink see ye mingle it,
As well ye may, and let his servants sit
O'er wine so honied at the feast to-night.
Then certes shall their sleep not be so light, 920
That bare feet pattering quick across the floor,
Or unused creaking of an open door,
Shall rouse them; though no deadly drug it is,
But bringer of kind sleep and dreamy bliss.

"But now, what think'st thou? Are your hearts so good,
That ye will dare to shed your father's blood
That he may live for ever?—then is he
The luckiest of all men. But if ye
Draw back now, after all my prayers and tears,
Then were it best that ye should end your fears 930
By burning me with quick fire ere to-night.
And yet not thus should ye lead lives aright,
And free from fear; because the sandalled queen
Doth ever keep a memory fresh and green
For all her faithful servants—ye did see
Late in the green-wood how she loveth me.—

"Therefore be wise, and when to-night ye draw
The sharp-edged steel, glittering without a flaw,

Cast fear and pity from you. Pity him
I bid you rather, who with shrunken limb
And sunken eyes, remembers well the days
When in the ranks of war he garnered praise,
Which unarmed, feeble, as his last year ends,
Babbling amongst the elders now he spends.
Such shall not Pelias be, but rather now
The breath of new life past misdeeds shall blow
Adown the wind, and, taught by his old life,
Shall he live honoured, free from fear or strife."

"Fear not," Eradne said, "our will to-night,
For all thy bidding will we do outright,
Since still a Goddess thou dost seem to be
To us poor strugglers with mortality.
And for the secret spot this night we need,
Close to the sea a place I know indeed,
Upon the outskirts of this palace fair;
And on this night of all nights, close by there
My father sleeps, as oft his custom is,
When he is fain a Mysian girl to kiss,
Sea-rovers sold to him three months agone.
There after midnight we shall be alone
Beyond all doubt, since this place by the sea
A temple is of some divinity,
Whose very name men now have clean forgot,
And, as folk think, ill spirits haunt the spot:
So all men fear it sore, but soothly we
Fear nought of all these things, being led by thee."

She ceased, and from the Colchian won much praise,
And promises of many happy days.

Then as upon the door she laid her hand,
Medea said: "When midnight hides the land, 970
Come here to me, and bring me to that place;
Then look the last upon your father's face
As ye have known it for these eighteen years,
Furrowed by eld and drawn by many fears;
But when ye come, in such guise be ye clad
As in the wood that other night ye had."
Then did Eradne leave her, and the day
Through sunshine and through shadow passed away.

But with the midnight came the sisters three,
To lead her to that temple by the sea, 980
And in black raiment had they hurried there,
With naked feet, and unadorned loose hair,
E'en as the other night Medea bade,
Except that each one had a trenchant blade
Slung round her neck, wherewith to do the deed.
Of these Alcestis trembled like the reed
Set midmost of some quickly running stream,
But with strange fire Eradne's eyes did gleam,
And a bright flush was burning on her cheek,
As still her fingers the sharp steel did seek; 990
While tall Amphinome, grown pale and white
Beyond all measure, gazed into the night
With steady eyes, as with the queen they went
To that lone place to work out their intent.
So when all courts and corridors were passed,
Unto the ancient fane they came at last,
And found it twofold; for below there stood

Square marble pillars, huge, and red as blood,
And wrought all o'er with fretting varying much;
Heavy they were, and nowise like to such   1000
As men built in the lands Medea knew,
Or in the countries fate had led her through:
But they, set close and thick, aloft did hold
A well-wrought roof, where still gleamed scraps of
    gold,
That once told tales of Gods none living praise;
And on this roof some king of later days
Had built another temple long before
The Minyæ came adown unto that shore
From fair Orchomenus, of whose rites indeed
And to what Gods the victim then did bleed,   1010
Men knew but little; but therein there rose
Fair slim white pillars set in goodly rows,
And garlanded with brazen fruit and flowers,
That gleaming once, through lapse of many hours,
Now with black spirals wrapt the pillars white.
But this fair fane was open to the night
On one side only, toward the restless sea;
And there a terrace, wrought full cunningly,
Clear of the pillars hung above the sand.
   Now went those maids, groping with outstretched
    hand   1020
Betwixt the pillars of the undercroft,
Until they reached a stair that led aloft
Into the windy, long-deserted fane
Of younger days; but when their feet did gain
The open space above the murmuring sea.

In whispers did the queens of Thessaly
Show to the Colchian where the great pile was,
Built 'neath a vessel of bright polished brass,
And many water-jars there stood around;
And as they spoke, to them, the faint low sound   1030
Of their own whispered voices seemed as loud
As shouts that break from out the armed crowd
Of warriors ready for the fight.
                            But she
Spoke with no lowered voice, and said: "O ye!
Be brave to-night, and thenceforth have no fear
Of God or man since ye to me are dear.
Light up the torches, because certainly
Those that may see them gleaming o'er the sea
Will think they light but spirits of the air."
Then presently the torches out did flare,   1040
And lighted up the smile upon her face
And the tall pillars of the holy place,
And the three sisters gazing at her there,
Wild-looking, with the sea-wind in their hair,
And scant black raiment driven from their feet.
  But when her eyes their fearful eyes did meet,
With wild appealing glances as for aid,
S me little pity touched the Colchian maid,
Some vague regret for their sad destiny.
But to herself she said: "So must it be,   1050
And to such misery shall such a king
Lead wife and child, and every living thing
That trusts him." Then she said, "Leave me alone,
And go and do that which were better done

Ere any streak of dawn makes grey the sky.
And come to me **when ye have seen him lie**
Dead to his old life of misdeeds and woe."

   Then voiceless from the torchlight did they go
Into the darkness, and she, left **alone,**
Set by the torches till the **deed was done**　　　1060
Within the pillars, and turned back again
With eager eyes to gaze across the main,
But nothing she beheld by that starlight
But on the beach the line of breakers white,
And here and there, above the unlit grey,
Some white-topped billow dotting the dark bay.
   Then, sighing, did she turn herself around
And looked down toward the plot of unused ground,
Whereby they passed into that fateful place,
And gazed thereon with steadfast wary face,　　1070
And there the pavement, whitened by the wind,
Betwixt the turf she saw, and nigh it, twined
About a marble image carelessly,
A white wild-rose, and the grey boundary
Of wind-beat stone, through whose unhinged door
Their stealthy feet had passed a while before.
   Nought else she saw for a long dreary hour,
For all things lay asleep in bed or bower,
Or in the little-lighted mountain caves,
Or 'neath the swirling streams and toppling waves. 1080
   She trembled then, for in the eastern sky
A change came, telling of the dawning nigh,
And with swift footsteps she began to pace

Betwixt the narrow limits of the place;
But as she turned round toward the close once more
Her eyes beheld the pavement by the door
Hid by some moving mass; then joyfully
She waved her white arms toward the murmuring sea,
And listened trembling, and although the sound
Of breakers that the sandy sea-beach ground   1090
Was loud in the still night, yet could she hear
Sounds like the shuffling steps of those that bear
Some heavy thing, and as she gazed, could see
The thin black raiment of the sisters three
Blown out, and falling backward as they bent
Over some burden, and right slowly went;
And 'twixt their arms could she behold the gleam
Of gold or gems, or silver-broidered seam,
Till all was hidden by the undercroft.
And then she heard them struggling bear aloft   1100
That dreadful burden, and then went to meet,
With beating heart, their slow ascending feet,
Taking a half-burnt torch within her hand.

   There by its light did she behold them stand
Breathless upon the first stone of that fane,
And with no word she beckoned them again
To move on toward the terrace o'er the sea,
And, turning, went before them silently.

   And so at last the body down they laid
Close by the caldron, and Eradne said :—   1110
   "O thou, our life and saviour! linger not,
We pray thee now! because our hearts are hot
To see our father look with other eyes

Upon the sea, the green earth, and the skies,
And praise us for this seeming impious deed."
  Not heeding her, Medea saw the weed
She erst beheld all glittering in the hall,
And that same mantle as a funeral pall
Which she had seen laid over either knee,
The wonder of King Æson's treasury,   1120
Which wise Phœnicians for much coined gold,
And many oxen, years agone had sold
To Æson, when folk called him king and lord.
  Then to the head she went, and with no word
The white embroidered linen drew away
Over the face of the dead man, that lay
As though she doubted yet what thing it was,
And saw indeed the face of Pelias.

  Then o'er her pale face a bright flush there came,
And, turning, did she set the torches' flame   1130
Unto the dry brands of the well-built pyre,
And, standing back, and waving from the fire
The shuddering girls, somewhat thereon she cast,
Like unto incense: then with furious blast
Shot up a smokeless flame into the air,
Quivering and red, nor then did she forbear
To cry aloud, in her old Colchian tongue,
Proud words, and passionate, that strangely rung
Within the poor bewildered sisters' ears,
Filling their hearts with vague and horrid fears. 1140
  "O love!" she said, "O love! O sweet delight!
Hast thou begun to weep for me this night,

Dost thou stretch out for me thy mighty hands—
The feared of all, the graspers of the lands?
Come then, O love, across the dark seas come,
And triumph as a king in thine own home,
While I, the doer of a happy deed,
Shall sit beside thee in this wretched weed;
That folk may know me by thine eyes alone
Still blessing me for all that I have done.   1150
Come, king, and sit upon thy father's seat,
Come, conquering king, thy conqueror love to meet."

But as she said these words the luckless three
Stared at her glowing face all helplessly,
Nor to their father's corpse durst turn their eyes,
While in their hearts did fearful thoughts arise.
But now Medea, ceasing, fed the fire
With that same incense, and the flame rose higher,
A portent to the dwellers in the town,
Unto the shepherd waking on the down,   1160
A terror telling of ill things to be.

But from the God-built tower of Thessaly,
Grey Pelion, did the centaur Cheiron gaze,
And when he saw that ruddy flame outblaze,
He smiled, and said: "So comes to pass the word
That in the forests of the north I heard,
And in such wise shall love be foiled, and hate,
And hope of gain, opposing steadfast fate."
So to the flowery eastern slopes he gat,
Waiting the dawn, nor hoped for this or that.   1170

BOOK XVI.

The landing of the heroes—Jason is made king in Iolchos, and the Argonauts go to their own homes.

BUT other watchers were there on that night,
Who saw the birth of that desired light
From nigh green Cicynethus' woody shore.
 For in mid-channel there, with every oar
Run out, and cable ready for the slip,
Did Jason hold his glorious storm-tossed ship,
While in the top did keen-eyed Lynceus stand,
And every man had ready to his hand
Sharp spear, and painted shield, and grinded sword.
Thus as they waited, suddenly the word   10
Rang out from Jason's mouth, and in the sea
The cable splashed, and straight the Minyæ
Unto their breasts the shaven ash-trees brought,
And, as the quivering blades the water caught,
Shouted for joy, and quickly passed the edge
Of Cicynethus, green with reed and sedge.
And whitening the dark waters of the bay,
Unto Iolchos did they take their way.
 Meanwhile the Colchian queen triumphantly
Watched the grey dawn steal forth above the sea, 20
Still murmuring softly in the Colchian tongue,
While o'er her head the flickering fire yet hung,

And in the brazen caldron's lips did gleam;
Wherefrom went up a great white cloud of steam,
To die above their heads in that fresh air.
But **Pelias'** daughters, writhing in despair,
Silent for dread of her, she noted nought,
Nor of the dead man laid thereby she thought.

  At last came forward tall Amphinome,
And said: "O Queen, look o'er the whitening sea, 30
And tell us now what thing it is we lack
To bring our father's vanished breathing back
With that new life, whereof thou spak'st to us."
So in a broken voice and piteous
She spoke; but when no answer came at all,
Nor did Medea's grey eyes on her fall,
She cried again: "O, art thou pitiless?
Wilt thou not note our measureless distress?
Wilt thou not finish that thou hast begun?
Lo, in a little while the piercing sun 40
Shall find us slayers of our father here.
Then if thou hast no pity, hast thou fear?
We are king's daughters still, and with us still
Are men who heed nought but to do our will;
And if thou fall'st into the hands of these,
Thou shalt lament the gloomy northern trees
And painless death of threescore years and ten,
And little shall thy beauty help thee then."

  So cried she shrilly in her gathering ire;
But when Medea answered **not**, the fire 50
Burnt **out** within her heart, and on her knees
She fell, and cried: "O crown of Goddesses,

Forgive these impious words, and answer me,
Else shall I try if the green heaving sea
Will hide from all these impious blood-stained hands,
Or bear them far away to savage lands,
That know no good or evil; O speak, speak!
How can I pray thee when all words are weak?
What gifts, what worship, shall we give to thee?"

 E'en as she spoke, Medea seemed to see   60
A twinkling light far off amidst the bay,
Then from the suppliant hand she drew away,
Nor turned to her; but looking seaward still,
She cried: "O love! yet shalt thou have thy fill
Of wealth, and power, and much desired fame,
Nor shall the Grecian folk forget my name
Who dearly bought these for thee; therefore come,
And with the sun behold thy wished-for home."

 So spoke she, and no less the wretched three
Beheld that light grow greater o'er the sea,   70
And therewithal the grey dawn coming fast,
And from them now well-nigh all hope had passed.
But fair Alcestis, grovelling on the ground,
And crying out, cast both her arms around
Medea's knees, and panting, and half-dead,
Poured forth wild words, nor knew the words she said.
While the two others, mad with their despair,
Ran wailing through the pillars here and there,
Nor knew indeed what thing had come on them,
For now, at last, fair Argo's plunging stem   80
Medea saw in the still gathering light,
And round about her the sea beaten white

With steady oars; then she looked down, and said:
"What! art thou praying for the newly dead,
For him who yesterday beheld the sun?
And dost thou think that I am such an one
That what the Gods have unmade I can make?
Lo! with the dead shall Pelias awake,
And see such things as dead men's eyes may see."

   Then as Alcestis, moaning wretchedly,   90
Fell back upon the pavement, thus she said :—
"Take comfort yet, and lift again thine head,
O foolish woman! Dost thou think that fate
Has yet been stopped by any love or hate,
Or fear of death, or man's far-shouted fame?
And still doubt not that I, who have to name
The wise Medea, in such ways as this
Have long been struggling for a life of bliss
I shall not gain; and thus do all men do,
And win such wages as have happed to you.   100

   "Rise up and gaze at what the fates have wrought,
And all the counsels they have brought to nought
On this same morn. Hearken the dash of oars
That never more ye thought would brush these shores;
Behold the man stand on the high-raised prow
That this dead man so surely dead did know.
See how he raises in his conquering hand
The guarded marvel of the Colchian land,
This dead king deemed hid death and unknown woe.
See how his folk ashore the grapnels throw;—   110
And see, and see! beneath the risen sun,
How fair a day for this land is begun.

And let king Pelias rise if now he can,
And stop the coming of the half-shod man."

E'en as she spoke, the keel had touched the sand,
And catching up her raiment in her hand,
She ran with speed, and gained the temple close,
Made fragrant with that many-flowered white rose,
And o'er its daisied grass sped toward the beach;
But when her feet the wrinkled sand did reach,   120
There, nigh the ship, alone did Jason stand,
Holding two spears within his ready hand;
And right and left he peered forth warily,
As though he thought some looked-for thing to see.
But when he saw her hurrying him to meet,
With wild wind-tangled hair, and naked feet,
And outstretched hands, and scanty raiment black,
But for one moment did he start aback,
As if some guardian spirit of the land
Had come upon him; but the next, his hand   130
Had caught her slim wrist, and he shouted out:
"Ashore, O heroes! and no more have doubt
That all is well done we have wished were done;
By this my love, by this the glorious one,
The saviour of my life, the Queen of Love,
To whom alone of all who are above,
Or on the earth, will I pour wine, or give
The life of anything that once did live."

Then all men shouting, leapt forth on the sand,
And stood about them, shield and spear in hand,   140

Rejoicing that their mighty task was done;
But as he saw the newly-risen sun
Shine on the town, upon their left that lay,
Then, smiling joyously, did Jason say:—
"O heroes, tell me, is the day not won?
Look how the sun's rays now are stealing on,
And soon will touch that temple's marble feet
Where stood the king our parting keel to greet,
But the great golden image of the God
Holds up, unlighted yet, his crystal rod,   150
And surely ere the noon shall gleam on it
Upon my father's throne his son shall sit,
Hedged round with spears of loyal men and true,
And all be done that we went forth to do."

  But, 'midst their shouting, spoke the queen again:—
"Jason, behold hereby this ancient fane—
Amidst its pillars let the heroes go
Until a marble stair they come unto,
And thereby mount into a pillared place,
At end whereof, upon an open space   160
Hung o'er the beach, that fire shall they see
That lighted you to finish gloriously
Your glorious journey; and beside the fire
There shall they find the slayer of thy sire,
Who, soothly, shall not flee from them to-day,
Nor curse the men who carry him away."

  Then forth Menœtius and Nauphius stood,
Lynceus the keen, and Apheus of the wood,
To do the thing that she would have them do,
While unto Argo did Medea go,   170

And for the last time scaled the sea-beat side;
There 'midst her silken curtains did she hide,
And taking forth the fairest weed she had,
In many a fragrant fold her body clad,
And on her feet bound golden sandals fair,
And set a golden garland on her hair.

  But when again she reached the shell-strewn sand
She saw the shielded heroes wondering stand
About the new-slain body of the king,
Not knowing yet whose hands had wrought the thing.
For, scared amid their woe and misery,   181
By clash of arms, the wretched sisters three
Were lurking yet within the undercroft,
Amongst the close-set pillars, thinking oft
That now the whole round world should be undone.

  But while they trembled, Æson's glorious son
Bade men make onward toward the market-place,
That there he might the wondering townsfolk face
For war or peace whichever it might be;
But first upon a great oar carefully   190
They bound a spar crosswise, and hung thereon
That guarded marvel that their arms had won,
And as a banner bore it well aloft.
And fair Medea, upon cushions soft,
Laid upon spear-staves did they bear along,
Hedged round with glittering spears and bucklers strong,
And unarmed, fearless, mighty Jason led
Their joyous march, next whom, the man just dead,

The strong-armed heroes upon spear-shafts bore,
With dark blue sea-cloaks deftly covered o'er.   200
  So, following up the poor unkingly bier
Of him who erst, for love of gain and fear,
Had sent them forth to what he deemed their end,
They through the palace courts **began to** wend,
Not stayed of any, since the guards indeed
Still slept, made heavy by the drowsy weed
Eradne in their wine erewhile did steep.
And other folk, just risen from their sleep,
Looked from the windows 'mazed; and like a dream
The queen, enthroned on golden cloths did seem,   210
And like a dream the high-raised, glittering Fleece,
And that new-slain long-hated pest of Greece.
And some indeed there were who saw full well
What wondrous tale there would be now to tell;
Who the glad setting forth did not forget,
Unto whose eyes more fair, more glorious yet
The heroes showed, than when the sunny bay
First felt their keel upon a happy day.
Then, crying out for joy, beheld the Fleece,
And that fair Helper who had saved for Greece   220
The godlike heroes, and amidst of these
Seemed not the least of heavenly Goddesses.
  Withal they reached at last the brazen gate
Of Æson's house, outside of which did wait
Men armed and shouting, for that dawn a man
None knew, a fisher on the water wan,
From house to house among the folk had gone,
Who said, that being in his own boat alone,

Casting his nets a little time before
The dawn, he heard the sound of many an **oar,**   230
And looking round, beheld a glittering prow
That he for Argo's armed beak did know;
And as he gazed, her many-coloured side
Dashed past him like a dream with flood of tide,
As for the far-off ancient fane she made;
And **that** thereon his anchor straight he weighed,
And made good haste the landing-place to gain.
"**For** certes," said he, "Pelias is slain,
And we are free once more." So saying, he passed
From house to house, and reached the gates at last; 240
Nor any saw him more on land or sea,
And, certes, none but clear-voiced Mercury
Spoke in that man by helpful Juno made,
No body, soothly, but a hollow shade.

  Now, therefore, when the gates were open wide,
Shouting, the folk drew back on either side,
All wild with joy; but when they did behold
The high-raised Fleece of curling ruddy gold,
And the glad heroes' mighty heads beneath,
And throned Medea, with her golden wreath,   250
And folded hands, and chiefest thing of all,
The godlike man who went beside the pall,
Whereon the body of their tyrant lay,
Then did their voices fail them on that day,
And many a man of weeping there was fain.

  At last did Jason set his foot again
Upon the steps of that same ivory throne
Where once he fronted Pelias all alone,

And bare of friends : but now he turned about,
And, 'mid the thunder of the people's shout,
Scarce heard his fellows' spears : and by his side
There stood his gold-adorned Colchian bride,
With glad tears glistening in her sweet grey eyes :
And dead, at end of foiled treacheries,
There lay his foe, the slayer of his kin.
  Then did he clasp the hand that lay within
His mighty and sword-hardened fingers brown,
And cried aloud above the shouting town :—

  "Tell me, O people of my father's land,
Before whose ivory well-wrought throne I stand,
And whose fair-towered house mine eyes behold,
Glittering with brazen pillars, rich with gold?

  "A while ago we sailed across the sea,
To meet our deaths, if so the thing must be,
And there had died, had not the kind Gods been,
Who sent to us this lovely Colchian queen
To be our helper : many a land we saw
That knoweth neither tongue of man, or law
Of God or man : oft most things did we lack
That most men have, as still we struggled back
Unto the soft wind and the Grecian sea,
Until this morn our keel triumphantly
Furrowed the green waves of the well-known bay.
There to yon palace did I take my way,
As one who thought his father's face to see ;
Yet landing on the green shore warily,

(Since times may change, and friendship come to
    nought)
To this dead man straightway my feet were brought,
Whose face I knew, the face of Pelias.

  " Then still more warily thence did we pass,   290
Till we met folk who told us everything,
Both of the slaying of the godlike king,
Æson, my father, and of other folk,
And how the whole land groaned beneath the yoke
Of this dead man, whom sure the Gods have slain
That all our labour might not be in vain,
Nor we, safe passing through the deadly land,
Lie slain in our own country at his hand.
So have the Gods wrought, therefore am I here,
No shield upon mine arm, no glittering spear   300
In my right hand, but by my unarmed side
This Colchian Queen, by many sorrows tried.
Therefore, no fear of you is in my heart,
And if ye will, henceforth will I depart,
Nor take mine own; or if it please this town
To slay me, let them lay my dead corpse down,
As on his tomb my father's image lies,
Like what he was before these miseries
Fell on his head. But in no wise will I
Take seat beneath this golden canopy,   310
Before ye tell me, people of this land,
Whose throne this is before the which I stand,
Whose towered house this is mine eyes behold,
Girt round with brazen pillars, bright with gold."

Then, ere he ceased, the people's shouts broke in
Upon his speech: "Most glorious of thy kin!
Be thou our king—be thou our king alone,
That we may think the age of iron gone,
And Saturn come with every peaceful thing:—
Jason for king! the Conqueror for king!"   320
  Therewith the heroes clashed their spears and shields,
And as within the many-flowered fresh fields
This way and that the slim-stalked flowers do bend,
When sweeping gusts the soft west wind doth send
Among their hosts, so moved the people then,
When ceased the shouting of the armed men.
For each unto the other 'gan to speak,
And o'er the tall men's heads some dame would seek
To raise her child to look upon the king.
And as with smiles and laughter many a thing   330
They chattered through the great square joyously,
Each careless what his neighbour's words might be,
It sounded like some February mead,
Where thick the lustred starlings creep and feed,
And each his own song sings unto his mate,
Chiding the fickle spring so cold and late.
  But through the happy clamour of the folk,
At Jason's bidding, the great trumpet broke,
And great Echion's voice rang clear and strong,
As he cried silence; then across the throng,   340
Did Jason cry: "O people, thanked be ye,
That in such wise ye give yourselves to me.
And now, O friends, what more is there to say

But this? Be glad, and feast this happy day,
Nor spend one coin of all your store for this;
Nor shall the altars of the high Gods miss
Their due thankoffering: and She chief of all,
Who caused that this same happy time should fall,
Shall have a tithe of all that 'longs to me.

"And ye, O loved companions o'er the sea,
Come to my golden house, and let us feast,   350
Nor let time weary us this night at least;
O! be so glad that this our happy day
For all times past, all times to come may pay."

He ceased, and one more shout the people sent
Up to the heavens, as he descending went
With the fair Colchian through the joyous folk,
From whose well-ordered lane at times there broke
Some little child, thrust forward well to see
The godlike leader of the Minyæ;   360
Or here and there forth would some young man lean
To gaze upon the beauty of the queen
A little nearer, as they passed him by.

Then, in such guise, they went triumphantly
To all the temples of that city fair,
And royal gifts they gave the great Gods there,
But chiefest from the Queen of Heaven's close
The clouds of incense in the air uprose,
And chiefly thither were the white lambs led,
And there the longest, Jason bowed the head   370
Well garlanded with lily flowers white.
But She, when all these things were done aright,

And Jason now had turned to go away,
In midmost of that cloudless sunny day
Bade Iris build her many-coloured bow,
That She her favour to the king might show.

Then still more did the royal man rejoice,
And o'er the people, lifting up his voice,
Cried: "See, Thessalians, who is on my side,
Nor fear ye now but plenty will abide 380
In your fair land, and all folk speak of it,
From places whence the wavering swallows flit,
That they may live with us the sweet half year,
To earth where dwells the sluggish white-felled bear."

So spake he, glad past words; and for the rest
Did Juno love him well since his great quest
Had brought home bitter death on Pelias,
And his love's words had brought the thing to pass,
That o'er that head was hanging, since the day
When from Sidero dead he turned away, 390
And as with Neleus down the steps he trod,
Thought things that fitted some undying God.

Thence to his father's tomb did Jason go,
And found the old man's body laid alow,
Within a lone, unkingly grave, and bade
That straightway should a royal tomb be made
To lay him in, anigh the murmuring sea,
Where, celebrating their great victory,
They might do honour to his head recrowned,
And 'mid their shouts all mourning might be drowned,
Nor would they gladden Pelias' lonely shade 401
By weeping o'er the slaughter he had made.

 Therefrom unto his own house Jason came,
He had not entered since the night his name
Rang 'twixt the marble walls triumphantly,
And all folk set their hearts upon the sea.
So, now again, when shadows 'gan to fall
Still longer from the west, within that hall
Once more the heroes sat above their wine,
Once more they hearkened music nigh divine,   410
Once more the maidens' flower-scattering hands
Seemed better prizes than well-peopled lands.

 Glorious and royal, now the deed was done,
Seemed in that hall the face of every one,
Who, 'twixt the thin plank and the bubbling sea,
Had pulled the smooth oar-handle past his knee.
Tuneful each voice seemed as the heroes told
The marvels that their eyes did erst behold,
Unto some merchant of the goodly town,
Or some rich man who on the thymy down   420
Fed store of sheep, and in whose lush green mead
The heavy-uddered cows were wont to feed.

 And she who all this world of joy had made,
And dared so many things all unafraid,
Now sat a Queen beside her crowned King.
And as his love increased with everything
She did or said, forgot her happy state
In Æa of old times, ere mighty fate
Brought Argo's side from out the clashers twain,
Betwixt the rainbow and the briny rain.   430
Yet in the midst of her felicity
She trembled lest another day should see

Another fate, and other deeds for these,
Who hailed her not the least of Goddesses.

  Yet surely now, if never more again,
Had she and all these folk forgotten pain,
And idle words to them were Death and Fear;
For in the gathering evening could they hear
The carols of the glad folk through the town,
The song of birds within the garden drown;   440
And when the golden sun had gone away,
Still little darker was the night than day
Without the windows of the goodly hall.

  But many an hour after the night did fall,
Though outside, silence fell on man and beast,
There still they sat, nor wearied of the feast;
Yea, ere they parted glimmering light had come
From the far mountains, nigh the Colchian's home,
And in the twilight birds began to wake.

  But the next morn, for slaughtered Æson's sake 450
The games began, with many a sacrifice,
And, these being all accomplished, gifts of price
The heroes took at Jason's open hands,
And, going homewards, unto many lands
They bore the story of their wandering.

  And now is Jason mighty lord and king,
And wedded to the fairest queen on earth,
And with no trouble now to break his mirth;
And, loved by all, lives happy, free from blame,
Nor less has won the promised meed of fame. 460
So, having everything he once desired

Within the wild, ere yet his heart was fired
By Juno's word, he lives an envied man,
Holding these things that scarce another can,
Ease, love, and fame, and youth that knows no dread
Of any horrors lurking far ahead
Across the sunny, flowered fields of life :—
—Youth seeing no end unto the **joyous strife.**

And thus in happy days, and rest, and peace,
Here ends the winning of the Golden Fleece.   470

BOOK XVII

*Jason at Corinth —The wedding of Glauce—The **death of Jason.***

SO ends the winning of the Golden Fleece,
   So ends the tale of that sweet rest and peace
That unto Jason and his love befell;
Another **story** now my tongue must tell,
And tremble in the telling. **Would that I**
Had but some portion of that mastery
That from the rose-hung lanes of woody Kent
Through these five hundred years such songs have sent
To us, who, meshed within this smoky net
Of unrejoicing labour, love them yet.   10
And thou, O Master !—Yea, my Master still,
Whatever feet have scaled Parnassus' hill,

Since like thy measures, clear, and sweet, and strong,
Thames' stream scarce fettered bore the bream along
Unto the bastioned bridge, his only chain.—
O Master, pardon me, if yet in vain
Thou art my Master, and I fail to bring
Before men's eyes the image of the thing
My heart is filled with: thou whose dreamy eyes
Beheld the flush to Cressid's cheeks arise, 20
When Troilus rode up the praising street,
As clearly as they saw thy townsmen meet
Those who in vineyards of Poictou withstood
The glittering horror of the steel-topped wood.

Ten years have passed, since in the market-place
The hero stood with flushed and conquering face,
And life before him like one happy day;
But many an hour thereof has passed away
In mingled trouble and felicity.
And now at Corinth, kissed by either sea, 30
He dwells, not governed now or governing,
Since there his kinsman Creon is a king.
And with him still abides the Colchian,
But little changed, since o'er the waters wan
She gazed upon the mountains that she knew,
Still lessening as the plunging Argo flew
Over the billows on the way to Greece.
But in these ten sweet years of rest and peace
Two fair man-children has she borne to him,
Who, joyous, fair of face, and strong of limb, 40
Full oft shall hear the glorious story told

Y

Of Argo and the well-won Fleece of Gold,
By some old mariner; and oft shall go
Where nigh the sea the wind-swept beech-trees grow,
And with a grey old woman tending them,
Shall make an Æa of some beech-tree's stem,
About whose roots there stands the water black.
Nor of the fleece shall they have any lack,
For in the bushes hangs much tangled wool
From wandering sheep who seek the shadow cool; 50
And for the dragon shall there be thereby
A many-coloured snake, with glazed dull eye,
Slain by the shepherd; so shall pass their days,
Whom folk look soon to gather wealth and praise.

And 'midst these living things has Argo found
A home here also; on the spot of ground
'Twixt Neptune's temple and the eastern sea,
She looks across the waves unceasingly;
And as their ridges draw on toward the land,
The wind tells stories of the kingly band. 60
There, with the fixed and unused oars spread out
She lies, amidst the ghosts of song and shout,
And merry laughter, that were wont to fill
Her well-built hollow, slowly dying still,
Like all that glorious company of kings
Who in her did such well-remembered things.
But as the day comes round when o'er the seas
She darted 'twixt the blue Symplegades,
And when again she rushed across the bar,
With King Æetes following her afar, 70

And when at length the heroes laid adown
The well-worn oars at old King Æson's town,—
When, year by year, these glorious days came round,
Bright with gay garments was that spot of ground,
And the grey rocks that o'ertop Cenchreæ,
Sent echoes of sweet singing o'er the sea.

For then the keel the maidens went about
Singing the songs of Orpheus, and the shout
Of rough-voiced sea-folk ended every song;
And then from stem to stern they hung along   80
Garlands of flowers, and all the oars did twine
With garlands too, and cups of royal wine
Cast o'er her stem; and at the stern a maid,
Clad like to Juno, on the tiller laid
Her slender fingers, while anigh the stem
Stood one with wings and many-coloured hem
About her raiment, like the messenger
Who bears the high Gods' dreadful words with her,
And through the sea of old that stem did lead.

Lo, in such wise they honoured that great deed, 90
But Jason did they reverence as a God;
And though his kinsman bore the ivory rod
And golden circlet, little could he do
Unless the great Thessalian willed it too.

Yet therefore Creon nowise bore him hate,
But reverencing the wise decrees of fate,
Still honoured him the more; and therewith thought,
Would that this man by some means might be brought
To wed my daughter, since, when I am dead,

By none but him the people shall be led. 100
And on this thought he brooded more and more,
And 'gan to hate the Colchian very sore,
And through the place, as lightly he might do,
He spread ill tales of false things and of true,
And unto Jason's self such words did say
As well he thought might turn his heart away
From faith and truth; and as such words will **come,**
When wise men speak them, to a ready home,
So here they did; though soothly for his part,
He knew it not, nor yet his restless heart. 110

   But on a day it fell that as they sat
In Creon's porch, and talked of this **or that,**
The king said unto Jason: "Brave thou art,
But hast thou never fear within thine heart
Of what the Gods may do for Pelias?"
"Nay," Jason said, "let what will come to pass,
His day is past, and mine is flourishing,
But doubtless is an end to everything,
And soon or late each man shall **have his day."**
   Then said the king: "Neither did thine hand
      slay 120
The man thyself, or bring his death about;
Each man shall bear his own sin without doubt.
Yet do I bid thee watch and take good heed
Of what the Colchian's treacheries may breed."
   Then quickly Jason turned his head around
And said: "What **is there** dwelling above ground
That loveth me as this one loveth me?
O Creon! I am honoured here as thee;

All do my will as if a God I were;
Scarce can the young men see me without fear,   130
The elders without tears of vain regret.
And, certes, had this worshipped head been set
Upon some spike of King Æetes' house,
But for her tender love and piteous,
For me she gave up country, kin, and name,
For me she risked tormenting and the flame,
The anger of the Gods and curse of man;
For me she came across the waters wan
Through many woes, and for my sake did go
Alone, unarmed, to my most cruel foe,   140
Whom there she slew by his own daughters' hands,
Making me king of all my father's lands:
Note all these things, and tell me then to flee
From that which threateneth her who loveth me."

  "Yea," said the king, "to make and to unmake
Is her delight; and certes for thy sake
She did all this thou sayest, yea, and yet more.
Seeing thee death-doomed on a foreign shore,
With hardy heart, but helpless; a king's son,
But with thy thread of life well-nigh outrun;   150
Therefore, I say, she did all this for thee,
And ever on the way to Thessaly
She taught thee all things needful, since ye were
As void of helpful knowledge as of fear.
All this she did, and so was more than queen
Of thee and thine: but thou—thine age is green,
Nor wilt thou always dwell in this fair town,
Nor through the wild wood hunt the quarry down—

Bethink thee—of the world thou mayst be king,
Holding the life and death of everything,
Nor will she love thee more, upon that day
When all her part will be but to obey;
Nor will it then be fitting unto thee
To have a rival in thy sovereignty
Laid in thy bed, and sitting at thy board."

Now somewhat Jason reddened at that word,
But said: "O Creon, let the thing be so!
She shall be high the while that I am low,
And as the Gods in heaven rule over me,
Since they are greater, in such wise shall she,
Who as they gave me life, has given me life,
And glorious end to seeming hopeless strife."

Then Creon said: "Yea, somewhat good it were
If thou couldst lead that life, and have no fear."
Laughing he spoke; but quickly changed his face,
And with knit brows he rose up from his place,
And with his hand on Jason's shoulder, said:—
"O careless man, too full of hardihead!
O thou ease-loving, little-thinking man,
Whate'er thou doest, dread the Colchian!
She will unmake thee yet, as she has made,
And in a bloody grave shalt thou be laid."

Then turning, to his palace went the king,
But Jason, left alone and pondering,
Felt in his heart a vague and gnawing fear,
Of unknown troubles slowly drawing near,
And, spite of words, the thing that Creon said
Touched in his heart that still increasing dread,

And he was moved by that grave elder's face,
For love was dying in the ten years' space. 190

  But Creon, sitting in his chamber, thought,
"Surely I deem my hero may be brought
To change his mate, for in his heart I see
He wearies of his great felicity,
Like fools, for whom fair heaven is not enough,
Who long to stumble over forests rough
With chance of death: yet no more will I say,
But let the bright sun bring about the day."
  Now such an one for daughter Creon had
As maketh wise men fools, and young men mad, 200
Who yet in Corinth at this time was not,
But dwelt afar upon a woody spot
Anigh Cleonæ; whither oft before
Had Jason gone for chasing of the boar
With Creon and his folk; and on a day
With the old king again he took his way
To that dark wood, whereto, about the noon,
They came, well harbingered by thrushes' tune.
And there straight fell to hunting of the boar;
But, either through default of woodland lore, 210
Or bidden by the king, huntsmen and all
The king's stout servants from the chase did fall,
And Jason with him soon was left alone.
And both saw that the day should soon be done,
For 'midst the thick trees was it nigh twilight,
Then Jason said: "Surely our bed to-night
Will be beneath these creaking boughs and black."

"Nay," said the king, "surely we shall not lack
Soft golden beds such as old men desire,
Nor on the hearth the crackling of the fire,   220
For hereby is a little house of mine
Where dwells my daughter Glauce, near the shrine
Of round-armed Juno; there, with two or three,
Matrons or maids, she guardeth reverently
The altar of the Goddess."

       With that word
Forward his jaded horse old Creon spurred,
And Jason followed him; and when the sun
His burning course that day had well-nigh done,
The king and Jason came anigh the place
Where stood the house upon a swarded space   230
Amidst thick trees, that hedged it like a wall,
Whose shadows now o'er half the place did fall,
While, 'twixt their stems the low sun showed like fire,
And in the east the still white moon rose higher.

 But midmost there a glittering roof of gold
Slim shafts of pale blue marble did uphold,
And under it, made by the art divine
Of some dead man, before a well-wrought shrine,
The Goddess stood, carved out of purest gold,
That her fair altar thence she might behold,   240
And round that temple was a little close
Shut by a gilded trellis of red rose
From off the forest green-sward; and from thence
Carried by winds about the beech wood dense,
The scent of lilies rose up in the air,
And store of pea-fowl was there roosting there,

Or moving lazily across the grass.
 But from the temple did the two kings pass
Unto a marble house that was thereby,
Not great indeed, but builded cunningly,   250
And set about with carven images,
Built in a close of slim young apple-trees;
A marble fountain was there nigh **the door,**
And there the restless water trickled o'er
A smooth-hewn basin coloured like a shell,
And from the wet pink lip thereof it fell
By many a thin streak into a square pool,
From whence it ran again, the grass to cool,
In a small stream o'er sand, and earth, and flint,
Edged all about with fragrant blue-flowered mint, 260
Or **hidden** by the flat-leaved quivering sedge.
But from the pool's smooth-wrought and outmost edge
There went a marble step the fount to meet,
Well worn **by many a** water-drawer's feet.
 And thereon now they saw a damsel stand,
Holding the basin's lip with either hand,
While at her feet a brazen ewer stood;
But when she heard them coming from the wood,
She turned about, and, seeing men near by,
Caught up the brazen vessel hastily,   270
And swiftly ran towards the marble house;
But Creon, in his voice imperious,
Cried: "Hither, Glauce, am I grown so old,
That without fear thou canst no more behold
Thy father, Creon? Nay, come near, O child,
And bid us welcome to the forest wild."

Then straight she stopped, and setting down the urn,
Unto her father and his guest did turn,
While o'er his saddle-bow old Creon bent,
Rejoicing in her beauty as she went; 280
And for one moment every scheme forgat,
For raising this thing and abasing that;
As well he might, for as in poor array
She drew towards them at that end of day,
With raiment fluttering in the evening breeze,
She **seemed** like Her, the crown of Goddesses,
Who, o'er the dark sea, at the sunset came
To be in heaven a joy, on earth a flame.
Blushing, she came to Creon's saddle-bow,
And kissed him, who said, smiling: "Fearest thou 290
Thy father, grown the oldest of old men?
How wilt thou look upon this stranger then,
Who **is** no God, though such he seems to be,
But Jason, leader of the Minyæ?"
Somewhat she started at the glorious name,
And o'er her face deeper the red flush came,
As she, with upraised face and shamefast eyes,
Said: "Welcome, winner of the guarded prize!
Good hap it is indeed that thou art come
Unto my little-peopled woodland home. 300
Come then, my lords, to what awaits you here;
Not Mæonean wine or dainty cheer
Your lips shall taste, but of fair simple flowers,
Plucked at the edges of the beechen bowers,
Your drink shall savour, and your meat shall be
Red-coated squirrels from the beechen tree."

Then fain to hide her eyes and blushing face,
She turned from them, and at a gentle pace
Unto the pillared porch she led the twain.
There they, alighting, the dark house did gain,   310
And there they ate and drank, making such cheer
As fasting men will do; and still anear
Was Glauce to them, telling every maid
How such and such a thing should be arrayed;
And ever the Thessalian's eager eyes
Did follow her, and to his heart did rise
Vague feelings of a new-found happiness.

But now as the round moon was growing less,
And waxing brighter, and of fitting food
The kings had eaten as they thought it good,   320
Then Creon said: "O daughter, rise and take
This full cup to the hero for my sake,
And bid him drink thereof, and tell thee all
That unto him at Æa did befall,
And what fate did as still he journeyed home."

Then unto Jason did the maiden come,
Bearing the cup, and when he saw her thus,
The lapse of time seemed strange and piteous;
For he bethought him of that other tide,
When certain-seeming death he did abide   330
In King Æetes' hall; and when she drew
Anigh unto him, back the past years flew,
And he became that man entrapped again,
And newly felt, as then, that joyous pain,
And in his hand as then the cup he took,
With the warm fingers, and as then her look

Sent fire throughout his veins; yea, and as then
He had no heed of any Gods or men.

Therewith her musical sweet voice he heard,
Speaking again the king her father's word:—   340
"O Jason, if it please thee, tell me all
That unto thee at Æa did befall,
And what thou sawedst as thou journeydst home,
And how it happed thee to thy land to come."

But ever as she spake she gazed at him,
And with new thoughts her simple eyes did swim,
Thinking her happy that this man had wed;
And therewithal she turned from pale to red,
And red to pale. Then said he: "Thou shalt know,
O fair king's daughter, all I have to show."   350
And so the story of the Fleece began,
And how fair Argo crossed the water wan;
While from his glittering eyes, deep sunk with eld,
The **wily** king those beauteous folk beheld,
As still from Jason's lips poured forth the tale,
And she sat listening, whiles with cheeks grown pale
And parted lips, and whiles with downcast eyes
And blushing for the thoughts that would arise
Uncalled for; and thus passed that eve away
Till time of rest came. Then until the day,   360
In his fair silken bed did Jason dream
Of Argo struggling with the unknown stream,
And all the wonders of their long-past quest,
And well-known faces long time laid to rest.

But when the night was past, and the great sun

Another day for all things had begun,
The kings, arising, unto Corinth rode.
But ere they left the woodland fair abode,
Unto the Goddess did they sacrifice,
And on her altar in such woodland wise 370
As huntsmen use, their offerings did they lay.
With them was Glauce on that dawn of day,
Upon the left hand of the ancient king,
Unto the reverend Goddess ministring.
But when they turned once more unto the town,
The half-quenched censer did she lay adown,
And holding still the fresh-plucked flower-wreath,
Bade them farewell.

    Then by thick wood and heath
They rode, and on their journey Jason said
Few words and wandering; for still that maid 380
Did he behold before his waking eyes,
And with the oft-recurring memories
Of days and things a long time passed away
Her image mixed, and words that she did say.
 But when upon the threshold of his house
He met Medea, who, with amorous
And humble words, spoke to him greetings kind,
He felt as he whose eyes the fire doth blind,
That presently about his limbs shall twine,
And in her face and calm grey eyes divine 390
He read his own destruction; none the less
In his false heart fair Glauce's loveliness
Seemed that which he had loved his whole life long,
And little did he feel his old love's wrong.

Alas for truth! each day, yea, hour by hour,
He longed once more to see the beechen bower,
And her who dwelt thereby. Alas, alas!
Oft from his lips the hated words would pass:—

"O wavering traitor, still unsatisfied!
O false betrayer of the love so tried! 400
Fool! to cast off the beauty that thou knowst,
Clear-seeing wisdom, better than a host
Against thy foes, and truth and constancy
Thou wilt not know again whate'er shall be!"

So oft he spoke words that were words indeed,
And had no sting, nor would his changed heart heed
The very bitterest of them all, as he
Thought of his woodland fair divinity,
And of her upturned face, so wondering
At this or that oft-told unheeded thing. 410
Yet whiles, indeed, old memories had some power
Over his heart, in such an awful hour
As that, when darksome night is well-nigh done,
And earth is waiting silent for the sun;
Then would he turn about his mate to see,
From lips half open, breathing peacefully,
And open, listless, the fair fingers laid,
That unto him had brought such mighty aid.
Then, groaning, from her would he turn away,
And wish he might not see another day, 420
For certainly his wretched soul he knew,
And of the cruel God his heart that drew.
But when the bright day had come round again,
With noise of men, came foolish thoughts and vain,

And, feeding fond desire, would he burn
Unto Cleonæ his swift steps to turn.

  Nor to these matters was the Colchian blind,
And though as yet his speech to her was kind,
Good heed she took of all his moody ways,
And how he loved her not as in past days;   430
And how he shrunk from her, yet knew it not,
She noted, and the stammering words and hot,
Wherewith, as she grew kinder, still he strove
To hide from her the changing of his love.

  Long time she tried to shut her eyes to this,
Striving to save that fair abode of bliss;
But so it might not be; and day by day
She saw the happy time fade fast away;
And as she fell from out that happiness,
Again she grew to be the sorceress,   440
Worker of fearful things, as once she was,
When what my tale has told she brought to pass.

  So, on a weary, hopeless day, she said:—
"Ah! poor Medea, art thou then betrayed
By that thou trustedst? Art thou brought to nought
By that which erst, with wonders strangely wrought,
Thou madest live through happy days and long?
Lo, now shall be avenged those poor maids' wrong,
Who, in that temple o'er the murmuring sea,
Ran maddening here and there; and now shall be   450
That word accomplished that I uttered then,
Nor yet believed—that to all earthly men,
In spite of right and wrong, and love and hate,

One day shall come the turn of luckless fate.
Alas! then I believed it not, when I
Saw Argo's painted prow triumphantly
Cleave the grey seas, and knew that I it was,
My very self, who brought those things to pass,
And lit those eyes unseen. How could I know
Unto what cruel folly men will grow?" 460

 She wept therewith—and once more on that night
She stole abroad about the mirk midnight,
Once more upon a wood's edge, from her feet
She stripped her shoes and bared her shoulder sweet.
Once more that night over the lingering fire
She hung with sick heart famished of desire.
Once more she turned back when her work was done;
Once more she fled the coming of the sun;
Once more she reached her dusky, glimmering room;
Once more she lighted up the dying gloom; 470
Once more she lay adown, and in sad sleep
Her weary body and sick heart did steep.
Alas! no more did tender Love come down
And smooth her troubled face of fear and frown;
No more with hope half-opened lips did smile.

 Not long she slept, but in a little while,
Sighing, she rose, when now the sun was high,
And, going to her wallet wearily,
Took forth a phial thence, which she unstopped
And a small driblet therefrom slowly dropped 480
Upon a shred of linen, which straightway
In the sun's gleaming pathway did she lay;
But when across it the first sunbeam came,

Therefrom there burst a colourless bright flame,
Which still burnt on when every shred was gone
Of that which seemed to feed the flame alone;
Nor burnt it less for water, that she threw
Across it and across. Thereon she drew
A linen tunic from a brazen chest,
Wherein lay hid the fairest and the best   490
Of all her raiment; this she held, and said:—
"**Jason,** thy love is fair by likelihead,
Pity it were to hide her over-much,
And when this garment her fair limbs shall touch,
So will it hide them as the water green
Hid Citheræa, when she first was seen."

  Soothly she spoke, because the web was fair
And thin, and delicate beyond compare,
And had been woven in no common loom,
For she herself within her fair-hung room   500
Had set the warp and watched the fine weft glide
Up from the roller, while from side to side,
Scarce seen, the shuttle flew from fingers thin
Of a dark Indian maid, whom gold did win
From some Phœnician, that loved nought but gold.

  But sighing now the raiment to behold,
She poured into a well-wrought bowl of brass
The thing that in the phial hidden was,
And therein, fold by fold, the linen laid,
Then for a little while her hands she stayed,   510
Till it had drunk the moisture thoroughly;
Whereon she took it forth and laid it by,
Far from the sunlight, on her royal bed,

z

Saying: "O thou who hast the hardihead,
Whoe'er thou art, to take from me mine own,
It had been better for thee that of stone
Thy limbs were wrought, nor made to suffer pain,
If this morn's deed has not been quite in vain."

 So saying, did she mutter moodily,
Watching the spread-out linen slowly dry;   520
At last she took it and within a bright
Fair silver casket hid it from the sight.
 This done, about the noble house she went,
And bitterly full oft her eyes she bent
On man and maid, and things grown old and dear,
'Midst hope of rest, no longer hoped for there.

 And, meantime, Jason, by the wily king
Still watched, had little joy in anything,
For while with fierce desire his heart still burned,
Yet now again for rest and peace he yearned,   530
Nor praise of other men yet counted nought,
And somewhat of the coming days he thought,
And helpless eld with many memories
Beset, and pictures of reproachful eyes;
Yet thinking of the chain of days and nights
Stretched out all barren of once-hoped delights,
A sorry thing life seemed to him to be,
And one path only from that misery
Seemed open to him—where the fair girl stood,
Within the shadow of the beechen wood.   540
 But while he wavered thus 'twixt love and fear,
And something of the old time grown too dear

To cast off lightly, Creon noted all,
And surely now had hope that should befall
He long had wished for, and in such wise wrought
That all unto an ending soon be brought.

 Therefore it happed that on a July morn,
Jason at last, by many troubles torn,
Mounted his horse, and toward Cleonæ turned.
But as with pale face, and a heart that burned   550
To end all things in sweet love at the last,
He by the palace of King Creon passed;
There Creon stood before the door, and said:—
" Where goest thou, O Jason? By my head,
Wilt thou not sit at our high feast to-day?
What do'st thou then, upon the stony way
That leads to Argolis?"

       " O King," said he,
" I am not meet for your solemnity,
Because the Gods to-day have made me sad;
Nor knew I yet what feast here should be had,   560
But thought to-day to see my arrows fly
Within the green glades of the woods hereby."

 " Nay," said the king; " full surely many a day
Of summer will there be to play this play,
But on this day to Citheræa's house
Folk go, both maids and young men amorous;
Yea, elders like to me will hold this feast,
Who in their foolish hearts can mourn at least
For days and things that never come again.
Yet, for myself, I shall not feast in vain,   570
For on this day my daughter comes to me,

That nigh Cleonæ erewhile thou didst see,
And she too goes with flower-bearing hands
To kiss the foot that on the tortoise stands."

So saying, did his ancient wily eyes
Behold the blood to Jason's brow arise,
And inwardly he laughed; but Jason said:—
"Yea, then, O King, to chase my drearihead,
This were a fair sight for mine eyes to see,
And since thou willest, I will go with thee."   580

Then 'lighting from his horse, beside the king
He stood, and talked of this or that light thing,
And saw meanwhile full many a broad-wheeled wain,
Filled with fair flowers plucked from the unshorn plain,
Go toward the temple of the Cyprian queen,
And youths and maidens, wreathed about with green.
Pass singing carols through the listening street.

At last the king said: "Come, and let us meet
This joyous band within the very fane."
So forth they went, and soon the place did gain,   590
Where the fair temple of the Goddess rose
From 'midst a grassy apple-planted close.
But each side of the door a maid there stood,
Clad in thin silken raiment red as blood,
Who had by her a gilded basket light,
Filled full of flowers woven for delight,
Wherefrom unto the passing kings they gave
Wreaths bound with gold, that somewhat they migh
    have
To offer to the dread divinity,
Whose image, wrought of silver cunningly,   600

Stood 'neath a canopy of gleaming gold
Midmost the place, where damsels fair did hold
Baskets of flowers, or swung rich censers high;
Then to the precious shrine they drew anigh
And forth stood Creon, and the fragrant wreath
Laid on the altar, and beneath his breath
Some prayer he muttered; and next Jason laid
His gift by Creon's, but of much afraid,
And hoping much, he made not any prayer
Unto the Goddess; then amid the fair   610
Slim pillars did he stand beside the king,
Confused as in a dream, and wondering
How all would end.   But as they waited thus,
Within that fragrant place and amorous,
Languid grew Jason with the roses' scent
And with the incense-cloud that ever went
Unto the half-seen golden roof above,
Amongst whose glimmering the grey-winged dove
Hung crooning o'er his wrongs; moreover there
The temple-damsels passed them, shy and fair,   620
With white limbs shining through their thin attire,
And amorous eyes, the hearts of men to fire,
Beneath their heavy crowns of roses red;
And veiled sweet voices through the place did shed
Strange fitful music, telling more than words,
Confused by twitter of the restless birds
Within the temple-eaves, and by the doves,
Who 'mid the pillars murmured of their loves.

   But when the pleasure of that temple fair
Had sunk into his soul, upon the air   620

Was borne the sound of flutes from folk outside,
And soon the greatest doors were opened wide,
And all the rout of worshippers poured in,
Clad in fair raiment, summer-like and thin,
And holding wreaths, part twined of fragrant flowers—
The children of the soft, sweet April showers—
And part of blossoms wrought in ruddy gold.
Now back the incense from the altar rolled
At their incoming, driven by the wind,
And round the pillars of the place it twined,   640
Enwrapping Jason, so that faint and dim
The fair show of the maidens was to him,
As each upon the altar laid adown
The blossoms mingled with the golden crown,
And prayed her prayer, then passed behind the shrine.
  At last from 'midst that cloud did Venus shine
Before the eyes of the Thessalian,
Who, with fixed eyes, and lips grown thin and wan,
Stared at the image, little though he saw,
But at her feet a sweet face, grave with awe,   650
Just bending over toward the silver feet,
Which Glauce with a timid kiss did greet,
And this being done, drew backward murmuring
Her prayer to Venus: "Goddess, a small thing
Before this altar do I ask of thee,
That I my hero and my love may see,
That I"—but therewithal her face she raised,
And met his hungry eyes that on her gazed,
And stopped all trembling, letting fall adown
The hand that held the gold-enwoven crown.   660

Yet little anger Venus had therefore,
But rather smiled to see her learn her lore
Within her house upon her festal day.
  But now upon the altar did she lay
Her offering, and yet she finished not
Her prayer begun, though in her poor heart, hot
With thoughts of love, full many a prayer she prayed.
  And now was all that pageant well arrayed
To pass about the temple, and her place
Did Glauce take with flushed and eager face;   670
But on her finger did she loose a ring,
Which that same day the wise Corinthian king
Had given her, therewith she went along,
Murmuring faint words amidst her fellows' song.
  Then past the kings the long procession swept,
And somewhat from the pillars Jason stepped,
Seeking a sign from that desired face;
And when the damsels at a gentle pace
Went by him, and for fear of him and awe
Shrunk back, and with their slender hands did draw
Closer about them the thin fragrant weed;   681
Still nought of all their beauty did he heed,
But as the amorous army passed him by
Into sweet Glauce's eyes appealingly
He gazed, who, trembling like some snow-trapped dove,
From her soft eyes sent forth one look of love,
Then dropped the lids, as, blind with love and shame,
Unto the place where stood the kings she came.
And there her hand that down beside her hung
She raised a little, and her faltering tongue   690

Just framed the words: "O love, for thee, for thee!"
And with that word she trembled piteously,
In terror at the sound of her own voice.
And much did wily Creon then rejoice,
Looking askance, and feigning to see nought,
When he beheld those hands together brought.

   But Jason, when those fingers touched his own,
Forgat all joys that he had ever known;
And when her hand left his hand with the ring,
Still in the palm, like some lost, stricken thing   700
He stood and stared, as from his eyes she passed.
And from that hour all fear away was cast,
All memory of the past time, all regret
For days that did those changed days beget,
And therewithal adown the wind he flung
The love whereon his yearning heart once hung.

   Ah! let me turn the page, nor chronicle
In many words the death of faith, or tell
Of meetings by the newly-risen moon,
Of passionate silence 'midst the brown birds' tune, 710
Of wild tears wept within the noontide shade,
Of wild vows spoken, that of old were made,
For other ears, when, amidst other flowers,
He wandered through the love-begetting hours.
Suffice it, that unhappy was each day
Which without speech from Glauce passed away,
And troublous dreams would visit him at night,
When day had passed all barren of her sight.
And at the last, that Creon, the old king,

Being prayed with gifts, and joyful of the thing, 720
Had given a day when these twain should be wed.

  Meanwhile, the once-loved sharer of his bed
Knew all at last, and fierce tormenting fire
Consumed her as the dreadful day drew nigher,
And much from other lips than his she heard,
Till, on a day, this dreadful, blighting word,
Her eyes beheld within a fair scroll writ,
And 'twixt her closed teeth still she muttered it :—

  "Depart in peace! and take great heaps of gold,
For nevermore thy body will I fold 730
Within these arms. Let Gods wed Goddesses
And sea-folk wed the women of the seas,
And men wed women ; but thee, who can wed
And dwell with thee without consuming dread,
O wise kin of the dreadful sorceress!
And yet, perchance thy beauty still may bless
Some man to whom the world seems small and poor,
And who already stands beside his door,
Armed for the conquest of all earthly things.

  "Lo, such an one, the vanquisher of kings, 740
And equal to the Gods should be thy mate.
But me, who for a peaceful end but wait,
Desiring nought but love—canst thou love me?
Or can I give my whole heart up to thee?

  "I hear thee talk of old days thou didst know—
Are they not gone?—wilt thou not let them go,
Nor to their shadows still cling desperately,
Longing for things that never more can be?

"What! wilt thou blame me still that the times
    change?
Once through the oak-wood happy did I range,   750
And thought no ill; but then came over me
Madness, I know not why, and o'er the sea
I needs must go in strife to win me fame,
And certes won it, and my envied name
Was borne with shouts about the towns of Greece.

"All that has vanished now, and my old peace,
Through lapse of changing years, has come to me.
Once more I seem the woodland paths to see,
Tunes of old songs are ringing in mine ears,
Heard long ago in that place free from fears,   760
Where no one wept above his fellow dead,
And looked at death himself with little dread.
The times are changed, with them is changed my heart,
Nor in my life canst thou have any part,
Nor can I live in joy and peace with thee,
Nor yet, for all thy words, canst thou love me.

"Yet, is the world so narrow for us twain
That all our life henceforth must be but vain?
Nay, for departing shalt thou be a queen
Of some great world, fairer than I have seen,   770
And wheresoe'er thou goest shalt thou fare
As one for whom the Gods have utmost care."

Yea, she knew all, yet when these words she read,
She felt as though upon her bowed-down head
Had fallen a misery not known before,
And all seemed light that erst her crushed heart bore,

For she was wrapped in uttermost despair,
And motionless within the chamber fair
She stood, as one struck dead and past all thought.
 But as she stood, a sound to her was brought   780
Of children's voices, and she 'gan to wail
With tearless eyes, and, from writhed lips and pale,
Faint words of woe she muttered, meaningless,
But such as such lips utter none the less.
Then all at once thoughts of some dreadful thing
Back to her mind some memory seemed to bring,
As she beheld the casket gleaming fair,
Wherein was laid that she was wont to wear,
That in the philtre lay that other morn,
And therewithal unto her heart was borne   790
The image of two lovers, side by side.
 Then with a groan the fingers that did hide
Her tortured face slowly she drew away,
And going up to where her tablets lay,
Fit for the white hands of the Goddesses,
Therein she wrote such piteous words as these.

 " Would God that Argo's brazen-banded mast
'Twixt the blue clashing rocks had never passed
Unto the Colchian land! Or would that I
Had had such happy fortune as to die   800
Then, when I saw thee standing by the Fleece,
Safe on the long-desired shore of Greece!
Alas, O Jason! for thy cruel praise!
Alas, for all the kindness of past days!
That to thy heart seems but a story told

Which happed to other folk in times of old.
But unto me, indeed, its memory
Was bliss in happy hours, and now shall be
Such misery as never tongue can tell.

"Jason, I heed thy cruel message well,   810
Nor will I stay to vex thee, nor will stay
Until thy slaves thrust me thy love away.
Be happy! think that I have never been—
Forget these eyes, that none the less have seen
Thy hands take life at my hands, and thy heart
O'erflow in tears, when needs was we should part
But for a little; though, upon the day
When I for evermore must go away,
I think, indeed, thou wilt not weep for this;
Yea, if thou weepest then, some honied kiss   820
From other lips shall make thy grey eyes wet,
Betwixt the words that bid thee to forget
Thou ever hast loved aught but her alone.

"Yet of all times mayst thou remember one,
The second time that ever thou and I
Had met alone together—mournfully
The soft wind murmured on that happy night,
The round moon, growing low, was large and bright,
As on my father's marble house it gleamed,
While from the fane a baneful light outstreamed,   830
Lighting the horror of that prodigy,
The only fence betwixt whose wrath and thee
Was this poor body. Ah! thou knowest then
How thou beheldst the shadows of thy men
Steal silently towards Argo's painted head.

Thou knowest yet the whispered words I said
Upon that night— thou never canst forget
That happy night of all nights.   Ah! and yet
Why make I these long words, that thou the more
Mayst hate me, who already hat'st me sore,   840
Since 'midst thy pleasure I am grown a pain.

  " Be happy! for thou shalt not hear again
My voice, and with one word this scroll is done—
Jason, I love thee, yea, love thee alone—
God help me, therefore!—and would God that I
Such as thou sayst I am, were verily,
Then what a sea of troubles shouldst thou feel
Rise up against thy life, how shouldst thou steel
Thy heart to bear all, failing at the last,
Then wouldst thou raise thine head, o'erwhelmed,
         downcast,   850
And round about once more shouldst look for me,
Who led thee o'er strange land and unknown sea.

  "And not in vain, O dearest! not in vain!
Would I not come and weep at all thy pain,
That I myself had wrought? would I not raise
Thy burdened head with hopes of happy days?
Would I not draw thee forth from all thy woe?
And fearless by thy side would I not go,
As once I went, through many unknown lands
When I had saved thee from my father's hands?   860

  " All would I do, that I have done erewhile,
To have thy love once more, and feel thy smile,
As freed from snow about the first spring days
The meadows feel the young sun's fickle rays.

"But I am weak, and past all, nor will I
Pray any more for kindly memory;
Yet shalt thou have one last gift more from me,
To give thy new love, since men say that she
Is fairer than all things man can behold.

"Within this casket lies in many a fold
Raiment that my forgotten limbs did press,
When thou wert wont to praise their loveliness.
Fear not to take it from the sorceress' hands,
Though certainly with balms from many lands
Is it made fragrant, wondrous with a charm
To guard the wearer's body from all harm.

"Upon the morn that she shall make thee glad,
With this fair tunic let her limbs be clad,
But see that no sun falls upon its folds
Until her hand the king, her father, holds,
To greet thine eyes: then, when in godlike light
She shines, with all her beauty grown so bright,
That eyes of men can scarcely gaze thereon—
Then, when thy new desire at last is won—
Then, wilt thou not a little think of me,
Who saved thy life for this felicity?"

She ceased, and moaning to herself she said :—
"Ah! when will all be ended? If the dead
Have unto them some little memory left
Of things that while they lived Fate from them reft,
Ere life itself was reft from them at last,
Yet would to God these days at least were past,
And all be done that here must needs be done!

"Ah! shall I, living underneath the sun,
I wonder, wish for anything again,
Or ever know what pleasure means, and pain?—
—And for these deeds I do; and thou the first,
O woman, whose young beauty has so cursed
My hapless life, at least I save thee this—
The slow descent to misery from bliss,   900
With bitter torment growing day by day,
And faint hope lessening till it fades away
Into dull waiting for the certain blow.
But thou, who nought of coming fate dost know,
One overwhelming fear, one agony,
And in a little minute shalt thou be
Where thou wouldst be in threescore years at most,
And surely but a poor gift thou hast lost.
The new-made slave, the toiler on the sea,
The once rich fallen into poverty,   910
In one hour knows more grief than thou canst know;
And many an one there is who fain would go
And try their fortune in the unknown life
If they could win some ending to this strife,
Unlooked-for, sudden, as thine end shall be.
Kindly I deal with thee, mine enemy;
Since swift forgetfulness to thee I send.
But thou shalt die—his eyes shall see thine end—
Ah! if thy death alone could end it all!

"But ye—shall I behold you when leaves fall,   920
In some sad evening of the autumn-tide?
Or shall I have you sitting by my side

Amidst the feast, so that folk stare and say,
'Sure the grey wolf has seen the queen to-day.
What! when I kneel in temples of the Gods,
Must I bethink me of the upturned sods,
And hear a voice say: 'Mother, wilt thou come
And see us resting in our new-made home,
Since thou wert used to make us lie full soft,
Smoothing our pillows many a time and oft?   930
O mother, now no dainty food we need,
Whereof thou once wert wont to have such heed.
O mother, now we need no gown of gold,
Nor in the winter time do we grow cold;
Thy hands would bathe us when we were thine own,
Now doth the rain wash every shining bone.
No pedagogue we need, for surely heaven
Lies spread above us, with the planets seven,
To teach us all its lore.'
       Ah! day by day
Would I have hearkened all the folk would say.   940
Ah! in the sweet beginning of your days
Would I have garnered every word of praise.
'What fearless backers of the untamed steed,'
'What matchless spears, what loyal friends at need,'
'What noble hearts, how bountiful and free,'
'How like their father on the troublous sea!'
 "O sons, with what sweet counsels and what tears
Would I have hearkened to the hopes and fears
Of your first loves: what rapture had it been
Your dear returning footsteps to have seen   950
Amidst the happy warriors of the land;

But now—but now—this is a little hand
Too often kissed since love did first begin
To win such curses as it yet shall win,
When after all bad deeds there comes a worse;
Praise to the Gods! ye know not how to curse.

"But when in some dim land we meet again
Will ye remember all the loss and pain?
Will ye the form of children keep for aye
With thoughts of men? and 'Mother,' will ye say, 960
'Why didst thou slay us ere we came to know
That men die? hadst thou waited until now,
An easy thing it had been then to die,
For in the thought of immortality
Do children play about the flowery meads,
And win their heaven with a crown of weeds.'

"O children! that I would have died to save,
How fair a life of pleasure might ye have,
But for your mother:—nay, for thee, for thee,
For thee who might'st have lived so happily; 970
For thee, O traitor! who didst bring them here
Into this cruel world, this lovely bier
Of youth and love, and joy and happiness,
That unforeseeing happy fools still bless."

Amid these wild words had the evening come
Of the last day in that once happy home;
So, rising, did she take the casket fair,
And gave it to a faithful slave to bear,
With all those wailing words that she had writ
To Jason, her love once; then did she sit 980
Within that chamber, with her heavy head

Laid on her arms, and scarce more than the dead
She moved, for many hours, until at last
A stupor over her some kind God cast,
So that she slept, and had forgetfulness
A little while from fury and distress.

   But Jason, when he read that bitter word
Was sore ashamed, and in his ears he heard
Words that men durst not speak before his face;
Therewith, for very shame, that silver case   990
And what it held he sent unto his bride,
And therewithal this word: "Whatso betide,
Let not the sun shine on it till the hour
When thou hast left for aye thy maiden bower,
And with the king thou standest in the hall,
Then unto thee shall all good things befall."

   So to his rest he went, but, sooth to say,
He slept but little till the dawn of day,
So troubled was his mind with many a thing,
And in his ears long-spoken words did ring.   1000
"Good speed, O traitor! who shall think to wed
Soft limbs and white, and find thy royal bed
Dripping with blood and burning up with fire."
   So there, 'twixt fear and shame and strong desire,
Sleepless he lay until the day began—
The conqueror, the king, the envied man.

   But on the chamber where sweet Glauce lay,
Fair broke the dawning of that dreadful day,
And fairer from her bed did she arise,

And looking down with shamefast timid eyes, 1010
Beheld the bosom that no man had seen,
And round limbs worthy of the Sea-born Queen.
With that she murmured words of joy and love,
No louder than the grey, pink-footed dove,
When at the dawn he first begins his tale,
Not knowing if he means a song or wail.

   Then soon her maidens came, and every rite
That was the due of that slim body white,
They wrought with careful hands; and last they took
Medea's gift, and all the folds outshook, 1020
And in a cool room looking toward the north,
They clad the queen therewith, nor brought her forth
Till over all a gold cloak they had laid.
Then to King Creon did they bring the maid,
Rejoicing in the greatness of her love,
Which well she thought no lapse of time could move,
And on the daïs of the royal hall
They waited till the hour should befall
When Jason and his friends would bear her thence
With gentle rape and tender violence, 1030
As then the manner was, and the old king
Sat there beside her, glad at every thing.

   Meanwhile the people thronged in every way,
Clad in gay weed, rejoicing for that day,
Since that their lords had bidden them rejoice,
And in the streets was many a jocund voice,
That carolled to the honour of the twain
Who on that day such blissful life should gain.

   But Jason set out from his pillared house,

Clad in rich raiment, fair and amorous, 1040
Forgetful of the troubles of the night,
Nor thinking more of that impending blight,
Nor those ill words the harpies spoke of old,
As with his fellows, glittering with gold,
Towards Creon's palace did he take his way,
To meet the bride that he should wed that day

But in the hall the pillars one by one
Had barred the pathway of the travelling sun,
As toward the west he turned, and now at last
Upon the daïs were his hot rays cast, 1050
As they within heard the glad minstrelsy
Of Jason to his loved one drawing nigh.

Then Creon took fair Glauce by the hand,
And round about her did her damsels stand,
Making a ring 'gainst that sweet violence,
That soon should bear their lovely mistress thence.
While Glauce, trembling with her shamefast joy,
With the gold mantle's clasp began to toy,
Eager to cast that covering off, and feel
The hero's mighty arms about her steal. 1060

Meanwhile, her lover through the court had passed,
And at the open door he stood at last,
Amidst his friends, and looking thence, he saw
The white arms of the damsels round her draw
A wall soon to be broken; but her face
Over their flower-crowned heads made glad the place:
Giddy with joy one moment did he gaze
And saw his love her slender fingers raise

Unto the mantle's clasp—the next the hall
Was filled with darting flames from wall to wall,　1070
And bitter screams rang out, as here and there,
Scorched, and with outspread arms, the damsels fair
Rushed through the hall; but swiftly Jason ran,
Grown in one moment like an old worn man,
Up to the daïs, whence one bitter cry
He heard, of one in utmost agony,
Calling upon his once so helpful name;
But when unto the fiery place he came,
Nought saw he but the flickering tongues of fire
That up the wall were climbing high and higher;　1080
And on the floor a heap of ashes white,
The remnant of his once beloved delight,
For whom his ancient love he cast away,
And of her sire who brought about that day.

　Then he began to know what he had done,
And madly through the palace did he run,
Calling on Glauce, mingling with her name
The name of her that brought him unto fame,
Colchian Medea, who, for her reward,
Had lonely life made terrible and hard,　1090
By love cast back, within her heart to grow
To madness and the vengeance wrought out now;
But as about the burning place he ran,
Full many a maid he met and pale-faced man,
Wild with their terror, knowing not what end
That which their eyes had seen might yet portend:
But these shrunk backward from his brandished sword,
And open shouting mouth, and frenzied word,

As still from chamber unto chamber fair
He rushed, scarce knowing what he sought for
    there,   1100
Nor where he went, till his unresting feet
Had borne him out at last into the street,
Where armed and unarmed people stood to gaze
On Creon's palace that began to blaze
From every window out into the air,
With strange light making pale that noontide fair.
    But they, bewildered sore, and timorous,
Gazed helplessly upon the burning house,
And dreaded yet some hidden enemy,
Thinking indeed a dreadful God to see,   1110
Bearing a fresh destruction in his hand.
    But now, when Jason with his glittering brand
Broke in upon them from the growing fire,
With wild pale face, and half-burnt rich attire,
They fell back shuddering as his face they knew,
Changed though it was, and soon a murmur grew:—
"Death to the sorceress, the Colchian!"
But he, unheeding still, from 'midst them ran,
Until unto his own fair house he came,
Where gazed his folk upon the far-off flame,   1120
And muttered low for fear and woefulness.
    Then he knew not his own, but none the less,
Into the court he passed, and his bright sword
Cast down and said: "What feeble, timid lord
Hides here when all the world is on a blaze,
And laughing, from their heaven the high Gods gaze
At foolish men shut in the burning place?"

With that he turned about his haggard face,
And stared upon his own fair-sculptured frieze,
Carved into likeness of the tumbling seas, 1130
And Argo, and the heroes he had led,
And fair Medea. Then he cried, and said:—
"Lo, how the Gods are mocking me with this,
And show me pictures of my vanished bliss,
As though on earth I were, and not in hell;
And images of things I know full well
Have set about me. Can I die again,
And in some lower hell forget the pain
My life is passed in now?"

                        And with that word
He cast his eyes upon his glittering sword, 1140
And caught it up and set it to his breast,
And in one moment had he been at rest
From all his troubles, when a woman old,
His nurse in past times, did the deed behold,
And ran and caught the hero's mighty hand,
And hanging round about him did she stand,
And cried: "Ah, Jason! ah, my lord, let be!
For who can give another life to thee?
And though to-day the very sun looks black,
And wholesome air the whole world seems to lack,
Yet shalt thou yet have wealth of happy days, 1151
And well fulfilled desires, and all men's praise,
Unless the Gods have quite forgotten thee.
O Jason! O my child! come now with me,
That I may give thee sweet forgetfulness
A little while of sorrow and distress."

Then with the crone did Jason go along,
And let her thin hand hold his fingers strong,
As though a child he were in that old day,
Ere in the centaur's woodland cave he lay.   1160
But through the house unto a distant room,
Dark-hung, she brought him, where, amidst the gloom,
Speechless he lay, when she had made him drink
Some potion pressed from herbs plucked by the brink
Of scarce-known lakes of Pontus; then she said,
As she beheld at last his weary head
Sink on the pillow: "Jason, rest thee now,
And may some kind God smooth thy wrinkled brow.
Behold to-morrow comes, and thou art young,
Nor on one string are all life's jewels strung;   1170
Thou shalt be great, and many a land shalt save,
And of thy coming life more joy shalt have
Than thou hast thought of yet."
       He heard her words,
But as the far-off murmur of the birds
The townsman hears ere yet the morn is late,
While streets are void and shut is every gate;
But still they soothed him, and he fell asleep,
While at his feet good watch the crone did keep.

But what a waking unto him shall be!
And what a load of shameful misery   1180
His life shall bear! His old love cast away,
His new love dead upon that fearful day,
Childless, dishonoured, must his days go by.
For in another chamber did there lie

Two little helpless bodies side by side,
Smiling as though in sweet sleep they had died,
And feared no ill. And she who thus had slain
Those fruits of love, the folk saw **not again**,
Nor knew where **she** was gone; yet she **died not**,
But fleeing, somehow, **from that fatal spot**,   1190
She came to Athens, and there long **did dwell**,
Whose after life I list not here to tell.

But as for Jason;—**Creon now** being slain,
And Corinth kingless, every man was fain,
Remembering **Jason's** wisdom and sharp sword,
To have the hero for their king and lord.
So on his weary brows they set the crown,
And he began to rule that noble town.
And 'midst all things, somewhat his misery
Was **dulled unto him, as the days went by,**   1200
And he began again to cast his eyes
On lovely things, **and hope began** to rise
Once more within his heart.
                              But on a day
From out the goodly town he took his way,
To where, beneath the cliffs of Cenchreæ,
Lay Argo, looking o'er the ridgy sea.
Being fain once more to ponder o'er past days,
Ere he should set his face **to winning** praise
Among the shouts of men and clash of steel.

But when he reached the well-remembered keel,
The sun was far upon his downward way,   1211
At afternoon of a bright summer day.

Hot was it, and still o'er the long rank grass,
Beneath the hull, a widening shade did pass;
And further off, the sunny daisied sward,
The raised oars with their creeping shadows barred;
And grey shade from the hills of Cenchreæ
Began to move on toward the heaving sea.

  So Jason, lying in the shadow dark
Cast by the stem, the warble of the lark,   1220
The chirrup of the cricket, well could hear;
And now and then the sound would come anear
Of some hind shouting o'er his laden wain.
But looking o'er the blue and heaving plain,
Sailless it was, and beaten by no oar,
And on the yellow edges of the shore
The ripple fell in murmur soft and low,
As with wide-sweeping wings the gulls did go
About the breakers crying plaintively.

  But Jason, looking out across the sea,   1230
Beheld the signs of wind a-drawing nigh,
Gathering about the clear cold eastern sky,
And many an evening then he thought upon
Ere yet the quays of Æa they had won,
And longings that had long been gathering
Stirred in his heart, and now he felt the sting
Of life within him, and at last he said:—
"Why should I move about as move the dead,
And take no heed of what all men desire?
Once more I feel within my heart the fire   1240
That drave me forth unto the white-walled town,
Leaving the sunny slopes, and thick-leaved crown

Of grey old Pelion, that alone I knew,
Great deeds and wild, and desperate things to do.
"Ah! the strange life of happiness and woe
That I have led, since my young feet did go
From that grey, peaceful, much-beloved abode,
But now, indeed, will I cast off the load
Of memory of vain hopes that came to nought,
Of rapturous joys with biting sorrows bought. 1250
The past is past, though I cannot forget
Those days, with long life laid before me yet.
"Ah, but one moment, ere I turn the page,
And leave regret to white hairs and to age.
"Once did I win a noble victory,
I won a kingdom, and I cast it by
For rest and peace, and rest and peace are gone.
I had a fair love, that loved me alone,
And made me that I am in all men's eyes;
And like my hard-earned kingdom, my fair prize, 1260
I cast my tender heart, my Love away;
Yet failed I not to love, until a day,
A day I nigh forget, took all from me
That once I had.—And she is gone, yea, she
Whose innocent sweet eyes and tender hands
Made me a mocking unto distant lands:
Alas, poor child! yet is that as a dream,
And still my life a happy life I deem,
But ah! so short, so short! for I am left
Of love, of honour, and of joy bereft— 1270
And yet not dead—ah, if I could but see
But once again her who delivered me

From death and many troubles, then no more
Would I turn backward from the shadowy shore,
And all my life would seem but perfect gain.

"Alas! what hope is this? is it in vain
I long to see her? Lo, am I not young?
In many a song my past deeds have been sung,
And these my hands that guided Argo through
The blue Symplegades, still deeds may do.   1280
For now the world has swerved from truth and right,
Cumbered with monsters, empty of delight,
And, 'midst all this, what honour I may win,
That she may know of and rejoice therein,
And come to seek me, and upon my throne
May find me sitting, worshipped, and alone.
Ah! if it should be, how should I rejoice
To hear once more that once beloved voice
Rise through the burden of dull words, well-known;
How should I clasp again my love, mine own,   1290
And set the crown upon her golden head,
And with the eyes of lovers newly wed,
How should we gaze each upon each again.

"O hope not vain! O surely not quite vain!
For, with the next returning light will I
Cast off my moody sorrow utterly,
And once more live my life as in times past,
And 'mid the chance of war the die will cast.

"And surely, whatso great deeds have been done,
Since with my fellows the Gold Fleece I won,   1300
Still, here, some wild bull clears the frightened fields;
There, a great lion cleaves the sevenfold shields;

There, dwells some giant robber of the land;
There, whirls some woman-slayer's red right hand.
Yea, what is this they speak of even now,
That Theseus, having brought his conquering prow
From lying Crete, unto the fairwalled town,
Now gathers folk, since there are coming down
The shielded women of the Asian plain,
Myriads past counting, in the hope to gain   1310
The mastery of this lovely land of Greece?
So be it, surely shall I snatch fair peace
From out the hand of war, and calm delight
From the tumultuous horror of the fight."

So saying, gazing still across the sea,
Heavy with days and nights of misery,
His eyes waxed dim, and calmer still he grew,
Still pondering over times and things he knew,
While now the sun had sunk behind the hill,
And from a white-thorn nigh a thrush did fill   1320
The balmy air with echoing minstrelsy,
And cool the night-wind blew across the sea,
And round about the soft-winged bats did sweep.

So 'midst all this at last he fell asleep,
Nor did his eyes behold another day,
For Argo, slowly rotting all away,
Had dropped a timber here, and there an oar,
All through that year, but people of the shore
Set all again in order as it fell.
But now the stempost, that had carried well,   1330

The second rafter in King Pelias' hall,
Began at last to quiver towards its fall,
And whether loosed by some divinity,
Or that the rising wind from off the sea
Blew full upon it, surely I know not—
But, when the day dawned, still on the same spot,
Beneath the ruined stem did Jason lie
Crushed, and all dead of him that here can die.

What more?—Some shepherd of the lone grey slope,
Drawn to the sandy sea-beach by the hope   1340
Of trapping quick-eared rabbits, found him there,
And running back, called from the vineyards fair,
Vine-dressers and their mates who through the town
Ere then had borne their well-filled baskets brown,
These, looking on his dead face, straightway knew
This was the king that all men kneeled unto,
Who dwelt between the seas; therefore they made
A bier of white-thorn boughs, and thereon laid
The dead man, straightening every drawn-up limb;
And, casting flowers and green leaves over him,   1350
They bore him unto Corinth, where the folk,
When they knew all, into loud wailing broke,
Calling him mighty hero, crown of kings.
  But him ere long to where the sea-wind sings
O'er the grey hill-side did they bear again.
And there, where he had hoped that hope in vain,
They laid him in a marble tomb carved fair
With histories of his mighty deeds; and there
Such games as once he loved yet being alive,

They held for ten days, and withal did give   1360
Gifts to the Gods with many a sacrifice,
But chiefest, among all the things of price,
Argo they offered to the Deity
Who shakes the hard earth with the rolling sea.

And now is all that ancient story told
Of him who won the guarded Fleece of Gold.

THE END.

www.ingramcontent.com/pod-product-compliance
Lightning Source LLC
Chambersburg PA
CBHW020219240426
43672CB00006B/355